Mercy on Trial

Mercy on Trial

WHAT IT MEANS TO STOP AN EXECUTION

AUSTIN SARAT

PRINCETON UNIVERSITY PRESS

PRINCETON AND OXFORD

Published by Princeton University Press, 41 William Street, Princeton,
New Jersey 08540
In the United Kingdom: Princeton University Press, 3 Market Place, Woodstock,
Oxfordshire OX20 1SY

Second printing, and first paperback printing, 2007
Paperback ISBN: 978-0-691-13399-7

The Library of Congress has cataloged the cloth edition of this book as follows

Sarat, Austin.
Mercy on trial : what it means to stop an execution / Austin Sarat.
p. cm.
Includes index.
ISBN 0-691-12140-0 (hardcover: alk. paper)
1. Clemency—Illinois. 2. Pardon—Illinois. 3. Capital Punishment—Illinois.
4. Ryan, George H. I. Title.
KFI1785.S27 2005
345.773'077—dc22
2005005904

British Library Cataloging-in-Publication Data is available

This book has been composed in Sabon

Printed on acid-free paper. ∞

press.princeton.edu

Printed in the United States of America

3 5 7 9 10 8 6 4 2

TO STEPHANIE AND MR. B

A pardon is an act of mercy flowing from the fountain of bounty and grace. . . . Although laws are not framed on principles of compassion for guilt; yet when Mercy, in her divine tenderness, bestows on the transgressor the boon of forgiveness, Justice will pause, and forgetting the offense, bid the pardoned man go in peace.

—Judge Harold Erskine, *United States v. Athens Armory* 24 Fed. Cas, 878, 884, 885 (1868)

Contents

Acknowledgments

My interest in clemency was sparked by my friend and colleague Nasser Hussain with whom I wrote two articles on the subject. Nasser saw the importance of this subject both for legal theory and for America's public life long before I did. I am grateful to him for opening my eyes to it and for his generous and inspiring intellectual companionship. I also gratefully acknowledge my research assistant, Penelope Van Tuyl. Penelope is truly remarkable. This book could not have been written without her help. Along with Nasser, Conor Clarke, Jennifer Culbert, Patricia Ewick, Timothy Kaufman-Osborn, and Stuart Scheingold, each read an earlier draft of this manuscript and provided just the right balance of encouragement and constructive criticism. Thanks also to Ian Malcolm of Princeton University Press for his support of this project and skilled editorial hand.

Parts of this book were presented in several venues: the 2004 annual meetings of the Association for the Study of Law, Culture, and the Humanities and of the Law and Society Association; The Symposium on Punishment and Its Purposes, Stanford Law School; the conference on The Impact of the Death Penalty on Victims' Families, Skidmore College; The Symposium on Legal Borderlands, the Hart Institute, Pomona College; the conference on law and literature, Northwestern Law School; The Institute for the Humanities, University of Illinois, Chicago; Wayne State University School of Law; New York Law School; the University of Denver College of Law; the Ohio State University College of Law; Suffolk University School of Law, and the University of Rhode Island. I am grateful to participants in those events for their helpful comments. Thanks also to Amherst College dean of faculty, Gregory Call, and to the Axel Shupf Fund for Intellectual Life for generous financial support.

As in all I do, I owe my greatest debt to Stephanie, Lauren, Emily, and Mr. B for being generous in their grants of clemency, merciful in their judgments, and constant in their love.

Parts of this book have previously appeared in different forms elsewhere. Chapters 3 and 5 include portions of "On Lawful Lawlessness: George Ryan, Executive Clemency, and the Rhetoric of Sparing Life," 56 *Stanford Law Review* (2004), 1307–44 (reprinted with permission of Stanford law Review) and of "Putting a Square Peg in a Round Hole: Victims, Retribution, and George Ryan's Clemency," 82 *North Carolina Law Review* (2004), 1345–76.

Mercy on Trial

CHAPTER 1

Mercy, Clemency, and Capital Punishment

THE ILLINOIS STORY

If we simply use the term "mercy" to refer to certain of the demands of justice (e.g., the demand for individuation), then mercy ceases to be an autonomous virtue and instead becomes part of . . . justice. It thus becomes obligatory, and all the talk about gifts, acts of grace, supererogation, and compassion becomes quite beside the point. If, on the other hand, mercy is totally different from justice and actually requires (or permits) that justice sometimes be set aside, it then counsels injustice. In short, mercy is either a vice (injustice) or redundant part of justice.

—*Jeffrie Murphy*

No one who has never watched the hands of a clock marking the last minutes of a condemned man's existence, knowing that he alone has the temporary Godlike power to stop the clock, can realize the agony of deciding an appeal for executive clemency.

—*Michael DiSalle*

Death is power's limit, the moment that escapes it.

—*Michel Foucault*

ON JANUARY 10 AND 11, 2003, Governor George Ryan emptied Illinois's death row. Exercising his clemency powers under the state constitution, he first pardoned 4 and then commuted 167 condemned inmates' sentences in the broadest attack on the death penalty in decades. Ryan's act was a compelling moment in our society's continuing turmoil about crime and punishment, appearing, at first glance, to be a rare display of mercy in distinctly unmerciful times. As a seemingly humane, compassionate gesture in a culture whose attitudes toward punishment emphasize strictness not mercy, severity not forgiveness, it ran against the grain of today's tough-on-crime, law-and-order politics. In the controversy that it occasioned, Ryan's clemency put mercy on trial, forcing us to consider anew when and to whom it should be accorded.

It was, in addition, the single sharpest blow to capital punishment since the U.S. Supreme Court declared it unconstitutional in1972.[1] Because Ryan pardoned or commuted the sentences of sadistic rapists and murderers as well as those who seemed more sympathetic candidates for mercy and those whose convictions were questionable, his decision produced an explosive reaction among people who believe that death is both a morally appropriate and necessary punishment. They demonized Ryan and denounced his clemency in the strongest possible terms, claiming that he had dishonored the memory of murder victims, inflicted great pain on their surviving families, made the citizens of Illinois less safe, and abused his power. For opponents of capital punishment, Ryan became an instant hero. His decision, they claimed, would be a signal moment in the evolution of a "new abolitionist" politics.[2] They hoped it would mark a turning point on the way toward the demise of state killing.

That Ryan acted with two days left in his term and in the face of vocal opposition from citizens, the surviving families of murder victims, prosecutors, and almost all of Illinois's political establishment only compounded the drama. In addition, and even to many opponents of capital punishment, Ryan's action was a worrying reminder of the virtually unchecked powers of chief executives at the state and federal level to grant clemency. In a society committed to the rule of law, to the idea that all of the government's actions should be governed and disciplined by rules, that all government powers should be checked and balanced, that those who govern always should be accountable for their acts, what Ryan did exposed a gaping hole in the fabric of legality. It seemed to push to, and beyond, the limits of law's ability to regulate executive power, and, like the actions of the president in times of national emergency, hinted at the specter of power out of control, a dangerous, undemocratic, unaccountable power lying dormant and waiting for an occasion to be exercised.[3]

George Ryan hardly seemed typecast for such a dramatic part in our contemporary history. Prior to becoming governor, Ryan had had a long career in Illinois politics, serving in the state legislature from 1973 to1983, as lieutenant governor from 1983 to 1991, and as secretary of state in 1991. Because Ryan embodied a rather unremarkable combination of familiar midwestern Republican positions—fiscally conservative, moderate in his social views—his 1998 election as governor was barely noticed nationally and greeted with little fanfare locally. This white-haired, sixty-nine-year-old former pharmacist from Kankakee, Illinois, did not fit anyone's stereotype of either demon or hero, much less of the kind of national and international celebrity his clemency decision would make him. Nothing in his personality, or prior political record, suggested he would make much of a splash during his gubernatorial term or become a key national anti–death penalty activist. Ryan himself noted, "I mean, I am a Republican pharmacist from Kankakee. All of a sudden I've got gays and lesbians by my side. African-Americans. Senators from Italy, groups from around the world. It's a little surprising."[4]

Throughout his career in government he had been an outspoken supporter of capital punishment, and in his gubernatorial campaign he had restated his belief in the appropriateness of the death penalty. "I believed some crimes were so heinous," Ryan said of his long-held position on capital punishment, "that the only proper way of protecting society was execution. I saw a nation in the grip of increasing crime rates; and tough sentences, more jails, the death penalty—that was good government." In 1977, after the Supreme Court lifted its ban on execution, a bill to reinstate the death penalty came before the state legislature in Springfield. When an anti–death penalty legislator asked his colleagues to consider whether they personally would be willing to throw the switch, "Ryan rose to his feet with 'unequivocal words of support' for execution—words he now regrets. The truth, though, was that Ryan never thought about capital punishment much before that vote or for more than twenty years afterward, except as an abstract idea of justice. 'I supported the death penalty, I believed in the death penalty, I voted for the death penalty.' "[5]

During his tenure as governor his views about capital punishment were radically transformed, with the result that he took two particularly dramatic actions: the first a statewide moratorium on executions, which he announced in February 2000; the second his mass clemency. These two acts helped to galvanize and change the national discussion about capital punishment.

The Shifting Terrain

By the time Ryan became governor, voices at both the national and state level had begun to raise new and disturbing questions about state killing. To take but one particularly important example, in February 1997 the American Bar Association issued a call for a nationwide moratorium on executions. The ABA proclaimed that the death penalty as "currently administered" was not compatible with central values of our Constitution. Thus it called

> upon each jurisdiction that imposes capital punishment not to carry out the death penalty until the jurisdiction implements policies and procedures . . . intended to (1) ensure that death penalty cases are administered fairly and impartially, in accordance with due process, and (2) minimize the risk that innocent people may be executed.[6]

In the report accompanying its call for a moratorium, the ABA pointed to three glaring flaws in the death penalty process.[7] First was the failure of most states to guarantee competent counsel in capital cases. Because those states have no regular public defender systems, indigent capital defendants are frequently assigned lawyers with no interest, or experience, in capital litigation.[8] The result is often an incompetent defense that is all the more damaging in light of rules preventing defenses not raised, or waived, at trial from being raised on appeal or in habeas proceedings.[9] The ABA thus called for the appointment of "two experienced attorneys at each stage of a capital case."[10]

The second basis for the ABA's recommended moratorium was a significant erosion in postconviction protections for capital defendants caused by the passage of the Anti-Terrorism and Effective Death Penalty Act of 1996. Contradicting the provisions of that act, the ABA said that "federal courts should consider claims that were not properly raised in state court if the reason for the default was counsel's ignorance or neglect and that a prisoner should be permitted to file a second or successive federal petition if it raises a new claim that undermines confidence in his or her guilt or the appropriateness of the death sentence." Third, the ABA called for a moratorium because of the persistence of "longstanding patterns of racial discrimination . . . in courts around the country."[11] The ABA cited research showing that defendants are more likely to receive a death sentence if the victim is white rather than black,[12] and that in some jurisdictions African Americans tend to receive the death penalty more than do white defendants.[13] The report urged the development of "effective mechanisms" to eliminate racial prejudice in capital cases.

Following the ABA's recommendation, activists mounted a statewide moratorium campaign in Illinois,[14] and legislators introduced bills in the state legislature calling on then-governor Jim Edgar to stop executions and appoint a commission to conduct a comprehensive review of the state's death penalty system.[15] The Chicago Council of Lawyers joined in the call for a moratorium, citing especially the fact that between 1993 and 1997 seven death row inmates had been freed after it was discovered that they were convicted and sentenced to death for crimes they did not commit. In July 1997 Governor Edgar signed into law a bill providing funds for postconviction DNA testing of inmates on death row. And late in that year, the Illinois State Bar Association formed a special committee to study the state's capital case process and to recommend needed reforms.

During the 1990s the increasingly availability of DNA testing throughout the country and in Illinois resulted in dramatic exonerations of inmates condemned to death, like those cited by the Chicago Council of Lawyers. Among the most striking and important of these cases was the exoneration in February 1999 of Anthony Porter. Porter, an African-American man with an IQ of 51, had been convicted and sentenced to die for the double homicide of Marilyn Green and Jerry Hillard in 1982. His conviction and sentence were later upheld on appeal by both the Illinois and the U.S. Supreme Court. However, forty-eight hours before his scheduled execution in 1998, a judge entered a stay to allow for a hearing on the question of whether Porter's IQ was so low that he should not be executed.

After the stay was entered, the case against Porter began to unravel when a key prosecution witness signed an affidavit saying that he lied under oath during the trial. In early 1999 an inmate in state prison admitted that his uncle and he "took care" of Green and Hillard because of a drug debt. Finally, a private investigator working on the Porter case with a Northwestern University journalism professor and his students obtained a videotaped confession from the uncle acknowledging that he had committed the murders.[16]

The Porter case quickly came to symbolize what death penalty opponents had long claimed about rampant problems in the administration of capital punishment, and it spurred calls for change. Newspaper editorials, the Illinois State Bar Association's Section on Criminal Justice, and many public officials called on Ryan to immediately stop all executions and launch a thoroughgoing review of the capital punishment system in Illinois. Yet Ryan at first refused. Instead, a spokesperson for the governor noted at the time of Porter's release that Ryan would "review death penalty case[s] on a case-by-case basis, just as the Supreme

Court does, and will make an appropriate decision on each at an appropriate time."[17]

Ryan's initial reaction to the Porter case echoed his predecessors' reactions to earlier exonerations. As his spokesperson put it, "I know people use these reversals as an argument for a moratorium . . . but an argument can also be made that the system is working as designed."[18] In Ryan's view, Porter's exoneration proved that the system worked.[19] As he said at the time, "I still support the death penalty, and there's no question it ought to be applied fairly and accurately and I'm willing to work with anyone to ensure that process goes on. We're still looking for the best way to do that."[20]

Later, reflecting on the transformation of his views about the death penalty, Ryan put a different spin on the Porter case. "I was caught completely off-guard. Maybe I shouldn't have been, but I was. That mentally retarded man came within two days of execution, and but for those students Anthony Porter would have been dead and buried. I felt jolted into reexamining everything I believed in."[21] Nonetheless, a conflicted Ryan still resisted a full-fledged review of Illinois's capital apparatus, though he endorsed one reform: an $18 million capital-crimes litigation fund to ensure that defendants like Porter, as well as prosecutors, have access to investigative resources.

In the meantime, a month after Porter's exoneration, Ryan received a clemency request in the capital case of Andrew Kokoraleis, who had been convicted and sentenced for his role in the kidnapping, rape, and mutilation murder of a twenty-one-year-old woman. Referring to himself as the "guy who pushes the plunger," Ryan publicly agonized about his decision, but, in the end, decided to let the execution proceed.[22] He explained his denial of clemency by saying that "some crimes are so horrendous and so heinous that society has a right to demand the ultimate penalty."[23]

Within three months of the Kokoraleis execution, two more Illinois death row inmates were exonerated: one by DNA evidence, the other when a jailhouse informant's testimony was discredited. The state judiciary began its own investigation,[24] and calls for a moratorium grew more frequent and intense. Still, Ryan recalled, "I was resisting." But one day, "the attorney general called seeking a new execution date for an inmate. In my heart at that moment, I couldn't go forward with it."[25] Ryan's critics suggested that his emerging doubts about capital punishment were less the product of a genuine change of heart than a political expedient designed to deflect attention from a brewing scandal and charges of corruption in the secretary of state's office during his tenure there.

Whatever its true motivation Ryan's transformation was facilitated by the publication in November 1999 of a four-part series in the *Chicago Tribune* entitled "The Failure of the Death Penalty in Illinois." Written by Ken Armstrong and Steve Mills, these articles painted a devastating picture of "a system so riddled with faulty evidence, unscrupulous trial tactics and legal incompetence" as to be unable to do justice reliably in capital cases. Armstrong and Mills documented numerous cases in which capital defendants were represented by incompetent lawyers. In addition, they reported that nearly half the state's death penalty cases were reversed on appeal, and many were marked by racial discrimination in jury selection. Their articles recounted case after case in which capital convictions were obtained on the basis of jailhouse snitches and confessions that police and prosecutors knew, or should have known, were of questionable value. The cumulative picture painted by the *Tribune* series was devastating. It exposed a system "so plagued by unprofessionalism, imprecision, and bias that . . . the state's ultimate form of punishment is its least credible."[26]

The Armstrong and Mills pieces marked a turning point for Ryan and Illinois.[27] Barely two months after they were published, Ryan reversed course and announced both a statewide moratorium on executions and the creation of a blue-ribbon panel to study the state's death penalty system. As he said at the time,

> I now favor a moratorium, because I have grave concerns about our state's shameful record of convicting innocent people and putting them on death row. I believe many Illinois residents now feel that same deep reservation. I cannot support a system, which, in its administration, has proven to be so fraught with error and has come so close to the ultimate nightmare, the state's taking of innocent life. Thirteen people have been found to have been wrongfully convicted. . . . How do you prevent another Anthony Porter—another innocent man or woman from paying the ultimate penalty for a crime he or she did not commit? Today, I cannot answer that question. Until I can be sure that everyone sentenced to death in Illinois is truly guilty, until I can be sure with moral certainty that no innocent man or woman is facing a lethal injection, no one will meet that fate. I am a strong proponent of tough criminal penalties, of supporting laws and programs to help police and prosecutors keep dangerous criminals off the streets. We must ensure the public safety of our citizens but, in doing so, we must ensure that the ends of justice are served. As Governor, I am ultimately responsible, and although I respect all that these leaders have done and I will consider all that they say, I believe that a public dialogue must begin on the question of the fairness of the application of the death penalty in Illinois.[28]

Several themes that would reemerge three years later when he announced his clemency decision stand out in this statement. First is the criticism of the *process* through which the death penalty is administered, not of capital punishment itself. Here Ryan presented himself as a new abolitionist interested in defending traditional legal values rather than in being merciful toward the condemned. New abolitionists do not oppose state killing because it is an affront to morality, nor do they claim that it is per se unconstitutional. Instead, new abolitionists, like Ryan, argue against the death penalty by claiming that it has not been, and cannot be, administered in a manner that is compatible with our legal system's fundamental commitments to fair and equal treatment.

Second is the characterization of his beliefs as following, not leading, public opinion. Here Ryan tried to side with what he saw as cultural common sense rather than presenting an elitist critique of the immorality of capital punishment. Third is a self-dramatizing emphasis on his own responsibility, an emphasis somewhat at variance with his effort to describe his decision as following the views of "many Illinois residents": "As Governor, I am ultimately responsible." Fourth is the articulation of an almost impossibly high burden of proof for the resumption of executions—what Ryan called "moral certainty." This standard would ultimately set the stage for his clemency decision. Finally, there is the emphasis, even as he stopped all executions, on his "tough on crime" credentials. It is indicative of the political and cultural context in which acts of mercy now exist that Ryan did not present the moratorium as motivated by, or as a form of, compassion for the condemned. In this way Ryan's initial step on the road to clemency was framed as fully compatible with a commitment "to help police and prosecutors keep dangerous criminals off the streets."

Unlike the controversy that would surround the clemency decision, there was surprisingly little in the way of outright public opposition in the immediate aftermath of the moratorium.[29] As the *Chicago Sun-Times* editorialized, "The moratorium is welcome—and long overdue,"[30] and many proponents of capital punishment quickly embraced it. Thus, Republican Senate President Philip Wood, longtime death penalty supporter and a key stumbling block in previous legislative efforts to impose a moratorium, said, "This is an opportunity for the legal community to review the death penalty process, not the death penalty."[31] Democratic House Speaker Michael Madigan, another longtime death penalty supporter, praised Ryan's action. Finally, Attorney General Jim Ryan, one of the governor's most persistent critics, joined in support, saying that everyone involved in administering the state's criminal justice system wants "to make sure capital punishment operates fairly."[32]

Five weeks after announcing the moratorium, Ryan unveiled the membership of his Governor's Commission. Comprised of leading politicians, prosecutors, public defenders, and well-known citizens, the commission was charged to review the entire death penalty system and make recommendations with the goal of ensuring that no innocent person would ever again be sentenced to death in Illinois. Referring to that system, one of the commission's cochairs said at the time, "We've got to find out why it's flawed, in what way it is flawed . . . and how it can be corrected."[33]

Two years later, as the Governor's Commission continued its work, and under the pressure of a growing federal investigation into allegations of corruption against Ryan, he announced that he would not seek reelection. During this same period, he occasionally voiced his own doubts about capital punishment, openly admitting that he was struggling with this issue. As he put it in a speech to the Association of the Bar of the City of New York, "I once believed that there were crimes that were so heinous that the death penalty sentence was the only proper societal response. . . . I believed in the death penalty and I thought it was the right thing. So I gave some words of unqualified support that I regret."[34] Later, talking about the impending execution of Oklahoma City bomber Timothy McVeigh, Ryan said, "I couldn't throw the switch on this guy, McVeigh, and he was a terrible guy. . . . I think there may be cause for the death penalty for a guy like him, but I don't know."[35]

At the same time, the terrain on which the death penalty debate proceeded in Illinois continued to shift. Thus in early 2001 the Illinois Supreme Court announced a revision of the Rules of Professional Conduct that guided capital litigation. It adopted new rules and amended existing ones to require, among other things, that prosecutors provide notice of intent to seek the death penalty within 120 days of arraignment and identify all evidence favorable to the defense prior to trial, that judges who preside in capital cases receive special training, and that lead attorneys in capital cases have at least five years of criminal litigation experience and training in the preparation and trial of capital cases in a course approved by the supreme court.[36]

The Road to Clemency

The start of 2002 brought with it anticipation of the forthcoming report of the Governor's Commission. The *Chicago Tribune* noted that the commission was "preparing a report containing scores of reforms as well as a controversial vote to abolish capital punishment."[37] However, the newspaper predicted that the final report would not contain a recommendation to end the death penalty since such a move would be seen by commissioners as going beyond their charge.

Looking forward to the completion of the Governor's Commission's work, Ryan began to talk openly about clemency. At the University of Oregon in March, Ryan told his audience that he was reviewing the cases of all inmates on death row to determine if any should have their sentences commuted. "I believe," he said, "there are probably some people we can commute [*sic*]. Believe me, it's been a topic of discussion."[38] This was his first public acknowledgment of the possibility of clemency, and opponents of capital punishment seized on it to urge him to consider commuting all death sentences in Illinois.[39]

In April the Governor's Commission issued its final report and recommendations. While stopping short, as the *Tribune* had correctly predicted, of urging abolition of the state's death penalty, the commission recommended eighty-five changes in the criminal justice system designed to improve the fairness and integrity of the death penalty system. Among other things, the commission suggested reduction of the list of twenty circumstances under which the death penalty could be imposed to five; that executing the mentally retarded be prohibited; that all police interrogations be videotaped; that juries consider a defendant's history of physical and emotional abuse when sentencing; that death sentences be banned when a defendant is convicted with only a single witness, a prison informant, or an accomplice whose testimony is not corroborated with other evidence; that judges be allowed to overrule a jury decision to impose a death sentence; and that a statewide panel of three prosecutors, an attorney general's representative, and a retired judge review each state's attorney's decision to seek the death penalty.

Illinois lawmakers and public officials reacted to the commission's recommendations with caution, some worrying about the cost of implementing its proposed changes.[40] Death penalty opponents saw them as a back door to abolition. "It is an effort, brick by brick, rock by rock, stone by stone, to create more burdens and restrictions upon the prosecution to have them say, 'Oh, the heck with it, What's the use? I'll just pursue it as a regular murder.'" And from the start, the commission's report and recommendations fueled talk about clemency. As Bill Ryan, president of the Illinois Death Penalty Moratorium Project, put it, the Governor's Commission's report is "the strongest case ever for the Governor to do the right thing and commute the sentences of the 160 or so people on death row. They were all convicted under a system rife with corruption."[41]

Through the following months of summer, increasing numbers of clemency petitions were filed with the state's Prisoner Review Board, which is charged with receiving and reviewing them and presenting nonbinding, confidential recommendations to the governor. As more petitions were filed, families of murder victims began publicly to voice their opposition to the prospect that the governor might pardon or commute death sentences. As one put it, "Why do we have the jury system? Why do we have the system we have if you're going to have a man who happens to be governor, and he can, with a twist of his pen, change the whole thing?"[42] Another said,

> We are the ones who have no rights as survivors. Our loved ones were not able to say which persons killed them. No. The death penalty is not going to bring our loved ones back, but it is a closure. People forget about the families that have to survive. None of us should have to go through this, but Governor Ryan is pushing this so he can go out with a big bang. How can he do it?

Newspaper commentators described the prospect of mass commutations as "appalling."[43] Others urged the governor not to "reverse years of honest work of jurors and judges and prosecutors . . . [and] to think of the heartbreak, the renewed grief, such an act would bring to those who have already suffered more than anyone deserves to suffer."[44]

That autumn brought with it the start of hearings convened by the Prisoner Review Board on the clemency petitions. Around the same time, Ryan began a period of public equivocation on the question of whether he would entertain the idea of a blanket clemency. Either everyone should have their sentences commuted or no one should, Ryan suggested. He wondered out loud whether it would be fair or right for him to "pick and choose" those whose lives should be spared: "That's why I have to determine whether it's going to be for everybody or nobody. I think that's probably what my decision is going to be. . . . How do you decide who's guilty and who isn't. The system right now is, you can flip a coin and determine who's going to live and die."[45]

Despite Ryan's ruminations about a possible all or nothing decision, the Prisoner Review Board went ahead with its hearings, held over a two-week period in Chicago and Springfield. As they began, critics again urged the governor not to put families of victims through the ordeal of the hearings if he was inclined to issue a blanket clemency. As one reporter noted, "Not since Pope John Paul II convinced Missouri Governor Mel Carnahan to spare the life of a triple murderer . . . has the issue of commuting sentences garnered such attention."[46]

The hearings themselves galvanized the state's attention, providing lead stories on local television news and in major newspapers. Against the abstract arguments of defense lawyers arguing about systemic flaws in the cases of their clients, families of victims presented gripping and emotionally compelling accounts of gruesome murders and of their shattered lives. Referring to those accounts and their impact, an advocate of blanket clemency said, "I would have to admit that we probably underestimated it. It's pretty much overpowering."[47] One newspaper described the twenty-three hearings held the first day as a "sad parade of victims' families, some of them wearing yellow ribbons in memory of their loved ones, saying they could hardly bear to again hear gruesome details of the cases."[48] Another reported that, "The issues that had defined the death penalty debate for more than two years—bad defense lawyering, police misconduct, the use of unreliable witnesses—have faded, at least for now."[49]

Columnists drew unflattering comparisons between Ryan and governors whose clemency considerations were plagued by corruption,[50] or held him personally responsible for what they called an "absurd Theatre of Pain." They said that the hearings were "a fraudulent process aimed at legitimizing a foregone conclusion."[51] The *Chicago Tribune* called them "disastrous" and worried that they had dealt "a political blow to the momentum of Illinois's reform movement."[52] As the *Tribune* predicted, the package of reforms arising from the recommendations of the Governor's Commission that Ryan had so enthusiastically sent to the legislature went nowhere. They were bogged down in the controversy surrounding the clemency hearings, Ryan's lame-duck status, and the usual end-of-term legislative logjam.[53]

As time went by, the chorus of criticism of the hearings included members of the Prisoner Review Board and witnesses testifying before it.[54] Many questioned Ryan's motives. "I really wish Governor Ryan was sitting here today and look[ing] in the eyes of the victims' families and see[ing] the hurt he's causing," one witness said. "He's using these victims' families as pawns in the debate on the death penalty."[55]

During and after the hearings Ryan was the subject of escalating pressure from all sides. In November and December 2002, first one group then another weighed in on the question of whether Ryan should commute any or all death sentences.[56] In response, he said that he had " 'pretty much ruled out' switching every death sentence to life in prison."[57]

Clemency as Mercy Beyond Law

When Ryan eventually announced his clemency, pardoning a few, commuting many sentences, and sparing the lives of the condemned, he exercised one of the great prerogatives of sovereignty. Indeed the original definition of "sovereignty" in the West comes from the Roman law maxim—*vitae et necis potestatem*—the power over life and death. Thus in the opening sentence of the final section of volume 1 of the *History of Sexuality*, Michel Foucault says that "for a long time, one of the characteristic privileges of sovereign power was the right to decide life and death."[58] The Anglo common-law tradition also contains elements of such a definition. The great English seventeenth-century common-law authorities, like Lord Coke, even as they tried to curb and contain such a power, acknowledged its existence, particularly for the new colonies attained by conquest. Hence in *Calvin's Case* Lord Coke suggested, "for if a King come to a Christian Kingdom by conquest, seeing that he hath *vitae et necis potestatem*, he may at his pleasure alter and change the laws of that kingdom."[59] In a modern constitutional democracy, the power over life and death is no longer associated with a king or a single authority. But as the continuing existence of capital punishment in the United States reminds us, that power is far from extinguished.

The context for the exercise of that power is, of course, quite different today than it was in the seventeenth century or even in the early twentieth century. Under the twin pressures of globalization and what Foucault calls "governmentality,"[60] state sovereignty and its prerogatives seem less secure, or at least more complicated, than they have been in the past. Just as the formation of nation-states was one of the defining characteristics of an earlier era, their rapid and often radical transformation is one of the defining characteristics of ours. Today state forms throughout the world alter and adapt, adding new functions, shedding old ones, refining institutional processes, developing new alliances within and beyond national borders, sometimes increasing democratic tendencies, sometimes weakening them. "There is a growing view, approaching conventional wisdom in some quarters, that the power of the nation state is being eroded by globalization. . . . [T]here is little doubt that the accelerating pace of structural transformations of the global economy places increasing strain on the adaptive capacity and hence the legitimacy of governments."[61]

The political theorist William Connolly lists "nonstate terrorism, the internationalization of capital, the greenhouse effect, acid rain, drug traffic, illegal aliens, the global character of strategic planning, extensive resource dependencies across state boundaries, and the accelerated pace of disease transmission across continents" as factors that "signify a widening gap between the power of the most powerful states and the power they would require to be self-governing and self-determining."[62] This gap, in turn, creates a dilemma for state sovereignty by undermining "the state's self-representation as an agency that is capable of efficaciously translating the will of the democratic electorate into coherent public policy."[63]

In addition, as Foucault famously warned, "in political thought and analysis, we still have not cut off the head of the king."[64] He advocated a theoretical beheading so that attention could shift to developments of the late modern era in which the state loses whatever monopoly it has on effective power in, and over, society. Governmentality designates a broad array of technologies—some public, some private, some official, some unofficial, some located in and around the state, some operating more or less autonomously from it. These technologies of power are characterized by a convergence of "the constitutional, fiscal, organizational and judicial powers of the state . . . (and by) endeavors to manage economic life, the health and habits of the population, the civility of the masses, and so forth."[65] The concept of governmentality directs attention to "the proliferation of alliances between state and nonstate bearers of expertise and authority aimed at regulating the conduct of diverse populations."[66]

Sociologist Nikolas Rose characterizes this proliferation of alliances as involving a shift from the social state to advanced liberal values—leading, in effect, to "a reconstruction of subjectivity": "National and international competitiveness," he notes, "was recoded, at least in part, in terms of the psychological, dispositional, and aspirational capacities of those who make up the labour force. Thus each individual is solicited as a potential ally of economic success."[67] In addition, neoliberal values seek to transform states by introducing market values into public processes. Laissez-faire once meant keeping the state out of the market; today neoliberalism means bringing the market into the state and transforming citizenship into another means for expressing and obtaining preferences. Just as competition is good within the market so too competition within and among state agencies is, in the neoliberal pantheon, something to be encouraged.

While globalization puts increased pressure on state sovereignty from outside its boundaries, governmentality and neoliberalism create pressure from within. Under these pressures, as political theorist Timothy Kaufman-Osborn says, "the authority of the late liberal state is now unsettled." And where sovereignty is most fragile, as it is today, dramatic symbols of its presence, like capital punishment, may be most important. The maintenance of the death penalty is, one might argue, essential to the demonstration that sovereignty still resides in nation-states. At a time when citizens are skeptical about the governing capacities of states, the death penalty provides one arena in which the state can redeem itself by taking action with clear and popular results.

Under pressure, state actors try to mobilize premodern symbols of sovereignty, one of the most important of which is the death penalty. They seek to "substantiate (the state's) mystical claim to sovereign authority via the carefully orchestrated drama of political power that is an execution."[68] Because a state unable (or unwilling) to execute those it condemns to die would seem too impotent to carry out almost any policy whatsoever, clemency, Ryan's act notwithstanding, has little place. In the drama of state sovereignty under conditions of globalization and governmentality, one form of prerogative—clemency—gives way before another: execution.

Much has been said and written about the power to kill within the confines of modern law;[69] death has been regarded as of a different order from other punishments, as the most robust and terrifying of law's dealings in pain and violence.[70] Such a sustained focus on the right to impose death sometimes eclipses the essential corollary of *vitae et necis potestatem*: the sovereign right to spare life.[71] In a modern political system this power to spare life remains in the form of executive clemency.[72] Executive clemency in capital cases is distinctive in that it is the only power that can *undo death*—the only power that can prevent death once it has been prescribed and, through appellate review, approved as a legally appropriate punishment.

Clemency is a general term referring to the legal authority of an executive to "intervene in the sentencing of a criminal defendant. . . . It is a relief imparted after the justice system has run its course."[73] Clemency is the reduction of punishment that is authorized by law. That it provides "relief" from legal justice strictly construed reminds us that not only has clemency traditionally been an important element of sovereign power, but it often has also been a vivid expression of mercy. As the law professor Robert Weisberg says, "the commutation of a death sentence (is) the most dramatic example of mercy."[74] Long ago William Blackstone described the relation between clemency and mercy by noting that the power to spare lives was "one of the great advantages of monarchy in general;

that there is a magistrate, who has it in his power to extend mercy, whenever he thinks it is deserved: holding a court of equity in his own breast, to soften the rigour of the general law, in such criminal cases as merit an exception from punishment."[75]

Recently scholars have tried to chart mercy's complex relations to forgiveness on the one hand and justice on the other,[76] some seeing irreconcilable tensions,[77] with others seeking to accommodate mercy with the virtues of forgiveness or the demands of justice.[78] In all of those efforts, certain aspects of mercy, the kind of mercy that may be shown in clemency, stand out. "Mercy is part of a larger notion of 'charity.' . . . Mercy entails a decision . . . either to forgo a right to punish or to reduce punishment because of compassion. . . . Mercy mitigates the punishment that an offender deserves. . . . Mercy is not earned or deserved but is given freely."[79] Charity, compassion—these moral sentiments are the essence of mercy and provide the impetus for the work it does in giving criminals less than they deserve.

Thus clemency has a contingent, not necessary, relation to mercy. The former may arise from, or express, a variety of sentiments of which mercy is only one. It may arise, as we will see, from a desire to correct injustices, spare the innocent from undeserved punishment, reward political allies, ameliorate political conflict, and so forth. Mercy, unlike clemency, always entails a particular motive and feeling toward the recipient: compassion (literally feeling "with" the other). The outcome of clemency and mercy is the same—the forgoing of some level of punishment—but mercy implies a particular orientation and relationship between grantor and grantee.[80]

The idea that clemency and mercy can be given (or withheld) "freely," together with Blackstone's "court of equity" language, highlight their complex and unstable relationship to law. Blackstone was undoubtedly thinking of the actual courts of equity in his time. They developed in distinction to the common-law courts with their elaborate, even Byzantine, system of rules, pleadings, and writs. And although by the time Blackstone wrote the *Commentaries*, equity had hardened into law, he knew well the common understanding that "Chancery was not a court of law but a court of conscience . . . (and) the essence of equity as a corrective to the rigour of laws was that it should not be tied to rules."[81] While the language of desert properly could be attached to it, the calculus of desert in clemency cannot be governed by rules; it remains purely discretionary.[82]

Like all sovereign prerogative, clemency's efficacy is bound to its very disregard of declared law. Thus more than half a century before Blackstone, John Locke called prerogative the "power to act according to discretion, for the public good, without the prescription of the Law, and sometimes even against it. . . . [T]here is a latitude left to the Executive power, to do many things of choice, which the Laws do not prescribe."[83] And mercy too extends beyond the reach of law. "The Rulers," Locke observed, "should have a Power . . . to mitigate the severity of the Law, and Pardon some Offenders: For the end of Government being the preservation of all, as much as may be, even the guilty are to be spared, where it can prove no prejudice to the innocent." Following Locke, John Harrison has recently defined clemency as "the power of doing good without a rule."[84]

Though the equity of which Blackstone speaks, or Locke's power to mitigate, springs from the body of sovereignty, as if originating well beyond any place the law could know or inhabit, the sovereign's right to intervene, like equity itself, "depends on the law getting a chance to get the right result; his actions are . . . derivative of the law, secondary, complementary, and equitable."[85] "Derivative," "secondary," "complementary," this language situates clemency at a fault line in the fabric of legality, waiting to do the work that law requires. While it entails the willing suspension of the right to punish, clemency serves, even as it mitigates punishment in an individual case or a group of cases, to affirm the general right to punish that law asserts. In this way clemency contributes to law's power and legitimacy even as it poses a challenge to it. It is, in this sense, law's necessary other.

What is this necessary other that the law seems incapable of holding within itself, the possibility of which nonetheless must always be present offstage? Pardon is like other prerogatives, which Locke had defined tout court as the embodiment of a necessary discretion, but it is also for Blackstone the "most amiable" of all the prerogative powers, as it is the only one that exercises mercy and compassion. And yet, crucially, Blackstone is aware of the possible dangers of designating the source of mercy and compassion outside the law: "Pardons (according to some theorists) should be excluded in a perfect legislation, where punishments are mild but certain: for that clemency of the prince seems a tacit disapprobation of the laws." Blackstone was willing to run such a risk rather than introduce an even more "dangerous power" by permitting judges and juries to apply the "criminal law by the spirit instead of the letter."[86]

Blackstone's reading of the prerogative clarifies, in a manner strikingly like the language of contemporary debates, essential quandaries in the act of clemency and the trial of mercy. For as he shows, it is certainly possible to judge a penal system by the standards of mercy and compassion—that is, one can speak of a penal system as more or less "*merciful.*" But there remains something in the act of *mercy* that invokes the ineradicable and perhaps necessary gap between law and justice, letter and spirit, rules and discretion.

On the Trial of Mercy: George Ryan Accused

Until George Ryan's clemency, the long-held constitutional right of chief executives to spare life seemed to have "died its own death, the victim of a political lethal injection and a public that overwhelmingly supports the death penalty."[87] Capital clemency also has been a victim of the rejection of rehabilitation as the guiding philosophy of criminal sentencing and the increasing politicization of issues of crime and punishment since the 1960s. Thus, at the outset of his administration,

Texas governor George W. Bush embraced a standard for clemency that all but ensured that few if any death sentences would be seriously examined. Writing about Bush's views, Alan Berlow noted,

> "In every case," [Bush] wrote in *A Charge to Keep*, "I would ask: Is there any doubt about this individual's guilt or innocence? And, have the courts had ample opportunity to review all the legal issues in this case?" This is an extraordinarily narrow notion of clemency review: it seems to leave little, if any, room to consider mental illness or incompetence, childhood physical or sexual abuse, remorse, rehabilitation, racial discrimination in jury selection, the competence of the legal defense, or disparities in sentences between co-defendants or among defendants convicted of similar crimes. Neither compassion nor "mercy," which the Supreme Court as far back as 1855 saw as central to the very idea of clemency, is acknowledged as being of any account. . . . During Bush's six years as governor 150 men and two women were executed in Texas—a record unmatched by any other governor in modern American history. . . . Bush allowed the execution to proceed in all cases but one.[88]

Similarly, then-governor Bill Clinton explained his reluctance to grant clemency by saying, "The appeals process, although lengthy, provides many opportunities for the courts to review sentences and that's where these decisions should be made."[89]

Today the Bush and Clinton views are the norm.[90] Mercy has been put on trial, and it has been found wanting. Governors are reluctant to substitute their judgment for those of state legislators and courts and, in death cases, to use clemency as an expression of mercy.[91] They seek, in Jonathan Simon's evocative phrase, to "govern through crime," to turn tough-on-crime policy into a strategy for building coalitions and strengthening the state.[92] Many have used the death penalty in their campaigns, promising more and quicker executions.[93] Simon's work suggests that the political power of governors depends

> in large part on their power to mobilize the state around crime fears. In numerous states and on many occasions the death penalty has been the venue for the assertion of a governor's power by campaigning for, or signing into law, a new death penalty statute . . . or signing a death warrant authorizing the execution of a particular prisoner. Clemency provides another occasion when, in effect, the Governor can assert his or her support for the death penalty (and empathy with ordinary citizens) by rejecting clemency.[94]

Perhaps because of the current political climate or his personal convictions, or both, Ryan's clemency did not focus on the morality of the death penalty as a punishment. Instead his decision was largely rooted in a critique of its application and administration.[95] By reducing punishment, he fulfilled one of the requirements of mercy, yet he showed no compassion toward those whose lives he spared. Instead of marking a revival of mercy, Ryan acted within the Bush-Clinton model of executive clemency, embracing what Justice Rehnquist has called a "fail safe" conception of the prerogative of power.[96] As a result, Ryan's commutations were fully compatible with our era's cramped conception of clemency.

Nonetheless Ryan's action generated intense controversy.[97] Interestingly, the distinction between rejecting capital punishment per se and criticizing its application was lost upon some who supported Ryan's decision.[98] "Governor Ryan has moved this nation in the direction of the other world democracies. The U.S. has been alone in the world in its use of the death penalty," said former Illinois senator Paul Simon. "What the families of the victims want is revenge, and that's understandable. But the role of government can't be about revenge. The role of government is to protect society—and there is no evidence at all that the death penalty protects society."[99] A spokesperson for Amnesty International said Ryan's decision marked a "significant step in the struggle against the death penalty" and urged governors in U.S. states still implementing the death penalty to follow suit.[100]

Neither Ryan's distinctions between opposition to the punishment and a more limited critique of the manner of its administration, nor his lack of compassion for the beneficiaries of his clemency, was of much solace to the victims' families. Cathy Drobney, whose daughter Bridget was murdered in 1985 by one of the people granted clemency, said of Governor Ryan, "He has killed them [the victims of those who had their sentences commuted] all over again."[101] John Woodhouse's wife, Kathy Ann, was raped and murdered in 1992; when he learned of Ryan's decision, Woodhouse complained that the death penalty debate in Illinois had become very one-sided because it focused on offenders rather than the victims and the harm done to their families. "The problem is the system, not the sentences," said Woodhouse. "If it's true—and it seems to be true—that the system is jailing and executing innocent people, well, fix the system. They had years and years to fix the flaws in the system. But don't destroy the sentences. Don't let murderers off the hook. This makes a mockery of my wife's life."[102]

Others were bitter. Seeing in Ryan's clemency an injury to themselves, they questioned his motivations. Sam Evans, whose sister and her children were murdered, complained, "He's seen to it that us and all the other families waiting will never have that final closure. . . . We've been robbed of our justice. He cannot state that there is any error whatsoever in our specific case. It was just wrong. There's no other way of putting it." Helen Rajca, whose two brothers were stabbed and shot to death in 1978, said, "I just think it's a political tactic. It's not right what he did. He's got too many things following him. This is just to blindside everyone from what he's done."[103] Or, as a newspaper article reviewing Ryan's term as governor put it, referring to the federal corruption probe that swirled around him and later resulted in his indictment for bribery and corruption, "Ryan is leaving office under such a cloud that his motives for commuting the sentences of all Death Row inmates will be debated for years to come. Was it rooted in personal conviction or merely an attempt to add at least a little varnish to a badly marred legacy?"[104]

Randy Odle, who lost five family members to a murder in 1985 committed by his cousin, said he might have been able to accept Ryan's decision if the governor had proceeded on a case-by-case basis. "There was never any question about Thomas Odle's guilt. He bragged about killing our family. He admitted it when the police arrived and he bragged about it in jail. This decision mocks our judicial system, and tells the jurors they did not do their jobs."[105]

Such criticism was not confined to the victim community.[106] In an editorial, the *Chicago Sun-Times* said that the governor reacted to the disturbing reality of wrongful conviction in Illinois with what it called "wrongful leniency." The newspaper criticized him for not issuing clemencies on a case-by-case basis. "We must bear in mind that there are also guilty people on Death Row—the majority. And it is not justice if their punishments are set aside because of the innocence of others or flaws in the system unrelated to their cases."[107] The Cook County state's attorney urged the legislature to limit the governor's clemency power,[108] and the attorney general and many state's attorneys filed suit alleging that Ryan did not have the authority to "grant clemency to 34 death row inmates who never sought to have their sentences reduced to life or for prisoners whose death sentences had been thrown out and who were awaiting resentencing."[109]

State Senator William Haine, who had helped convict two of those Ryan freed from death row during his tenure as a state's attorney, provided one of the most extensive critiques. He called Ryan's decision "a great wrong (and) . . . an extraordinary and . . . breathtaking act of arrogance." Advancing his own theory of clemency, Haine argued that it was meant to be used "sparingly to prevent clear miscarriages of justice" and "for an occasional act of mercy."[110] His analysis pointed in two somewhat different directions, one having to do with the place of clemency in a democratic political system, the other with its impact on the rule of law.

With regard to the first, "George Ryan," he said, "has severed the bond of trust between those who hold great power on behalf of the people and the people themselves."[111] Like Haine, other commentators also called Ryan's act antidemocratic. "Illinois Gov. George Ryan's commutation of the death sentences of all 167 inmates in Illinois prisons," columnist George Will wrote, "is another golden moment for liberals that underscores how many of their successes are tarnished by being explicitly, even exuberantly, anti-democratic." Will compared Ryan's act to the Supreme Court's abortion decision, "a judicial fiat that overturned the evolving consensus on abortion policy set by 50 state legislatures." Ryan's clemency decision will be remembered, Will continued, for its "disregard of democratic values" and "cavalier laceration of the unhealable wounds of those who mourn the victims of the killers the state of Illinois condemned."[112]

As to the rule of law, Senator Haine observed that Ryan "profoundly insulted his subordinates in the system—the state's attorneys, the police officers, the jurors and judges—with his pen and his reckless language. . . . [H]e may have irreparably injured the law itself. . . . It's not in the tradition of Abraham Lincoln, who believed in a government of law, not of men." Haine was angered that Ryan used his gubernatorial power to circumvent the state's legal system. "Even those who are opposed to the death penalty as an option must stand shocked at the use of raw power to cut down the law itself, the Constitution, to get at the end they desire—a state without a death penalty. . . . If they cheer him at Northwestern Law School (where Ryan announced his clemency decision), they are cheering the raw exercise of power against the law itself."

While the governor has "unfettered discretion," Haine continued,

> The bond between the governor and the citizens is that these great powers are to be used with constraint consistent with the

> law. George Ryan has, by his conduct, breached that ethic, which is as old as the Republic itself. . . . Every citizen should see this as an abuse of power. This was not intended by the framers of our Constitution. . . . I can't think of any analogy to compare it to other than the Civil War, when senators and military officers abandoned their oaths and took up arms against the United States. In the history of the Republic, I can't compare it to anything else, an act of this nature, where you simply take the position that the law doesn't mean anything.[113]

In this flood of criticism, two recurrent themes stand out: Ryan's personal arrogance, and the antidemocratic quality of his actions—an almost illegal usurpation of power. Perhaps such assertions are to be expected from those who so strongly disagree with Ryan's action, but what is striking about these criticisms is how at odds they are with the tone and content of Ryan's explanation for his decision. As we will see in chapter 5, that explanation is one marked by a language of humility and an effort to justify his action in terms of democratic responsibility.

In the chapters that follow, I move from Ryan's clemency to examine larger questions of sovereignty and state killing, clemency and constitutional democracy. I try to situate his decision in history, jurisprudence, and the philosophical debate surrounding clemency, showing the roots of today's trial of mercy. I argue that clemency in capital cases is in decline as political leaders respond to forces—for instance, victims rights and retributivism—that are increasingly powerful in American political culture. These forces reject mercy and compassion as legitimate responses to criminals. Thus even governors who grant clemency (such as George Ryan) do so in as unmerciful way as possible. I regret this trend and argue for recoupling clemency and mercy. Yet I recognize that there is something deeply mysterious and risky about mercy and its exercise. Learning to live comfortably with mystery and risk is perhaps the most important opportunity that today's trial of mercy offers.

In chapter 2 I look first at the history of gubernatorial clemency in capital cases in the twentieth century. Here I revisit the theme of clemency's recent decline and of the rejection of mercy that this decline reflects. This chapter provides background for Ryan's act, presenting three case studies of the use of clemency in capital cases. It examines the motivations of the governors granting clemency, the controversies surrounding their actions, and the way those controversies speak to contemporary concerns about clemency's lawlessness and compatibility with constitutional democracy.

Chapter 3 takes up Haine's critique of Ryan, "the raw exercise of power against the law itself." It explores the legal status of clemency in the United States for what it illustrates about the nature and limits of law. I see in the history of law's treatment of clemency an anxiety generated by its recognition of this power as necessarily beyond the reach of legal rules. As territorial boundaries erode in their distinctiveness, or become more permeable under the pressure of globalization, the temptation to seek other kinds of demarcation, what might be called "conceptual borders," intensifies.[114] Conceptual borders like those marked by adherence to the rule of law, mark a cultural and political geography, and are used in ongoing efforts to separate "self " from "other," "our nation" from "theirs."[115] Such borders, as law professor Margaret Montoya argues, are today particularly important as "an epistemic space for the exploration of cultural production."[116] More than ever they require critical examination.

Turning to mercy and executive clemency and their treatment in and by law provides one arena for such an effort, because, as I argue in chapter 3, here we see law authorizing a kind of lawlessness, or acknowledging the limits of the ability of rules to tell officials how, when, and why they may exercise the power accorded to them. In the jurisprudence of clemency we see law constructing and policing its own boundaries, boundaries within which, on its own account, prerogative power cannot be contained. In this jurisprudence we find law's borderland and, as in all borderlands, uncertainty and anxiety as well as possibility and opportunity.[117]

I develop this argument through an examination of cases from 1833, the year the first clemency case reached the U.S. Supreme Court, to the present, legal challenges brought after Ryan's decision. In addition, I discuss the theories of philosophers Georgio Agabem and Jacques Derrida as they illuminate clemency jurisprudence. The cases and theory suggest that clemency may contain in itself something—namely mercy—that is beyond the complete discipline or domestication of law, something essentially lawless. It is this lawlessness that law both authorizes and finds troubling.

Chapter 4 moves from history and jurisprudence to consider the recent rejection of rehabilitation as a governing theory of punishment and its consequences for a "redemptive" view of clemency. In so doing, it discusses some of the most important philosophical critiques of a mercy-based conception of clemency. In these critiques, scholars have responded to the mysteries and risks of mercy, and to the anxiety generated by clemency's ambivalent legal status, by offering what they see as a set of stabilizing prescriptions, philosophies, and guidelines to govern mercy and clemency. Taking off from Justice Rehnquist's idea that clemency should be used to remedy "miscarriages of justice," they have elaborated a retributive theory of clemency or, perhaps more accurately, tried to harmonize clemency with a retributive theory of punishment. Chapter 4 considers both the appeal and dangers of a retributive theory of clemency as well as efforts to respond to retributivism by seeking to rehabilitate mercy. I argue that law requires mercy of the kind that clemency can provide, that the dangers of a mercy gone bad are dangers that cannot be eliminated without driving mercy itself from the system of state killing.

Chapter 5 returns to Governor Ryan, taking a close look at what he said to justify his clemency and treating his rhetoric as an important event in the trial of mercy that his act precipitated. In this chapter I show how Ryan's decision was situated in an increasingly victim-centered political and legal environment as well as how it invokes and depends on retributivism. He tried to express a commitment to the interests of the victimized, and yet he embraced a retributive theory of clemency. In the first he sought to authenticate his act by identifying himself as a suffering subject, able in his suffering to know the pain that families of murder victims suffer at the hands of criminals and that they would suffer at his hands. In the second he painted himself as a reluctant actor, seeking to ensure that justice is done in a failing justice system and a political system in paralysis. This chapter argues that the embrace of victims and the logic of retributivism cannot coexist, and that Ryan's deployment of these contradictory justifications left little room for genuine compassion.

I end chapter 5 by arguing that, despite his inability to reconcile irreconcilable forces, Ryan's act was well within the bounds of contemporary understandings of clemency. In his preemptive strike against capital punishment, Ryan did the right thing. Yet far from disrupting the essential rhythms of American politics, in its emphasis on suffering and victimization, in its embrace of retributive principles, and in its demonstration of "energy in the executive," it gave new voice to ongoing trends in our political and cultural lives. If Ryan's was a form of clemency without compassion, it responded to the temper of our times even as it reverberated through our national debate about capital punishment. It was controversial because it seemed to be a lawless and arrogant act. I argue that if Ryan's use of clemency was an "injury to law itself," it was an injury that the law authorizes and requires, a form of lawful lawlessness without which the law would indeed by rendered meaningless.

In the concluding chapter I suggest that George Ryan's action reveals the precarious state in which clemency currently exists. It put mercy on trial and highlighted the trials of mercy in the killing state. Here I note that clemency has always needed a vigorous defense in the United States, and I discuss the kind of arguments that governors typically have used to defend it. I explore the fears that clemency and mercy evoke in a society dedicated to the rule of law and equal treatment under the law, and the way contemporary pardon tales speak to those fears. I argue that mercy and clemency always involve risks. Taking these risks means acknowledging the limits of law and justice, and of their ability to guarantee genuine moral deliberation rather than arbitrariness, fairness rather than discrimination.

CHAPTER 2

Capital Clemency in the Twentieth Century

PUTTING ILLINOIS IN CONTEXT

The danger is not, that in republics the victims of the law will too often escape punishment by a pardon; but that the power will not be sufficiently exerted in cases where public feeling accompanies the prosecution and assigns the ultimate doom to persons.

—*Joseph Story*

TODAY CAPITAL CLEMENCY is an endangered species. Yet this is not the situation with regard to other kinds of cases. To look first at what presidents have been doing, we see that Bill Clinton pardoned and/or commuted more than four hundred sentences during his two terms. Although this number is substantially lower than the number of clemencies issued by President Carter during his single four-year term (534), it is about the same as the number issued over two terms by President Reagan.[1] And in the states, the pattern seems uneven at best, with the number of clemencies rising in some places and falling in others. Thus, since 1996 Arkansas governor Mike Huckabee has granted 669 clemencies, 30 percent more than the previous three governors combined.[2] In contrast, Massachusetts has experienced a dramatic decline in the use of gubernatorial clemency.[3]

Whatever the pattern, clemency often has proven to be controversial and politically sensitive at both the federal and state levels. Typical was President Clinton's last-minute pardon of fugitive billionaire Marc Rich, whose ex-wife was one of Clinton's friends and campaign contributors. The Rich pardon ignited a firestorm of allegations and investigations. In response to charges of corruption and influence peddling, Clinton defended himself by saying, "I made the decision to pardon Marc Rich based on what I thought was the right thing to do. Any suggestion that improper factors including fund-raising for the [Democratic National Committee] or my library had anything to do with the decision are absolutely false."[4] Others explained his actions in ways that only elevated concerns about the integrity and abuse of clemency power. "The truth—as anyone who glances back into the history of the first Bush administration can quickly learn—is that Clinton hasn't done anything that his predecessor didn't do first and, in some cases, worse."[5]

Scandals surrounding gubernatorial grants of clemency occur with great frequency and are too numerous to catalog. However, one of the most notorious occurred during the administration of Governor Ray Blanton of Tennessee. Blanton led Tennessee from 1975 until 1979 and in many respects was an admirable chief executive. In his final days in office he pardoned or commuted fifty-two sentences. Around this time, three of his aides were charged with selling paroles for money. The governor was not charged and insisted on continuing to issue pardons even after this scandal broke. The result was that the state legislature cut short his term as governor by moving up the inauguration of his successor. Ultimately Blanton was convicted of extortion and conspiracy for selling a liquor license to a friend while in office. And as newspaper reporter Steve Neal puts it, "Blanton is still viewed with contempt and scorn by residents of Tennessee for his abuses of the criminal justice system."[6]

As deep as are the suspicions and controversies that often surround clemency, when that power is used to spare the lives of murderers, suspicions deepen and controversy becomes even more intense. In capital cases, public debate focuses less on issues of corruption and more on the wisdom of capital punishment itself. Thus it should not be surprising that politicians approach the question of capital clemency with kid gloves. The result has been that as the number of death sentences and executions increased in the last decade or so, the number of clemency grants decreased (see appendix B).[7] Because of the desire of state actors to deploy traditional symbols of state sovereignty to compensate for the loss of state power associated with globalization and governmentality, because of the rejection of rehabilitative approaches to criminal sentencing, and of because the fact that no politician wants to be seen as soft on crime or compassionate toward murderers, capital clemency has come to be both one of the most dramatic, and least often used, sovereign prerogatives.[8]

During the 1990s, from one to eight death row inmates had their sentences commuted every year—out of approximately twenty to ninety executions.[9] This represents a radical shift from several decades ago, when governors granted clemency in 20 to 25 percent of the death penalty cases they reviewed.[10] In Florida, for example, one of the states most firmly in the "death belt," governors commuted 23 percent of death sentences between 1924 and 1966, yet no Florida death penalty sentences were commuted in the 1990s. Similarly in Texas, since 1972 there only have been two commutations.[11]

The rarity of capital clemency is not just a southern, death-belt phenomenon. Thus "since at least 1965, no Washington Governor has intervened to overturn a death sentence, and in only one instance was an execution postponed by a Governor's action."[12] From 1964 to 2003, the year of Governor Ryan's clemency, clemency was granted in only one Illinois capital case. And in Pennsylvania, another state with a large death row population, the last death penalty commutation took place in the early 1960s.[13]

Rejecting appeals from the Pope, Mother Teresa, televangelist Pat Robertson, former prosecutors, and even judges and jurors in death cases, governors reserve their clemency power for "unusual" cases in which someone clearly has been unfairly convicted.[14] While during the 1950s and 1960s about 50 percent of the public supported the death penalty, today polls show the public overwhelmingly approves of it.[15] As Richard Dieter, executive director of the Death Penalty Information Center, observes, capital punishment is "the answer to the public's fear of crime, so (clemency) just goes against the grain."[16] Even as crime rates fell during the 1990s, fear of crime persisted, and, in this climate, mercy fell into disfavor, compassion went out of style.[17]

Yet in the United States this attitude toward clemency has not always been prevalent. During the early to mid-twentieth century, many governors took a broad view of their clemency power. Terry Sanford, former governor of North Carolina, provides one example of such a view.

> The courts of our state and nation exercise in the name of the people the powers of administration of justice. . . . The Executive is charged with the exercise in the name of the people of an . . . important attitude of a healthy society—that of mercy beyond the strict framework of the law. The use of executive clemency is not a criticism of the courts, either express or implied. I have no criticism of any court or any judge. Executive clemency does not involve the changing of any judicial determination. It does not eliminate punishment; it does consider rehabilitation. To decide when and where such mercy should be extended is a decision which must be made by the Executive. It cannot be delegated even in part to anyone else, and thus the decision is a lonely one. It falls to the Governor to blend mercy with justice, as best he can, involving human as well as legal considerations, in the light of all circumstances after the passage of time, but before justice is allowed to overrun mercy in the name of the power of the state. I fully realize that reasonable men hold strong feelings on both sides of every case where executive clemency is indicated. I accepted the responsibility of being Governor, however, and I will not shy away from the responsibility of exercising the power of executive clemency.[18]

Long before George Ryan, other governors had issued mass commutations (although none of Ryan's scale) or used their clemency powers to impose moratoriums in capital cases. Like Ryan they often acted against prevailing public sentiment in favor of capital punishment, but the rationale for most of those commutations was quite different from Ryan's: a principled, moral opposition to the death penalty. Thus Lee Cruce, Oklahoma governor from 1911 to 1915, commuted twenty-two death sentences to life in prison, boldly telling the state legislature, "The ground I take is that the infliction of the death penalty by the state is wrong in morals and is destructive of the highest and noblest ideals in government."[19] Speaking in the lofty terms of a confident sovereignty, Cruce asserted his right to spare lives on the grounds of his own principled disagreement with the state's policy.[20]

As he cleared Arkansas's death row with commutations at the end of his term in 1970, Governor Winthrop Rockefeller, like Governors Sanford and Cruce, used the rhetoric of high moralism to explain his grant of clemency: "I yearn to see other chief executives throughout the nation follow suit, so that as a people we may hasten the elimination of barbarism as a tool of American justice."[21] In 1986 Governor Toney Anaya of New Mexico, with just weeks left in office, commuted the death sentences of all five condemned men in his state. He called capital punishment "a false god that too many worship."[22] At the time of his commutation he had a hopeful vision: "I am dropping a pebble into a pond that will cause a ripple which I pray will be joined in other ponds across this great country, ripples that, coming together, will cause a rising tide."[23]

In the remainder of this chapter I examine in greater depth the uses of capital clemency by Governors Cruce, Rockefeller, and Anaya.[24] The stories of what they did, and why they did it, illuminate the traditions and historical context of executive clemency that framed George Ryan's actions. They also point to some of the conundrums intrinsic to those traditions and provide insight into how politics and personal morality play out when lives are on the line. Each highlights the trials of mercy in the killing state.

Lee Cruce: Governor of Oklahoma 1911–1915

When Lee Cruce became Oklahoma's second governor in 1911, no one expected this slight, unassuming, bookish man to take unprecedented action against the death penalty. Although Cruce had a fair amount of abolitionist company among other Progressive Era governors, he would act very differently than even his most ardently anti–death penalty colleagues. Other governors issued liberal reprieves while trying to convince the voters of their respective states to abolish capital punishment by referendum, but no one else so bluntly took on a public eager for executions. Others put aside their personal opposition to capital punishment and oversaw executions. Yet Cruce raised the stakes on gubernatorial action by refusing to allow any executions during his term and changing every sentence of death that came before him to a sentence of life without parole.

Born July 8, 1863, in Marion, Kentucky, Cruce was the fifth of six boys. His father died when Cruce was very young, leaving him and his brothers to run the family farm. From his modest childhood in a single-parent household in rural Kentucky to his achievements as prominent lawyer, politician, and businessman in neighboring Oklahoma, Cruce built a life full of noteworthy achievements. Quick-witted and passionate, though unassumingly so, he owed his educational achievement at least in part to the ill health he suffered through childhood and into young adulthood. Often housebound, he was an avid reader, bright and extremely self-disciplined in his studies. When his health later forced him to leave a pre-law program after one year at Vanderbilt University, he taught himself enough from reading books and working in his brother's law office to pass the Kentucky Bar in 1888. In 1891 he made junior partner in his brother's law firm and moved to the town of Ardmore in what was then known as Indian Territory.

After eight years practicing law in Ardmore, Cruce jumped into local politics as an alderman candidate and won narrowly. He intended to leave his law practice only temporarily, but when his term as alderman ended in 1901, he changed his mind and took a new job as a cashier at the recently opened Ardmore National Bank. Promoted just two years later to president of the bank, Cruce became active in the development and governance of the Oklahoma business sector, taking on the responsibilities of president of the Ardmore Commercial Club.

Cruce used this position as a business leader to campaign for Oklahoma statehood. He was also active in national politics during this period, serving as treasurer of the Oklahoma Territorial Democratic Committee during the 1904 presidential campaign. A popular figure in the territory, Cruce very nearly became the state's first governor, but lost narrowly in 1907. He ran again in 1911 and won. Despite his initial popularity, Cruce's style of governance and his stance on several key issues, not the least of which was capital punishment, earned him more than a few unhappy constituents and political foes. Like his abolitionist, clemency-granting peers who would follow later in the century, Cruce's term of office was stormy, marked by many legislative battles and ideological controversies.

The governor's difficulties did not, however, translate into political timidity when it came to pushing a legislative agenda. Perhaps because of his mild manner, or his slight appearance, state politicians underestimated Cruce when he took office in 1911. Much to the surprise and chagrin of many, his administration became well known for its unrelentingly moralistic agenda and its powerful political will in the face of whatever opposition stood in its way.[25] Reflected in nearly every one of his major policy stances was the belief that, "The chief concern of government is to bring about better moral, social, and educational conditions among the people."[26] This belief, born of his own religious convictions, shaped his legislative efforts on gambling, prohibition, education, and of course the death penalty. "The old order of 'an eye for an eye, and a tooth for a tooth,' as commonly interpreted, is not in harmony with modern civilization," Cruce insisted. "The infliction of the death penalty by the State is wrong on morals, and is destructive of the highest and noblest ideals of government."[27]

An ardent opponent of capital punishment on both philosophical and practical grounds, Cruce approached the question of executions in a politically risky fashion. He began commuting death sentences shortly after taking office, and continued to do so throughout his four years as governor. Moreover, acting unilaterally as governor, utterly against popular opinion, he unapologetically decried capital punishment, at great cost to his political career.

Though Cruce's opposition to capital punishment predated his election as governor, he did not come to office with a sure plan for what he would do with clemency requests. A few weeks after Cruce took office, officials in Tulsa carried out the sole execution of his term without consulting the governor. Lawyers for the executed black male defendant (he remained unnamed in the press; Oklahoma papers referred to him only as "the Negro")[28] failed to request clemency from the governor's office, and the execution was carried out without thought of mercy. Only when Oklahoma's next condemned man, John Henry Prather, stood before the hangman's noose the following summer did Cruce take his surprisingly bold stance against executions.

This time around, advocates for the defendant, including family members and Oklahoma judge J. T. Dickerson, successfully petitioned Cruce for clemency. "Talk about a battle with your conscience," Cruce later explained in an interview with the *Daily Oklahoman*, "that is when I had one. I don't think I slept a wink that night [before the Prather execution decision]. The question haunted me continually. I wanted to do the right thing, so I finally resolved all doubt in favor of the Fifth Commandment."[29]

July 28, 1911, the day of Prather's execution, saw a huge group gather to witness the hanging. As the *Daily Oklahoman* put it, "Prather had been shaved, bathed, and dressed for his journey into eternity . . . and a crowd of hundreds awaited the 'show.'"[30] But there would be no deadly "show" that day or any other during Cruce's governorship. The crowd was stunned when a dramatic, last-minute phone call from the governor's office brought the afternoon's "entertainment" to an abrupt halt. Prather would be moved to the state penitentiary, Governor Cruce decreed, where he would serve a life sentence without parole.

The dramatic spectacle of Prather's salvation generated enormous attention from the press and launched what would become a de facto moratorium. Cruce signed eight commutations his first two years in office, nearly doubling that number in the second half of his term with fourteen commutations between 1913 and 1915. He approved each of the petitions for clemency as it came along, without regard to the circumstances of the particular crime, the fairness of the trial, or the race of either criminal or victim.

Yet the issue of race was an important part of his opposition to capital punishment. Shortly after passing the Oklahoma bar exam, Cruce married a Chickasaw Indian woman and became a tribal citizen. It is a measure of his many complexities and somewhat puzzling self-contradictions that, despite a loving relationship with his wife (she passed away in 1903) and their daughter, Cruce campaigned for governor as the "white man's hope," berating his Republican opponent for opposing Jim Crow laws.[31]

This "white man's hope" was the same man who would be roundly criticized by citizens and public officials for his commentaries on racial disparities in capital sentencing and for granting clemencies equally to black men and white. After his commutation of Prather, a black man, Cruce wrote a letter to the Oklahoma County sheriff, pointedly raising the issue of racism. "If Prather had been a white boy," Cruce insisted, "I would have received thousands of letters asking mercy for him. As it is, he's never had an opportunity to make a man of himself. My conscience will not allow him to be hanged."[32]

The governor's argument did little to persuade the many Oklahomans who did not worry about executing black men and thought mercy a dangerous thing to grant black convicts. Objections to Cruce's use of clemency invariably included racist arguments. One eastern Oklahoma paper, simultaneously criticizing Cruce's moratorium while instilling fear in its white readership, wrote that "There is a large Negro population in this section of the state and a great many people entertain the conviction that the firm belief among the Negroes is that no Negro will be hanged so long as Cruce is governor. This is certain to result in a series of outrages which will result in a race riot."[33]

It was not the white readers who ought to have feared for their lives. As Cruce had made it clear that his would be a merciful administration, some particularly indignant white Oklahomans preferred to enact their own vengeance upon presumably guilty parties. During Cruce's term, mobs lynched more men (fifteen in all) than they did during the tenure of any other governor in the history of the territory.[34] While lynching in Oklahoma already outpaced that in all other states,[35] lynching, not race riots, became even more prevalent in the years Cruce spent in office.

Two of these lynchings took place immediately following the dramatic phone call from the governor's office that spared Prather's life. Accused men in the towns of Purcell and Durant were hanged by angry mobs that same night. Popular justification for the bloody violence made the pages of Oklahoma's papers, "If Cruce could have pity on a cold blooded killer like Prather, how could Oklahoma citizens be sure any other criminal would be properly punished?"[36] Cruce would have to confront arguments linking abolition to lynch-mob violence every time he spoke about the death penalty, but confront them he did, and with a painstakingly detailed defense of his opposition to state killing.

One such defense was presented on January 8, 1913, when Governor Cruce went before the state legislature and delivered a ten-thousand-word State of the State address. Capital punishment was featured at the start of the speech. At once broadly philosophical and defensive, Cruce laid out his moral case against the death penalty while refuting the pragmatic arguments leveled at the governor's office in support of executions. "The argument made in favor of capital punishment, that it prevents mob violence, is entirely fallacious," Cruce insisted, going on to cite local and national crime statistics. Having granted eight commutations in the previous two years, he reasoned, "It would seem that if there is potency in the argument that commutations lead to increased murders, [there would be] a regular saturnalia of crime in Oklahoma." Yet, as he was quick to point out, the homicide rate had actually fallen, albeit slightly, since he had taken office. Furthermore, the seven states in the United States then without capital punishment had no lynchings at all in 1911, while five of the ones *with* the death penalty had a combined total of twenty-nine lynchings that same year. "When a state sets the example of placing so cheap an estimate upon human life," Cruce concluded, "it is little wonder that the public adopts the same view of it."[37]

Cruce cited the examples of other states not only to make a point about deterrence, but also to set a standard for what he saw as higher degrees of civilization and sophistication. "The states of the Union in which capital punishment has been abolished are in the forefront of all activities of life and government that mean a better citizenship and a higher civilization," he argued. "Some of the best schools in the nation are located in their midst. A very low rate of illiteracy exists, and the noblest product of advanced civilization is to be found."[38]

On a more philosophical level, Cruce also used the speech to make a point about evolving standards of humane punishment and Christian behavior:

> The world has advanced immeasurably during the four thousand years intervening since the Code of Moses was given to the Jews. Of the multitude of offenses defined under his law as punishable by the infliction of the death penalty, in Oklahoma today only one of these crimes is visited with such punishment—the crime of murder. . . . The fact that we have abolished capital punishment for a number of offenses that were then considered sufficient to invoke the death penalty is very decided proof that civilization has advanced far beyond the period of development it had attained at the time these laws were originally promulgated.[39]

Cruce boldly drew a parallel between executions and slavery to highlight people's capacity to redefine morality. He encouraged his listeners to consider how a practice like slavery, so seemingly commonplace in certain contexts, can, in fact, be immoral and worthy of abolition as society evolves. "Capital punishment, like human slavery, has been practiced at one time or another by almost every government in the history of the world up until comparatively few years ago," Cruce pointed out. "In the years before the Civil War, every preacher and most everyone else for that matter in the south believed that human slavery was the right and proper thing and justified by divine law." He continued, "About all the advocates of capital punishment base their position upon is the 'eye for an eye, and a tooth for a tooth' doctrine, but there are a hundred places in the bible justifying human slavery to where there is one supporting capital punishment."[40]

In other contexts, Cruce, foreshadowing an argument that would emerge as crucial in the death penalty debate half a century later, complained about the arbitrariness of sentencing in Oklahoma, pointing out that the twenty-two men whose lives he spared were just a fraction of the eight hundred non–death row inmates also incarcerated for homicide statewide. Making this point about arbitrariness in one newspaper interview, Cruce declared, "The death penalty in murder cases is an exception rather than the rule."[41] Again foreshadowing "new abolitionist" arguments, Cruce warned of the fallibility of the criminal justice system. "Men," he said, "have been convicted in this state and sentenced to the gallows upon purely circumstantial evidence. . . . However, if it can be conceded that juries and courts are infallible in finding guilt, it does not change the situation in the least. . . . the infliction of the death penalty by the state is wrong in morals."[42]

Ironically, in spite of his vigorous use of the clemency power, Cruce was actually *not* a great champion of executive privilege. Quite the opposite, he actively shunned concentration of power in the governor's office. When a bill to establish the state's first Supreme Court Commission would have charged the governor with appointing the commissioners, Cruce lobbied against it, favoring appointments made by the justices of the Supreme Court instead. According to one journalist's account, "The power of making political appointments, long regarded as the method of paying debts and building political machines for self advancement, and the pardoning power, two of the most highly appraised prerogatives of the governorship, were to [Cruce] the most troublesome and objectionable duties of the office."[43]

Curiously, while Cruce's moralism led him to grant commutations liberally in capital cases, it inhibited him from granting pardons or paroles in any other circumstance. He opposed state-sponsored killing, but once criminals were condemned to a term of years, Cruce was utterly unsympathetic to pleas for clemency. During four years in the governor's mansion, Cruce did not grant a single pardon, and he only signed parole orders for two life-term offenders.[44] In fact, he clashed very publicly with his lieutenant governor on several occasions over the question of whether he should use his clemency power in noncapital cases. While the governor believed in using stiff, credible sentencing for lawbreakers as a means of effectively enforcing morality in Oklahoma, his lieutenant governor, J. J. McAlester, took every opportunity when Cruce was out of the state to sign pardons for hundreds of convicted criminals. It became such a problem that Cruce, enraged by what he called the "wholesale pardoning sprees of the Lieutenant Governor," vowed in 1913 to never again leave the state during his tenure.[45]

In contrast to Winthrop Rockefeller, whose belief in the rehabilitation and reintegration of criminals into society whenever possible informed his thinking about the death penalty, Cruce took a hard line on all forms of noncapital punishment. As the *Daily Oklahoman* reflected, "It was, and still is, Cruce's view of handling capital offenders, that the ends of justice can best be served without coming in conflict with conscientious scruples, based upon divine law, by condemning a man to life imprisonment at hard labor."[46]

Despite his tough-on-crime posture, critics called Cruce's blanket use of capital clemency a "chicken hearted policy," and many people believed that Cruce's actions signaled the beginning of a "riot of crime and a reign of wholesale murder . . . and that human life was no longer safe in Oklahoma."[47] Yet after the Prather commutation, Cruce reported that he had "received thousands of letters praising the action. I am perfectly pleased with the result." Nevertheless, according to one Oklahoma paper, "Almost without exception the attitude of the state press has been condemnatory of this position of the governor."[48] Indeed, by one historian's count, only four of the state's fifty main newspapers endorsed abolition of capital punishment.[49] "It is not protection for the criminal that Oklahoma needs," insisted the editors of the *Hollis Post-Herald*, "but a more rigid enforcement of its laws and a swift and a sure punishment for their violation."[50] In the wake of one particularly controversial commutation, granted to a man named John Cotton, the *Muskogee Times-Democrat* published an editorial loudly condemning Cruce's actions:

> The action of Governor Cruce in commuting the sentence of the Negro, while deserving of condemnation from the standpoint of public policy and legal ethics, becomes reprehensible considering the reason advanced by the governor in justifying his action. In explaining to Judge DeGaffenried why he saw fit to commute the sentence of the brutal Negro who took the life of a white man in cold blood, Governor Cruce said that it looked to him as if authorities in Wagoner County were trying to put one over on him, and in his opinion they proposed to hang Cotton without giving him a chance to be heard in the Criminal Court of Appeals.[51]

In addition to negative editorial response, Cruce faced harsh criticism from the state's elected and appointed officials. They pointed especially to what seemed to be Cruce's arrogant disregard for the law. Thus Judge DeGaffenried, the circuit court appeals justice in Cotton's jurisdiction, wrote an open letter to Cruce, faulting him for not specifically considering the merits of the case. "You commuted this Negro's sentence without seeing a line of testimony and without consulting with any officer who knew anything about the case." DeGaffenried complained, issuing what would subsequently become a familiar indictment of gubernatorial clemency in capital cases, "Governor, your position is that you are higher than the law, and when the enforcement of the law comes in conflict with your conscientious scruples, you will not permit the law to be executed. . . . I am disgusted to know that the chief executive of our state, sworn to enforce the law, has so little regard for its enforcement."[52]

Other justices of the Oklahoma Circuit Court of Appeals also lambasted Cruce for his position on capital punishment. "We think that capital punishment as the penalty for murder is essential to the security of society," argued Judge Thomas H. Doyle, "and we have no sympathy with the sickly, sentimental humanitarianism which, in the exercise of a mawkish sympathy for a heartless, unfeeling, felonious assassin, forgets and wholly ignores the innocent murdered victim." Chief Justice Henry M. Furman cited Old Testament justifications for capital punishment, and argued that while commutations have a rightful place in the criminal justice system, Cruce had abused his clemency power, which ought to be reserved for extraordinary situations. "No governor has the right to substitute his own view for the law on capital punishment or any other question," Furman declared.[53]

Cruce answered his critics as best he could, with references to the teachings of Jesus Christ and to the constitutional rationale for executive clemency. "Just as the appellate courts may reverse the decision of lower courts," he reasoned, "I, as governor, am permitted by the Oklahoma Constitution to alter the punishment of any convicted criminal for any reason I consider appropriate." When ministers across the state began to preach from the pulpit against the governor's commutation policy, Cruce replied, "I am glad that my reading of the Bible and the religion I believe in, is not a bloodthirsty, life demanding one. I have never been able to understand why many ministers whose mission in life is to try to save human souls should insist that it is right to take human lives."[54]

Cruce's refusal to allow executions led to calls for impeachment and demands for his resignation, but the governor never budged from his position, not even years after the fact, knowing what the consequences had been for his political career. "I am today more confirmed than ever," he told the *Daily Oklahoman* in 1927, "in my opposition to this ancient and uncivilized form of human punishment." He continued, reiterating his long-held view, "The death penalty has absolutely no effect upon the criminally inclined, as statistics prove, and therefore is unreasonable and unnecessary."[55] His beliefs did not convince his constituents, who turned Cruce out of office after a single term in part because of his anti-death-penalty stance. Lee Cruce passed away in 1933, having never returned to elected politics.

Winthrop Rockefeller: Governor of Arkansas, 1966–1970

Almost sixty years after Cruce left office, on December 30, 1970, Winthrop Rockefeller stood before the Arkansas press and announced an unprecedented decision concerning capital punishment in his state. Governors in other states had previously led abolition efforts, declared moratoriums, and granted large numbers of pardons, reprieves, and commutations, yet no one had ever granted a wholesale commutation to his state's entire death row. Though a Republican from an extraordinarily privileged background, Rockefeller's unwavering anti-death-penalty stance, combined with his willingness to use his prerogative power to oppose capital punishment, put him in the company of the Progressive Era populists like Lee Cruce. However, while these men took great political risks in staking out their stands against capital punishment, none went as far as Rockefeller.

After four years of refusing to sign execution warrants while prodding an opposition-dominated legislature to abolish capital punishment in Arkansas, the outgoing governor decided to take the fate of all fifteen men on death row into his own hands. When he announced his clemency decision, he expressed the hope that others might take similar action in their states, and, though none of his contemporaries did so, Rockefeller's clemency set an important precedent for future acts of gubernatorial activism in New Mexico and Illinois.

Rockefeller's governorship, like the rest of his life, reflected both great ambition and independent thinking. Born May 1, 1912, in New York City, Rockefeller was the fifth child of Standard Oil founder, John D. Rockefeller. While he enjoyed the same material and educational privilege as his sister and brothers, his unusual career choices would earn him a reputation as the "black sheep" of his generation of Rockefellers. After graduating from the Loomis Academy in Windsor, Connecticut, Rockefeller spent three years at Yale University, but left in 1934 to work in the Texas oil fields as a roustabout and roughneck. He never returned to complete his degree. His professional path thereafter was somewhat erratic, eventually leading him to Arkansas in 1953 where he started his own cattle farm on 927 acres of land one hour south of Little Rock.

Rockefeller became active in Arkansas politics only gradually. Two years after relocating to Little Rock, he was appointed to the Industrial Development Commission by then governor Orval Faubus. During his years on the commission, he became interested in redressing the lopsided party politics of his adopted state. A Republican in heavily Democratic Arkansas, Rockefeller soon was playing a leading role in efforts to boost Republican fortunes. Eventually those efforts led him to run for governor. In 1964 he lost, but in 1966 he ran again, this time successfully. Taking office in January 1967, he was the first Republican governor in Arkansas in nearly a century.

Rockefeller began his term with high hopes for changing the face of state government. Despite overwhelming Democratic opposition in the state legislature, he pushed a broad reform agenda. Among his proposals were sweeping prison reform as well as abolition of the death penalty. As to the former, he felt that prisons ought to serve as reformatories in the literal sense of the word, and he harbored a belief in the capacity of criminals to feel genuine remorse and to seek redemption and reformation if given the opportunity and the means. He soon created a new Department of Corrections to transform the state's prison system into a respectable and professional enterprise.

Compared to Cruce, Rockefeller's views about capital punishment were more rooted in an overall commitment to reforming his state's system of punishment. Despite the fact that Rockefeller took office during a time when abolitionist activity in the United States seemed to be growing, he made greater headway with his prison reforms than with his efforts to end the death penalty. Thus while the new Department of Corrections got off to a good start, a 1969 death penalty abolition bill was soundly defeated in the General Assembly.[56]

Rockefeller had succeeded a governor who presided over sixteen executions. A little over one year into his own first term, it appeared that the U.S. Supreme Court was close to ruling on the constitutionality of capital punishment. As a result he held off on issuing pardons and commutations. He later admitted that he had "been hoping that the Supreme Court would take a position that would clarify things."[57] And Rockefeller was not alone in harboring this hope or in acting to stop executions while he waited for the Court to act.[58] Governors of five states announced moratoria the same year he did and many more states observed "informal moratoria."[59]

Early in his term Rockefeller took the first of his sweeping actions against executions, ordering the state's electric chair dismantled and declaring a formal moratorium. In this way, Rockefeller sought relief from the life-or-death decisions that came with his office. "What earthly mortal has the omnipotence to say who among us shall live and who shall die?" he would later inquire. "I do not."[60]

Though they retained overwhelming control of the legislature all four years Rockefeller spent in the governor's mansion,[61] Democrats failed to unseat him when he came up for reelection in 1968. Two years later, however, they nominated one of the south's "New Democrats," Dale Bumpers. Much to Rockefeller's surprise, Bumpers won by a wide margin, bringing an abrupt end to four years of Rockefeller's maverick policies and reform agenda.

Unlike the trigger-happy successor Toney Anaya would face sixteen years later in New Mexico, Bumpers's position regarding the death penalty was nuanced. He opposed the death penalty save for "particularly heinous" criminals such as mass murderers and terrorists. He expressed interest in extending the moratorium and had doubts about the deterrent effects of capital punishment. Still he did not support its outright abolition. Not knowing whether Bumpers's misgivings about the death penalty were strong enough to prevent a resumption of executions, pleas for decisive clemency action began to reach the lame-duck governor's desk almost immediately following the November election. One such letter came from Reverend J. F. Cooley, civil rights leader, death penalty abolitionist, and longtime counselor to inmates awaiting execution in Arkansas. "After the election on November 3," Cooley wrote the governor, "the inmates on death row became (and still are) greatly disturbed. They feel their lives are finished with your going out of office."[62] With Rockefeller's departure from office imminent, he no longer could wait for the federal judiciary to determine the fate of those condemned to death in his state.

Three days before Christmas 1970, Governor Rockefeller called together a small group of aides and prominent death penalty opponents to help him decide how to proceed. Included in the discussion were George W. Howard Jr. and John W. Walker, lawyers representing several of the condemned men, and Anthony Amsterdam, constitutional lawyer and lead counsel on a pending Supreme Court case challenging the constitutionality of capital punishment.[63] John Himmelstein of the NAACP Legal Defense Fund also spent time at the governor's mansion making a case for clemency. Like the clemency hearings in Illinois held prior to Ryan's decision, these consultations drew attention from the media, heightening public anticipation about whether Rockefeller would take action or leave death row untouched. The press and the public expected that the governor would commute at least a few death sentences. Nevertheless, Rockefeller's advisors advocated blanket clemency.[64]

The day after his highly publicized meeting with death penalty opponents and aides, Rockefeller appointed a committee of five individuals to make official recommendations. Explaining that he wished to "keep the press off their backs," Rockefeller kept the identities of these five men secret, revealing only that the committee included "experts in psychology, law, and penology," not all of whom resided in Arkansas.[65] Some death penalty opponents thought it more politically expeditious for Rockefeller to grant clemency only in select, urgent cases. By doing so he would avoid the political repercussions bound to accompany any blanket action, while safely, they thought, leaving the rest to the courts because of the "favorable outlook for ending the death penalty."[66]

Media speculation focused on the impact Rockefeller's stand against the death penalty might have on future governors. Ernest Dumas, who covered the governor's office for the *Arkansas Gazette*, wrote, "Even if the courts do not stop executions, Mr. Rockefeller's successors are not likely to order their deaths. . . . It is hard to imagine succeeding governors reinstating a practice shunned so purposefully by their predecessors."[67] But Rockefeller was not so confident, and two weeks before leaving office, the governor informed the press that he had something important to announce to the people of Arkansas.

Flanked by several aides and the commissioner of correction, Robert Sarver, Rockefeller arrived half an hour late for an afternoon press conference he had called to announce his decision. Resolved to grant commutations to all fifteen men on death row, an unabashedly emotional Rockefeller said, "I cannot and will not turn my back on life-long Christian teachings and beliefs, merely to let history run out its course on a fallible and failing theory of criminal justice."[68] Anticipating outrage from death penalty supporters because of his sweeping use of executive power, the outgoing governor explained, "The law grants me authority to set aside the death penalty. . . . failing to take this action while it is within my power, I could not live with myself."[69]

In contrast to what would happen in Illinois thirty years later, Rockefeller did not focus on the reliability of convictions in capital cases, even though during his term the Arkansas Supreme Court had overturned the convictions of almost a third of those on the state's death row.[70] While local print media took note of this development, Rockefeller never publicly addressed the dilemma inherent in executing inmates under a death penalty system afflicted with so many erroneous convictions. He did, however, focus on the issue of racial disparity.

Eleven of the fifteen prisoners awaiting execution in Arkansas were black—six of those men having been convicted of raping white women. Asked in the days before his announcement if he believed discrimination influenced death sentences in his state, Rockefeller said, "I'm not going to philosophize on that. It's a fact." Yet, when he eventually granted clemency, he insisted he did so simply because he believed capital punishment to be morally reprehensible. "The records, individually or collectively, of the 15 condemned prisoners bear no relevance to my decision," Rockefeller explained. "It is purely personal and philosophical. . . . Justice is not served by . . . capital punishment."[71]

Responding to Rockefeller's decision to empty death row, many Arkansas papers expressed one degree of support or another. The *Arkansas Gazette* ran several editorials leading up to and following the commutations, speaking favorably of the governor's ability to make a "fair and judicious determination," and lauding him for his "act of conscience."[72] Like the *Gazette*, the *Jacksonville Daily News* was also supportive. "Putting a person to death is an act of revenge and not justice. . . . Executions by a government do nothing but lower the integrity of that government and it puts the government on the same moral level as those who are executed."[73] And public response directly to the governor's office was much more in support than against Rockefeller's actions, by a ratio of nearly five to one (324 telegrams of support, 73 objections).[74]

Curiously, media coverage of Rockefeller's clemency took no note of the abolitionist battles of Progressive Era governors like Lee Cruce or of their liberal use of the executive clemency privilege in Oklahoma and elsewhere. The *Arkansas Gazette* made cursory mention of the decisions of Governor Robert Holmes (Oregon, 1957–59) and Governor Endicott Peabody (Massachusetts, 1963–65) to commute death sentences case by case,[75] but Cruce's crusading abolitionism and maverick commutation policies went unmentioned by state papers, and even by the *New York Times*. Unlike coverage of George Ryan's commutations, which generally included some reference to related gubernatorial clemency controversies, the *Times* simply reported that Rockefeller's action was "believed to be the first time that any governor had reduced the sentences of all condemned men in the state at one time."[76] While it was true that Rockefeller's wholesale commutation was unprecedented in its scope and timing, the controversies raised over the legality or extra-legality of his move, his injection of personal moral beliefs into public office, and his compassion for prisoners mirrored the issues raised about Lee Cruce and anticipated the charges that thirty years later would be leveled against Ryan.

At the time the commutations were issued, governor-elect Dale Bumpers distanced himself from Rockefeller's action while maintaining his own delicate position on capital punishment. As the *Arkansas Gazette* reported, "During the campaign, Bumpers had said at one point that he would continue the moratorium on executions but that he believed the death penalty should be kept for the most atrocious crimes. . . . He said on Tuesday that he would not recommend taking the death penalty off the books but that he did not believe it was a deterrent to crimes of passion."[77] When asked by the media for his reaction to Rockefeller's decision, Bumpers offered neither praise nor condemnation. "I know [the governor] acted in accordance with his personal philosophy," Bumpers said. "I'm sure he had sufficient information to justify in his own mind the actions that he took."[78]

The most negative reactions came from state legislators, prosecutors, and circuit court judges, many of whom either took issue with the governor's injection of personal morality into public life or with his concern for prisoners rather than for crime victims. "I am greatly disturbed by the final action you took yesterday," wrote one of Rockefeller's own prosecutorial appointees. "My personal standards of morality or your personal standards of morality concerning capital punishment are immaterial—we are public officials who have sworn to obey the duly enacted laws of the state."[79] Rockefeller's critics took every opportunity to berate him for his decision and to mock him for the emotion that accompanied his announcement. Almost without exception, accounts of Rockefeller's commutation speech made reference to his "emotion-filled statement," "halting voice," his "misty eyes." "I expect to see the following ad in your paper," wrote one reader of the *Arkansas Gazette* after the paper ran a sympathetic editorial, "WANTED: Murderers and rapists. . . . Come to beautiful Arkansas. Guns will be furnished and also victims for the rapists. Also, the Governor will be misty-eyed as he haltingly proceeds to slap your hands for being a bad boy."[80]

Contemptuous of Rockefeller's sympathy for the fifteen condemned inmates, State Representative Grover "Buddy" Turner fumed, "I'd like to have his message to the victims now. I've seen his message to those on death row." State Senator Knox Nelson also criticized the governor's seemingly excessive concern for those on death row. "It appears that we are more concerned today about the criminal and what happens to him than what has happened to the victims—the people who were killed or raped."[81] Prosecutor Frank Wynnee was livid at what he saw as Rockefeller's callous disregard for the victims of crime. "The governor sits up there and he doesn't have to go out there and talk to the husband whose wife has been dragged out of her house . . . and into the woods and raped and raped again and then killed. . . . The governor and his advisors don't get the emotional impact that the prosecutor and the policemen have to deal with. If they had talked to the families of the victims and the people of the communities, he would have looked at it a long time before he would do away with the electric chair."[82]

Another criticism directed at the governor was that by choking off capital punishment in Arkansas, he was doing a disservice to law enforcement and inviting increased crime. As one angry citizen wrote,

> Who is he to say that he is superior to our courts, our jury system, and our entire system of law and justice? Winthrop never before displayed any religion, and I am wondering why he has not abolished the entire penal system in Arkansas since he has pardoned and freed so many of the inmates prior to this . . . why does he not go to the zoos and reptile farms and break the glass to set free all the snakes, alligators, tigers, lions, and bears? These are also "God's creatures. . . ." I would consider it a good swap to let these animals and reptiles free in exchange for Winthrop going back to New York.[83]

Prosecutor Bill F. Doshier lumped the governor's clemency action together with his prison reform efforts. "It looks like he's been trying to put law enforcement out of business since he's been in there," Doshier observed. "I don't understand it." A telegram to the governor's office from a constituent expressed similar frustration in more alarmist terms, accusing Rockefeller of opening the floodgates for the mafia to enter Arkansas.[84] Even those who were more measured in their response, such as Representative Paul Henry, felt Governor Rockefeller had damaged the credibility of the state's criminal justice system. "It's good to be tolerant and lenient and interested in social justice," he allowed, "but there has to be some accountability."[85]

Beyond the concerns about law enforcement and victims rights, the most virulent opposition combined indignation over Rockefeller's invocation of Christian morality to justify his actions with an acute sense that he had overstepped the boundaries of his legitimate power as the state's chief executive. While New Mexico governor Anaya would face a lawsuit arising from his use of clemency, discontent over Rockefeller's sweeping use of executive power and his Christian rhetoric never moved past editorial vitriol. Yet criticism from religious leaders and politicians alike was ruthless. In one letter to the editor, the pastor of Wakefield Baptist Church wrote:

> The manufacturers of Pepto-Bismol surely must have been elated at recent action of Governor Rockefeller as he mocked the integrity of our courts by obviating the death penalty for the men upon whom it had been sentenced. I am sure their sales soared to unparalleled heights as thousands of Christians in our state experienced acute nausea while they heard our chief executive blame his Christian beliefs as one of the primary reasons for the permissive action. . . . A man is conspicuously presumptuous to speak against a practice upon which Christ remained silent. The law of retribution saturates the bible from cover to cover. May I close by saying to Mr. Bumpers, if during your tenure of office you exercise your prerogative in changing the decisions of our courts, do so upon your convictions as one man—Do not use Christianity as your scapegoat.[86]

Like some of Ryan's and Cruce's critics, State Senator Virgil T. Fletcher objected to the lawless nature of the clemency power and to Rockefeller's willingness to take advantage of that privilege. "I'm bitterly opposed to the commutations," he complained. "I still believe in living with our courts. Every case had been confirmed by the Supreme Court. It was a broad use of the executive powers. I seriously doubt if he was up for reelection that he would have made that decision." Senator Olsen Hendrix expressed a similar point of view. "I've always felt the people who heard the evidence and the presiding judge should know more about how to handle a sentence than the chief executive. Those people violated the law and the law hasn't been repealed. I'm sure they had a fair trial and in the opinion of the juries they were guilty as charged."[87] Circuit court judge Elmo Taylor called Rockefeller's action "a gross abuse of executive power," yet his colleague Judge G. B. Colvin more closely reflected the sentiments of many when he said Rockefeller's decision to commute, "was his prerogative, but I don't agree with it."[88]

On New Year's Eve 1970, Rockefeller toured the Tucker Intermediate Reformatory and visited the fifteen men whose lives he had spared. After shaking hands and chatting with inmates, Rockefeller told reporters, "Even though I've been fired, I wanted them to know I've been thinking of them."[89] Rockefeller never again held elected office, yet he regularly defended his clemency and the right of other executives to follow suit. As he wrote in a *Catholic University Law Review* article published the year after he left office, "Essential at our moment in history is a greatly broadened understanding and acceptance of the fact that executive clemency, far from being an extra-legal device, is an intricate and necessary part of a fair and impartial system of justice."[90]

Toney Anaya: Governor of New Mexico, 1982–1986

Sixteen years after Rockefeller's clemency, Toney Anaya, the outgoing governor of New Mexico, made national headlines by commuting the sentences of all five men on his state's death row. After years of rumors that the governor might take such a step, Anaya acted in the face of strong public support for capital punishment both in his state and across the nation. Thus, sixty men were executed nationwide while Anaya was in office and not a single commutation was granted by any governor in the country.[91] Indeed since executions had resumed after the Supreme Court's 1976 decision in *Gregg v. Georgia,* only Governors George Busbee of Georgia and Bob Graham of Florida had granted clemency in capital cases.

Anaya announced and defended his decision in a speech delivered at a press conference in Santa Fe. While his statement contained elements of political pragmatism, like Rockefeller, Anaya stressed his religious beliefs and humane compassion above all else. "I call for the abolition of the death penalty," he declared, "because it is inhumane, immoral, anti-God, and is incompatible with an enlightened society."[92] Anaya called on governors across the country to join him in halting the "macabre national death march."

Toney Anaya had climbed from humble beginnings to make a successful career in law and politics. Born April 29, 1941, in Moriarty, New Mexico, he was the seventh of ten children in a Catholic family. He was raised in an adobe house with dirt floors, no indoor plumbing, and no electricity, but, after graduating high school in 1959, he earned a BA from Georgetown University in 1963 and a JD from American University in 1967. Before going into the private practice of law in 1978, he worked in state and federal offices, including the U.S. Department of State (as an executive assistant), the U.S. Senate (as legislative counsel), and the New Mexico governor's office (as assistant to Governor Bruce King). He also served as New Mexico's attorney general from 1975 to 1978. When sworn in as governor in 1982, Anaya became the highest-ranking elected Latino official in the United States.

Anaya's four years in the governor's mansion were marked by contentious battles with the state legislature and controversy over an agenda many New Mexicans came to regard as too liberal. He was criticized for, among other things, his extensive use of affirmative action in his political appointments, declaring New Mexico a sanctuary for Central American political refugees, and spending too much time on the national stage, campaigning for Walter Mondale. However, it was his opposition to capital punishment that would eventually give Toney Anaya lasting notoriety.

During his 1982 gubernatorial campaign, Anaya had made no secret of his strong anti-death-penalty stance. He first discussed how he would handle executions during the primaries, in a public forum that included all eight Republican and Democratic candidates. "Every one of the other candidates tried to outdo the others in terms of how tough they would be," he later told the

Los Angeles Times. "I indicated I would not permit anybody (on death row) to die during my term of office. It was kind of a spontaneous response."[93] That spontaneous response became a campaign promise and, subsequently, a political reality.

During his term as governor, he granted a stay of execution each time a death warrant crossed his desk. Yet he agonized over whether to commute death sentences altogether. Anaya considered issuing a blanket clemency for death row inmates several times. Ineligible for reelection thanks to a New Mexico law that, at the time, prohibited him from seeking a second term, a number of larger political considerations nonetheless restrained him from acting. "We've got many, many other issues that you've got to be concerned about," he explained. "Proper funding for education, day care, drug abuse, everything else. What do you give up for what you get if you commute?"[94] He worried about the impact granting clemency might have on his relationship with the Legislature, on other Democrats facing re-election battles in New Mexico, and on the fate of his judicial nominees and political appointments. He also feared setting off a campaign to curtail gubernatorial pardoning powers.[95]

Indeed, just as Anaya was beginning his second year in office, he made a statement to the *National Catholic Reporter* that stirred up a tempest in New Mexico's legislature. Anaya told the paper that he and his aides had launched "a review of policy . . . a step toward, perhaps, a policy of commuting sentences to life imprisonment."[96] This simple announcement, unaccompanied by any concrete action, spurred the legislature to debate two bills and a constitutional amendment that would have stripped the governor of his pardoning powers while making it easier to impose death sentences in the first place. Ultimately, debate deteriorated into battles over the budget for the legislation, and the measures never came to a vote.

The death penalty did, however, emerge as a key issue in the 1986 governor's race, with each candidate eager to prove the strength of his support for capital punishment. The eventual winner, Republican Garrey Carruthers, campaigned on the promise that he would reinstate executions as his *first* order of business. "Everybody was using [the capital punishment issue] who felt they could make hay out of it," Anaya later recalled. "It bothered me. The candidates were getting the people into the frenzy of a lynch mob."[97]

In comparison with Governor Ryan, whose position on the death penalty changed drastically during his term, Anaya stood with Lee Cruce and Winthrop Rockefeller as an unwavering opponent of capital punishment. However, Anaya did not follow Cruce and Rockefeller in leading a campaign to abolish capital punishment in his state *in addition* to granting reprieves and commutations. Not until his clemency announcement did Anaya propose a specific agenda for broad legislative action. Then he called on legislators to replace the death penalty with a "life without parole" statute and to enact more crime prevention programs, provide better resources for law enforcement agencies, more victim compensation and assistance programs, and a greater focus on prisoner rehabilitation.[98] Anaya's eleventh-hour plea for an overhaul of policy would be sharply criticized by Governor-elect Carruthers, who said "I believe a Governor is duty-bound to implement the law or aggressively seek to change it. Until today the incumbent chose to do neither."[99] And Anaya himself doubted that his plea would actually produce any legislative action.[100]

Anaya described the decision to clear death row as "a very lonely, gut-wrenching process to go through."[101] In one interview he commented, "There were times I would wake up at night. I would usually just lie in bed and think about all the pros and cons. . . . I wouldn't wake up my wife and discuss it with her. I wouldn't call a friend. . . . I would just keep my own counsel, keep my own conscience."[102] On November 26, 1986, he held a press conference in Santa Fe and announced his decision, taking pains to explain his logic and to justify moving beyond moratorium:

> While many can argue that I can leave office having already fulfilled my political campaign commitment that no one would be executed in the name of the state during my term of office, without my taking this action today, that argument rings hollow in view of the near frenzy that was created during the recent political campaigns in this state. . . . For me to simply walk away now would make me as much an accomplice as others who would participate in their execution.[103]

His speech was at once hopeful, well-reasoned, defensive, and lofty. While in some places he called for more merciful, enlightened governance, in others he tried to reassure voters that the guilty would still be duly punished. Using oratory that often sounded like a holiday sermon, Anaya said, "Born in thanksgiving for our blessings, and in anticipation of preparing to celebrate the birth of Christ, this action will result in a tidal wave of reform in our efforts to prevent crime, to realistically fight crime, to deter crime, to reform criminals that can be rehabilitated, to provide retribution as appropriate, and to assist the victims of crime in a compassionate and practical manner."[104]

In addition, Anaya argued that the state would be better off focusing its energy and resources on the root social causes of crime—poverty, abuse, poor education, and so forth—instead of responding to violence with deadly retribution. "Because of the clamor for capital punishment," he later argued, "society shackles itself and not criminals by giving us a false sense of security, a false sense of accomplishment, a hollow, empty, costly, temporarily-satisfying, vengeful outburst of emotions, yet accomplishing nothing in terms of establishing an effective crime prevention, crime-fighting strategy."[105]

Because "life without parole" did not then exist in New Mexico, a substantial portion of his speech went to explaining why life sentences for these five criminals (technically *with* the possibility of parole) would, in effect, produce the same result as life without parole. "These men will never again set foot in society,"

Anaya promised, and he went on to describe the "sentences and consequences" for each of the five men.[106]

Delivered during the "tough on crime" 1980s, and framed in the context of a post-*Furman* faith in "super due process," Anaya's abolitionist argument invoked some of the same arguments that George Ryan would deploy seventeen years later. Both emphasized the arbitrary, sometimes erroneous, application of the death penalty. Matching Illinois's record in post-*Furman* cases, New Mexico had actually experienced a 50 percent error rate on death penalty convictions between 1960, the year David Cooper became New Mexico's last execution of the twentieth century, and 1974, when New Mexico's death penalty statute was briefly declared unconstitutional, granting automatic life sentences to all seven men then on death row. In the decade that followed, four of these seven men were exonerated and let out of prison entirely.[107] Though he took note of this fact in his speech, Anaya chose not to justify his actions with the same "broken system" rhetoric that Ryan would employ in 2003. Unlike Ryan, Anaya's overarching justification for clemency was that it is fundamentally wrong for the state to kill.

His action garnered international attention from individuals and groups either enraged or overjoyed by the commutations. Favorable correspondence poured in from liberal groups with various civil rights, civil liberties, and anti–death penalty mandates. The National Coalition against the Death Penalty, the National Association for the Advancement of Colored People, the American Civil Liberties Union, and individual members of Amnesty International commended Anaya. Editorial boards of several national papers also applauded his move.[108]

Among his constituents the response was quite different. The *Los Angeles Times* reported that calls to the governor's office in the days following the commutations were running in the order of twenty to one opposed to his action. They also noted that his voter approval rating dipped to 12.2 percent by the end of his term, though they did not specify if the poll was taken after or before the commutations.[109] Anaya himself recalled being "pummeled [by] an outpouring of outrage from supporters of capital punishment."[110]

Some who opposed his actions were contemptuous of the national attention focused on Anaya, and they accused him of coveting the limelight. Critics said he had overreached his powers, broken faith with the voters, and acted callously toward the victims' families. The *New Mexican* called for the state bar to investigate Anaya's actions and ethics (not as a governor but as a licensed attorney sworn to uphold the law). That same paper also accused Anaya of excessive preoccupation with the rights of the guilty, particularly when he promised to commute the sentence of a sixth man, Terry Clark, if the courts sentenced Clark before the end of his term. "Not content to commute the sentences of all the murderers on New Mexico's Death Row," the paper's editorial seethed, "Gov. Toney Anaya now is going shopping for killers to save from the state's death penalty." Rumors of special efforts by the governor to assist Clark elicited indignation and disgust from many quarters. "The governor's actions have gone beyond that of an individual who is personally opposed to the death penalty," The *New Mexican* commented. "His actions have become those of a vindictive, petty politician who wants to rub the public's face in the vestiges of gubernatorial power in the last days of his administration."[111]

Anaya's attorney general, Paul Bardacke, with whom the governor had a fairly rocky working relationship, openly expressed disapproval of the commutations. In the week following Anaya's announcement, Bardacke met with a number of Republicans in the incoming administration, including the governor-elect, to explore possible ways to challenge the commutations in court. Acknowledging that Anaya was standing "on pretty solid ground," and calling any legal suit an "uphill battle," Bardacke nonetheless argued that an abuse-of-power case could be made on the grounds that by commuting the sentences based on his own religious beliefs, Anaya had violated the separation of church and state.[112]

Steven Schiff, district attorney in Bernalillo County (where three of the five men had been prosecuted) actually brought such a suit. Taking issue with Anaya's injection of personal morality into public life, Schiff argued, "The pardon power emanates from the constitution. It's not an absolute power in the hands of one individual." He alleged before the State Supreme Court that Anaya exceeded his legal authority in three ways: (a) failing to review the individual circumstances of each case, (b) violating the separation of church and state by basing his decision squarely on his religious beliefs, and (c) waiting until his last few weeks in office, thereby denying the legislature opportunity to impeach him.[113] Anaya responded to the second of these allegations by saying, "I personally believe very strongly in one of the Ten Commandments which says 'thou shall not kill' . . . but it's not an individualized moral viewpoint I'm espousing. It's the majority viewpoint on morality in the world."[114] The State Supreme Court ruled against Schiff very quickly—one week before Anaya left office—refusing, without comment, to overturn Anaya's commutations.

In the midst of the public outcry and Schiff 's legal action following Anaya's clemency, some called on the legislature to move again, as it had done in 1984, to restrict the governor's clemency power. But such legislation never materialized. In fact, some of the people who so vociferously accused Anaya of abusing his power—Governor-elect Garrey Carruthers, and District Attorney Steven Schiff—were the first to publicly oppose such legislative action. Schiff said that restricting the governor's authority to grant pardons would be "terrible," and Carruthers noted that, "The commutation process is part of governorships throughout the United States. The fact that one person abused the power does not mean the power should be curbed for future governors."

Though his own call for nationwide abolition of the death penalty went nowhere, Toney Anaya was heartened and impressed when, a decade and a half later, he learned of George Ryan's bold move to clear death row in Illinois. "I didn't believe any politician could have the courage do that," Anaya told a reporter in New Mexico. "It was one thing for me to commute five sentences. Could I have done it for 167? I don't know."[115] Setting forth a religious rationale (as opposed to Ryan's "broken system" rhetoric based on wrongful execution of the innocent) may indeed have made it harder for Anaya to defend a larger number of clemencies. It was difficult enough for him to weather the response to five.

Ironically, after all the criticism Anaya endured for giving religion such a prominent role in his decision, he felt abandoned by the nation's religious leaders in the wake of his clemency announcement. His gubernatorial papers contain letters of commendation from groups such as the Mennonite Committee, the Quakers, and Jewish Reform congregations, but his own Catholic Church issued only a brief message of tepid support, declining to take a strong stand against capital punishment, while acknowledging that Anaya's clemency helped to promote "a culture of respect for life."[116] Nearly ten years later, Anaya lamented this underwhelming support. "While supporters of capital punishment pummeled me, religious leaders remained ominously quiet. . . . Only when the religions of this country—all of whom have opposed capital punishment by various degrees—unite to change their followers' attitudes toward capital punishment by preaching from the pulpit, will the United States truly demonstrate that it is an enlightened country."[117]

Conclusion

For every governor who, during the twentieth century, opposed capital punishment, many more supported it. If, from early- to mid-century, governors who opposed capital punishment endangered the political coalitions on which their power was based, by century's end governors avoided that mistake by acting like prosecutors in order to cement these alliances. For every one who used his power to prevent state killing, many more made their political careers through an ardent embrace of it. If in those earlier periods there seemed to be different strategies from which chief executives could choose to do the work of governing, by the end of the twentieth century, Democrats as well as Republicans used crime as a major vector for doing that work.

Compared to the times in which Cruce, Rockefeller, and Anaya were in office, by the turn of the twenty-first century, capital clemency was in considerable disfavor, burdened as we will see in chapters 4 and 5 by a consolidation of pro-capital-punishment sentiment and the combined triumph of victims rights and retributivism. In that sense what George Ryan did was even more extraordinary than what was done by Cruce, Rockefeller, and Anaya. Yet when he announced his decision he took up their mantle, using clemency to stop state killing, putting himself and his political prospects in great jeopardy. As Edward M. O'Brien, a longtime member of the Massachusetts Governor's Council, which advises that state's governor on clemency petitions, put it, "If a guy gets a pardon, who's happy about it? Probably his wife and mother. The public is cynical and questions all actions of government that are not written in granite."[118]

However, while Cruce, Rockefeller, and Anaya linked their commutation with calls for the death penalty's abolition, Ryan did not. While they were each consistent and philosophical abolitionists, Ryan was not. While they made explicit appeals to others to join them in their crusade against capital punishment, Ryan did not. By refusing to limit themselves to individual grants of clemency in capital cases or their critiques to questions of procedure and fairness in the administration of the death penalty, Ryan's predecessors did more than suspend punishment or temporarily forgo a power that they conceded the state might, on other occasions, legitimately exercise. Their acts went beyond imposing a pause in the operations of the state's killing machine; they challenged the view that capital punishment could ever be reconciled with the demands of justice.

Despite these differences between Ryan and his abolitionist predecessors, each tried to put state killing in a larger context by linking their clemency decisions to a broader critique and agenda of reform in the death penalty system of their state. Each called a halt to executions in the face of widespread public support for the death penalty. Each was lionized by national elites and abolitionist groups yet was subject to virulent local criticism.

Similar kinds of criticism were directed at all of them, namely that they were insensitive to victims of crime or too solicitous of criminals, that their actions undermined the capacity of law enforcement to do its job and, as a result, posed a danger to public safety, and that it was arrogant and inappropriate to allow their personal moral or political convictions to override the considered judgments of legislatures, juries, or appellate courts. Like Ryan, Cruce, Rockefeller, and Anaya were all accused of abusing their power. And, especially prominent in all these cases were accusations that what these governors did threatened the fabric of legality. As their critics saw it, their actions were imperialistic and, above all, lawless.

CHAPTER 3

The Jurisprudence of Clemency

WHAT PLACE FOR MERCY?

Mercy cannot be quantified or institutionalized. It is properly left to the conscience of the executive entitled to consider pleas and should not be bound by court decisions meant to do justice.
—*Janice Rogers Brown*

Equity in law is the same that the spirit is in religion, what everyone pleases to make it. . . . Equity is a roguish thing. For law we have a measure. . . . Equity is according to the conscience of him that is the chancellor, and as that is larger or narrower so is equity.
—*John Selden*

WHEN STATE SENATOR WILLIAM HAINE labeled Governor Ryan's clemency "the raw exercise of power against the law itself" and said that it did not display "constraint consistent with the law,"[1] he joined a long line of people who have taken governors to task for using their prerogative to spare life. He also captured something close to the heart of all exercises of mercy, whether or not they take the form of executive clemency. Mercy always contains something beyond the complete discipline or domestication of law, something essentially lawless. This is what Haine recognized in Ryan's act and what others alleged about the clemency decisions of Governors Cruce, Rockefeller, and Anaya. The "unfettered discretion" which Haine attributed to Ryan, Blackstone says is a matter of what sits in the sovereign's "breast," in a realm of emotion rather than reason. As a monarchical prerogative or an executive action in a democracy, clemency appears to be outside of, or beyond, the law and thus a threat to a society dedicated to the rule of law.

Others share this view, emphasizing clemency's alleged lawlessness. "Historically," as Professor Colleen Klasmeier notes, "clemency's effectiveness depended on its unpredictability. . . . the sovereign might grant clemency for any reason or for no reason at all."[2] Clemency exists in a space of possibility beyond regulation, unpredictability exemplified. Thus pardon "does not belong to the juridical order. It does not stem from the same plane of the law. . . . Indeed pardon outruns the law as much through its logic as its end."[3] Law professor Henry Weihofen similarly contends that clemency "has always been the broadest and least limited of powers. By its very nature, it could not be subject to rules or restrictions. Its function was rather to break rules, wherever in the opinion of the pardoning authority mercy, clemency, justice, or merely personal whim dictated."[4]

But perhaps these renderings of a stark and complete antithesis of clemency and law miss something in both. Clemency exemplifies what legal theorist Peter Fitzpatrick describes as the condition of law itself. As Fitzpatrick argues, modern law is "stretched between stable determinism and responsive change." Fitzpatrick contends that determinism and responsiveness are antithetical, but that each entails the other, that "there can be neither position without responsiveness to what is always beyond it nor responsiveness without a position from which to respond." And when clemency is exercised to stave off death, confronting it head on and refusing its demand, it helps to mark death as the horizon of law, a supreme determinism and also "the opening to all possibility that is beyond affirmed order."[5] Clemency, too, opens possibility "beyond affirmed order."

It does not, however, completely abandon determination for responsiveness. Rather it exists in a continuous, if contingent, relation to both. Highlighting this, in the mid-twentieth century the attorney general of the United States issued a report on release procedures in the federal system, including the president's clemency power. Speaking in Blackstonian terms he described its relation to law as follows:

> Emerging from the field of mere arbitrary caprice or semi-magical folklore, pardon has become an institution which is part of, and yet above, the legal system. It has never been crystallized into rigid rules. Rather its function has been to break rules. It has been the safety valve by which harsh, unjust, or unpopular results of formal rules could be corrected. The almost wholly unrestricted scope of the power . . . has been the tool by which many of the most important reforms of the substantive criminal law have been introduced.[6]

"Part of yet above the law," a rule breaker that serves to improve the law—this language captures clemency's inside/outside relation to law.[7]

On Lawful Lawlessness: Sovereign Prerogative in Constitutional Democracy

Political theorist Giorgio Agamben suggests that sovereignty is the power to decide on an exception and exempt a subject from the reach of "regular" law.[8] In the use of such terminology, of course, Agamben draws on Carl Schmitt's famous definition: "[T]he sovereign is he who decides on the state of exception."[9] This definition reflects Schmitt's interest in the personal element of the decision and in the agonistic and borderline relation of exception and norm. Schmitt, who was a prominent legal and political theorist of Weimar and Nazi Germany, understood the exception in relation to a state of emergency, a situation of economic and political crisis that imperils the state and would require, for resolution, the suspension of regular law.

Executive clemency, of course, is not used only in times of imminent peril or collapse; its usual idiom is one of mercy and not danger. And yet the mercy and danger do have something in common. Neither the requirements of danger nor the circumstances that arouse feelings of mercy can be fully predicted or governed by specific, restrictive, and comprehensive codes.[10] Both capture "the essence of the state's sovereignty, which must be juridically defined correctly, not as the monopoly to coerce or to rule, but as the monopoly to decide."[11] At its core, sovereignty embodies a conception of power that is decisionist. Sovereignty cannot, of course, live without the concept of norm that it subtends and is parasitical upon, but that only leaves the matter more relational and agonistic—precisely the terms on which executive clemency exists in constitutional democracy.[12]

The sovereign exception is, as Agamben puts it, "a kind of exclusion," and, as if recapitulating the distinction between law and equity, he says that "[w]hat is excluded from the general rule is an individual case. . . . [W]hat is excluded . . . is not, on account of being excluded, absolutely without relation to the rule. On the contrary, what is excluded in the exception maintains itself in relation to the rule in the form of the rule's suspension. The rule applies to the exception in no longer applying, in withdrawing from it."[13] Acts of clemency create exceptions, exclusions, but as Agamben notes, the exception does not "subtract itself from the rule; rather the rule, suspending itself, gives rise to the exception and, maintaining itself in relation to the exception, first constitutes itself as a rule."[14] Acts of clemency are quintessentially sovereign acts. Even when they are authorized by law they are moments when officials can "decide who shall be removed from the purview of the law."[15]

Agamben's *Homo Sacer* points to the formative and continuing influence of a vision of sovereignty that is by no means completely extinguished by electoral democracy or the rule of law. However, he is distinctly less useful in understanding the historical mutations and contemporary arrangements of sovereign power under these conditions. One of the main transformations that Agamben neglects is that ideas of constitutionalism and the rule of law develop by essentially splitting *vitae et necis potestatem*. The power to punish (to authorize and to impose) is stripped away from the executive and vested in the legislature and courts. This is, of course, the well-known separation of powers that is constitutive of the very idea of limited government. Indeed, for the eighteenth-century philosopher Charles Montesquieu, the fact that "the king cannot judge" saved even an absolutist monarchy in the West from becoming "oriental despotism."[16] Blackstone also stresses this "splitting." "The King himself condemns no man; that rugged task he leaves to his courts of justice."[17] This splitting makes executive clemency today part of a received constitutional schema and not just some archaic residual of a once absolute power.

Recently French philosopher Jacques Derrida took up the subject of clemency, democracy, and law. Like Agamben, Derrida recognizes that clemency exists at several fault lines, fault lines that he describes in different ways starting with the matter of the pardoned themselves. "It is important," he says, "to analyze at base the tension . . . between on the one hand the idea . . . of the unconditional, gracious, infinite aneconomic pardon, accorded to the guilty precisely as guilty, without compensation, even to one who does not repent or ask for pardon, and on the other hand . . . a conditional pardon, proportionate to the recognition of fault, to remorse and the transformation of the sinner who asks, then, explicitly, for pardon." Clemency, as Derrida sees it, exists in the penumbra of the rule of reciprocity and the logic of exchange, always carrying with it an association with the unearned act of grace, even for those who appear to have earned our compassion. Thus the tension between the unconditional and the conditional is "irreconcilable and indissociable."[18]

Derrida also writes that it is never clear whether pardons are directed at acts or persons: "Does one pardon something," he asks, "a crime, a fault, a wrong, meaning an act or a moment which does not exhaust the incriminated person and at the limit is not confounded with the guilty who remains irreducible to it? Or rather does one pardon someone, absolutely, no longer marking then the limit between the wrong, the moment of the fault, and on the other hand, the person one holds responsible or guilty?"[19] This is a question that Derrida insists must be left open.[20]

He turns to law to describe, in yet another way, clemency's

indeterminacy. Like Agamben, he is fascinated by the relationship between sovereignty and law and sees in the pardon what he calls "the right of grace." To speak of such a right is to locate clemency on the terrain of law, that is to place it within the "order of rights."[21] Yet this right works precisely by inscribing in law "a power above the law."[22] Clemency, he says, is "Law above the law."[23] Like Agamben, Derrida thinks of the exception as an inscription in the field of law itself, at the boundary where lawlessness becomes lawful.[24]

Finally, Derrida considers clemency's compatibility with democracy by calling attention to the reappropriation of the "right of grace" and the idea of sovereignty in "the republican heritage." Democracies, he argues, claim to "secularize" clemency.[25] Yet the relation between democracy and clemency is, as the criticisms of Ryan and other governors who have commuted death sentences make clear, a troubled one.

Recognizing clemency's inside/outside relation to law may explain this trouble and suggest why Blackstone thought that "in democracies . . . this power of pardon can never subsist; for there nothing higher is acknowledged than the magistrate who administers the laws."[26] James Wilson, one of the signers of the Declaration of Independence, answered Blackstone's concerns by emphasizing that in a democracy the "supreme power" remains with the people who can hold those granting clemency accountable for their actions.[27] In a similar vein, former Supreme Court Justice Joseph Story insisted, in his classic *Commentaries on the Constitution of the United States*, that, "So far from the power of pardon being incompatible with the fundamental principles of a republic, it may be boldly asserted to be peculiarly appropriate, and safe in all free states; because the power can be guarded by a just responsibility for its exercise. . . . If the power should ever be abused, it would be far less likely to occur in opposition, than in obedience to the will of the people." Placing the clemency power in an executive who could override the considered judgments of the magistrates did not mean that it would be a lawless power since it could be contained within a framework of law that on Wilson's account "is higher" than those who administer it.[28] Yet Wilson conceded some territory to Blackstone by acknowledging that such a power, which allows executives "to insult the laws, to protect crimes, to indemnify, and by indemnifying, to encourage criminals," was indeed "extraordinary" in a democratic political system.[29]

The Trial of Mercy: Clemency in the Courts

Wilson's comments open up the question of how American law has regarded, and dealt with, that "extraordinary" power. What have the magistrates who interpret the law said about the place of mercy and clemency in our system of government? In fact, the United States has a long history of efforts by judges to come to terms with both, to name their relationship to democratic legality. Some believe that history to be marked by change from a less legalized to a more legalized conception, seeing an emergent, if not fully realized, triumph of law over clemency.[30] Yet a less legalized conception has in fact hardly been displaced. For every judge who finds resources to contain clemency's alegality in our legal tradition, others, in a Wilsonian way, continue to acknowledge and defer to that alegality.[31]

This fact highlights the place of pardon, commutation, and amnesty in law's barely chartable borderland. Law cannot quite contain the exception, nor can it renounce the effort to do so. The judicial corpus gives clemency its due as an opening, as a fissure in legal life, and seems to take some comfort in the fact that in granting clemency this status, it is asserting the continuing supremacy of law. This is what in another context literary critic Stanley Fish called law's "amazing trick," the ability of law to assert its supremacy even as it concedes ground to things beyond its purview. But it is perhaps less amazing than judges would like it to appear to be.[32] What is most apparent in the judiciary's efforts to pull off this trick is its inability to find a stable position from which to either tame or fully liberate clemency.

Instability has been present from the start. It is found in Chief Justice John Marshall's typically magisterial pronouncements in the first clemency case to reach the U.S. Supreme Court. *United States v. Wilson* brought to the Court President Andrew Jackson's pardon of a robber for "the crime for which he has been sentenced to death" and the question of what happened when Wilson, for breathtakingly inexplicable reasons, "did not wish in any manner to avail himself, in order to avoid the sentence in this particular case, of the pardon referred to."[33] Wilson's refusal put the courts in a bind of almost novelistic proportions, requiring them to determine whether a pardon could unseal the fate of a criminal against his wish to see it remain sealed.

To resolve such a question, Marshall found little in America's own nascent legal tradition and thus invoked the historical connection of the United States to England, "that nation whose language is our language." Adopting the "principles" and "rules" of English law, Marshall carved out an honored place for mercy. He described a pardon of the kind rendered by President Jackson as "an act of grace, proceeding from the power entrusted with the execution of the laws."[34] This grace is seemingly beyond the reach of legal compulsion or regulation; it is a grace freely given or withheld finding its only home, as Blackstone put it, in "a court of equity in . . . [the president's] own breast."[35]

Yet in the next moment of Marshall's opinion he describes pardons using legal language—promises, contracts, property. A pardon, he says, "is the private, though official act of the executive magistrate, delivered to the individual for whose benefit it is intended." Blurring the lines of public duty and private act, Marshall says that a pardon is "a constituent part of the judicial system" but that it is a "private deed." Sounding the offer and acceptance idiom of modern contract law, if a pardon is rejected by the person to whom it is "tendered," it cannot be valid; "we have discovered no power in a court to force it on him."[36] The force of law suddenly lacks force. The force from which the pardon is exempted and from which it seeks to exempt Wilson cannot save Wilson's life should he not wish it saved.[37] The sovereign's godlike prerogative to spare life is rendered impotent by his subject's humble refusal.

For Marshall the "public" interest in the pardon that President Jackson granted was insufficient to override a private, contractual transaction between the one who offers grace and the one who decides whether to accept it. While recognizing the majesty of the sovereign's mercy, he casually brushes aside the one legal authority that contests the language of offer and acceptance and so renders the king's pardoning power forceful regardless of the subject's consent, calling that authority "vague dictum." Marshall says that a pardon not pleaded by its intended recipient in a court "cannot be noticed by the judges."[38]

But judges "notice" pardons all the time, regularly repeating a ritual in which they ceremoniously accept jurisdiction, thereby asserting clemency's status as a legal act. Sometimes they confidently pronounce the law's ability to control clemency and the mercy that it provides. More often they avoid, defer, or refuse to use the "force" of the law to discipline, regulate, or regularize clemency and mercy.[39]

A little more than twenty years after *Wilson* the Supreme Court dealt with the question of whether the president could impose conditions on pardons. In *Ex Parte Wells*, a murderer under a death sentence received and accepted from President Filmore "a pardon of the offence of which he was convicted, upon condition that he be imprisoned during his natural life, that is, the sentence of death is hereby commuted to imprisonment for life in the penitentiary at Washington." The murderer subsequently sought habeas corpus review of his prison sentence. Taking up Justice Marshall's contractual imagery, Wells contended that his acceptance of the condition was invalid because it was undertaken while under the "duress" of imprisonment.[40]

The Court began its decision by acknowledging that, while the power to pardon was expressly provided for in the Constitution,[41] "[n]o statute has ever been passed regulating it in cases of conviction by the civil authorities. In such cases, the President has acted exclusively under the power as it is expressed in the constitution." And in an interesting assertion of law's dominion over pardon, Justice Wayne turned to language and usage, differentiating the way the term "pardon" is understood in "common parlance" from its legal meaning. In the former, "pardon"

> is forgiveness, release, remission. Forgiveness for an offence, whether it be one for which the person committing it is liable in law or otherwise. Release from pecuniary obligation, as where it is said, I pardon you your debt. Or it is the remission of a penalty, to which one may have subjected himself by the non-performance of an undertaking or contract, or when a statutory penalty in money has been incurred, and it is remitted by a public functionary having power to remit it.[42]

Yet "in the law," Wayne continued, "it has different meanings, which were as well understood when the constitution was made as any other legal word in the constitution now is."[43] Such a thing as a pardon "without a designation of its kind is not known in the law. Time out of mind, in the earliest books of the English law, every pardon has its particular denomination. They are general, special, or particular, conditional or absolute, statutory, not necessary in some cases, and in some grantable of course." Wayne continued, as if uncertain that enough had been, or could be, said to show the subservience of clemency to law,

> It [the Constitution] meant that the power was to be used according to law; that is, as it had been used in England, and these States when they were colonies; not because it was a prerogative power, but as incidents of the power to pardon particularly when the circumstances of any case disclosed such uncertainties as made it doubtful if there should have been a conviction of the criminal, or when they are such as to show that there might be a mitigation of the punishment without lessening the obligation of vindicatory justice. Without such a power of clemency, to be exercised by some department or functionary of a government, it would be most imperfect and deficient in its political morality, and in that attribute of Deity whose judgments are always tempered with mercy.[44]

Wayne's equation of clemency with mercy provides a touchstone for understanding law's ambivalent relation to clemency. Rules can, of course, authorize officials to grant mercy and/or assign that power to one institution or another, but mercy itself cannot be completely rule-governed.[45] It is precisely its status beyond the governance of rules that makes it an "attribute of Deity" and that means that it will always be accompanied by the anxiety that in any constitutional democracy accompanies the recognition of lawless power.[46]

The troubling quality of mercy reappeared when, in 1866, the Supreme Court again took up the president's power to pardon, this time upholding clemency for a confederate legislator who had been pardoned "for all offences by him committed, arising from participation, direct or implied, in the said Rebellion." The issue before the Court was whether that pardon exempted him from being subject to an act of Congress requiring persons wanting to practice law to swear that they had "not yielded a voluntary support to any pretended government, authority, power, or constitution, within the United States, hostile or inimical thereto."[47]

Speaking of the president's pardon power, Justice Stephen Field gave legal sanction to its lawlessness. "The power thus conferred," Field said,

> is unlimited, with the exception [in cases of impeachment]. It extends to every offence known to the law, and may be exercised at any time after its commission, either before legal proceedings are taken, or during their pendency, or after conviction and judgment. This power of the President is not subject to legislative control. Congress can neither limit the effect of his pardon, nor exclude from its exercise any class of offenders. The benign prerogative of mercy reposed in him cannot be fettered by any legislative restrictions.[48]

As for the effect of pardons, using almost theological terms, Field said that it transforms guilt into innocence, restores rights, and "makes him (the recipient), as it were, a new man."[49]

While "the benign prerogative of mercy" cannot, as Field conceives of it, be subject to rule in the normal sense of that word, he leaves unstated the scope of judicial review. His silence about the powers of courts in relation to pardons is most telling. In this silence he registers law's profound uncertainty and ambivalence about the place of mercy and of even the diminished form of prerogative left to executives in constitutional democracy, reserving for the courts an unstated, perhaps unstateable, role.

In the early twentieth century, the Supreme Court returned to clemency, again registering its uncertain legal status. In *Ex parte Grossman*, Chief Justice William Howard Taft conjured once more the merciful sovereign authorized by law to exercise an unfettered discretion.[50] Our Constitution, he said, "confers this discretion on the highest officer in the nation in confidence that he will not abuse it."[51] Two years later, in a case some commentators see as a turning point from Marshall's ambivalent conception of clemency as at once an act of grace and a kind of private contract, a unanimous Supreme Court joined Justice Oliver Wendell Holmes in rejecting the claim that commutation of a death sentence to one of life imprisonment "cannot be done without the convict's consent."[52] The Court rejected the idea that informed Marshall's view, namely that in order to be valid a pardon had to be presented to a court.

Holmes spoke in distinctly un-Marshallian terms, finally asserting, so it seemed, law's control over clemency by decoupling clemency from mercy and recharacterizing it from a contractual transaction to a matter of constitutional moment. "A pardon in our days," Holmes asserted, "is not a private act of grace from an individual happening to possess power. It is a part of the Constitutional scheme. When granted, it is the determination of the ultimate authority that the public welfare will be better served by inflicting less than what the judgment fixed."[53] Here the juxtaposition of the phrases "an individual happening to possess power" and "the ultimate authority" is particularly striking, seeming to move clemency fully within a legal order whose constant presence authorizes it. Rather than a court of equity in the sovereign's breast, clemency, as Holmes understood it, springs from a set of considerations by one expressly charged to act for the "public."[54]

In an imagined contest of wills between an authority intent on pardoning or commuting and a prisoner intent on taking the full measure of his judicially assigned punishment, Holmes quite explicitly dispenses with Marshall's simultaneous elevation and emasculation of sovereign prerogative. He first moves clemency from an act of grace to an act of authority under a constitution, and then affirms pardon's potency within that scheme. "Just as the original punishment," Holmes writes,

> would be imposed without regard to the prisoner's consent and in the teeth of his will, whether he liked it or not, the public welfare, not his consent, determines what shall be done. So far as a pardon legitimately cuts down a penalty, it affects the judgment imposing it. No one doubts that a reduction of the term of an imprisonment or the amount of a fine would limit the sentence effectively on the one side and on the other would leave the reduced term or fine valid and to be enforced, and that the convict's consent is not required. When we come to the commutation of death to imprisonment for life it is hard to see how consent has any more to do with it than it has in the cases first put. Supposing that Perovich did not accept the change, he could not have got himself hanged against the Executive order. Supposing that he did accept, he could not affect the judgment to be carried out. The considerations that led to the modification had nothing to do with his will.[55]

Holmes's reliance on a complete parallel between punishment and commutation misses the full impact of constitutional democracy on sovereignty that splits, as I have said, sovereign prerogative, reserving clemency for executive action, while removing punishment from its jurisdiction. Yet Holmes rightly reminds us that the power over death is not left with the individual whose life the government wishes to dispose of or preserve.[56] The sovereign right to spare life is preserved even as sovereignty is domesticated, and thus rendered less fearsome, by the requirements of due process.

Holmes was not alone in his effort to bring mercy and clemency fully within the law. Thus, almost a decade earlier, the Oklahoma Court of Criminal Appeals warned about the damage clemency can do to constitutional democracy and the rule of law. It suggested that there needed to be substantive limitations on the reach of the chief executive's power to pardon and commute duly imposed criminal sentences. It did so by juxtaposing clemency as an act of mercy (which it saw as compatible with both constitutional democracy and the rule of law) with a more sweeping exercise of clemency power (of the kind later exemplified in Governor Ryan's action).

While recognizing the governor's prerogative to extend a compassionate clemency in particular cases, the court warned that the "power to pardon, parole, or commute sentences cannot be arbitrarily exercised by any official." It differentiated uses of clemency in response to "special reasons" that might arise in individual cases from the use of clemency as a "wholesale suspension or repeal of any law or provision of law."[57] Here mercy is positioned as complementary to law, not threatening to a society's underlying commitment to legality. Mercy, in the court's view, begins with an acceptance of law's authority, even as it exempts someone from the full consequences of their breach of law. As such, mercy might involve an appropriate use of power. Wholesale clemency, in contrast, is an abuse of power.

Speaking openly about the sitting governor of Oklahoma—Lee Cruce—the court noted that Cruce "takes the position that all legal executions are judicial murder and . . . refuses to permit them to be carried into effect." It characterized Cruce's position as "utterly untenable" and urged him to use clemency only on particular defendants whose cases and circumstances made them good candidates for mercy. Governor Cruce's blanket opposition to capital punishment could not, the court said, "lawfully justify his action in a wholesale commutation of death sentences."[58]

Comparing gubernatorial clemency to jury service, the Oklahoma court cited a statute explicitly forbidding those with conscientious objections to capital punishment from serving as a jurors in capital cases. Moreover, it warned that the governor's contention amounted to a nullification of the rule of law itself. "If the Governor's position is correct," the court argued,

> then we do not have a government of law in Oklahoma, but a government of men only. If it were necessary for the Governor to approve such verdicts before they could be carried into execution, then the Governor should have made his views known before he was elected, and he should have refused to take the oath of office. There is no logical escape from this conclusion. The Governor's position can only be explained upon the hypothesis that he imagines himself to be a dictator, and that his will is supreme and above the law. In this the Governor is mistaken.[59]

The example of a governor interposing his personal objections against a valid law would, the court feared, fuel one of "the most mischievous tendencies of the present day," namely the "disposition manifest among the people to set their individual judgments up against the law, and to assert their right not to obey any law unless it meets their personal approval." While accepting such a view would be to invite "anarchy," reserving the prerogative to suspend or ignore any law with which he disapproved solely to the governor meant that "we have an empire in Oklahoma, and not a free state."[60]

Other courts have come close to the *Henry* position, asserting for example, that pardon or commutation must be "exercised in a lawful and proper manner"[61] or that the clemency power is not "limitless" and that it must be exercised "in the public interest" and in a way that does not violate "the Bill of Rights which expressly reserved to the 'individual' certain fundamental rights."[62] Yet most courts have rejected the view put forward in *Henry*, holding that the law imposes no substantive limitations regarding the circumstances in which chief executives can offer mercy and grant clemency. In an 1872 Virginia case, that state's supreme court likened clemency to "the authority to suspend the operation of laws." Fifty years later, the Kansas Supreme Court said that "when the court's attention is called to pardon it will not inquire into the motives which prompted the pardoning official to issue the pardon, for to do so would be to usurp the pardoning power." It portrayed clemency as an act of mercy properly used to repair injustices that occasionally arise in "a just government," yet concluded that clemency always "is in derogation of the law."[63]

Thirty years later, in a case brought by the parents of a murder victim seeking a declaratory judgment that would "inform the Governor that he must not exercise his power to commute a sentence of death because of his conviction that the death penalty is wrong,"[64] the Supreme Court of Oregon also repudiated the *Henry* position. Acknowledging mercy's lawless quality, it held that the governor's discretion "can not be controlled by judicial decision. The courts have no authority to inquire into the reasons or motives which actuate the Governor in exercising the power."[65] Or, as the Supreme Court of Louisiana put it, "clemency is shrouded in mystery and often fraught with arbitrariness."[66]

Thus Justice Holmes's apparent success in bringing clemency fully within the law was at best fleeting. Courts repeatedly fall back, without explicitly repudiating Holmes, on Marshall's conception of clemency as an act of grace existing in the borderland of legality. Thus in a 1977 decision, the Supreme Court of Florida endorsed the following excerpt from *American Jurisprudence*:

> An executive may grant a pardon for good reasons or bad, or for any reason at all, and his act is final and irrevocable. Even for the grossest abuse of this discretionary power the law affords no remedy; the courts have no concern with the reasons which actuated the executive. The constitution clothes him with the power to grant pardons, and this power is beyond the control, or even the legitimate criticism, of the judiciary. Whatever may have been

> the reasons for granting the pardon, the courts cannot decline to give it effect, if it is valid upon its face, and no court has the power to review grounds or motives for the action of the executive in granting a pardon, for that would be the exercise of the pardoning power in part, and any attempt of the courts to interfere with the governor in the exercise of the pardoning power would be manifest usurpation of authority, no matter how flagrant the breach of duty upon the part of the executive, unless granted the power by competent authority or unless fraud has entered into the case.[67]

Or, as the U.S. Court of Appeals for the Sixth Circuit explained in a 1997 decision,

> The very nature of clemency is that it is grounded solely in the will of the dispenser. He need give no reasons for granting it, or for denying it. And there is no precedent in our law that the granter of clemency need do anything with a request for clemency—which McQueen (the petitioner), in reality, has never filed. The governor may agonize over every petition; he may glance at one or all such petitions and toss them away; he may direct his staff as to the means for considering them. Certainly, McQueen could not complain if a petition went into the Governor's office and simply came out stamped "Denied." He equally cannot complain that the governor has chosen to resolve his mind on these matters by considering cases by categories, nor that he has chosen to make an announcement of such reasoning. No more is the governor bound by such a statement. He may change his mind tomorrow, or he may grant clemency in the face of his own announced policy, without hindrance. Just as the citizenry would have no legal claim if the governor were to announce that he would, without contemplation, pardon all violators of a certain law, McQueen has no claim that the governor, without individual contemplation, has failed to give him the relief that is in the governor's sole discretion."[68]

Saying that clemency is rooted solely in "the will" of the dispenser seems to be about as straightforward an acknowledgment as one can imagine of the tension between it and the rule of law. But the uncertain history of law's relation with mercy did not end in these apparent judicial repudiations of Holmes. One of the most revealing statements of the continuing trouble that clemency poses for constitutional democracy, of the spectral presence of both Marshall and Holmes in law's attitude toward it, is found in another Oklahoma case that arose during Governor Cruce's troubled term in the early twentieth century. In that case, *Ex parte Crump*,[69] the Court of Criminal Appeals of Oklahoma explored the relationship of sovereignty and death, only here, as in *Henry*, the death imagined is the death of law at the hands of a sovereign's uncheckable prerogative power.

"A pardon," the court said, echoing Marshall as well as Holmes, "is an act of grace and mercy bestowed by the state, through its chief executive, upon offenders against its laws. Yet a pardon properly granted is also an act of justice, supported by a wise public policy. While the power to pardon, parole, reprieve, or commute after conviction for offenses against the state is a matter of executive discretion, this discretion should be exercised on public considerations alone." This lawless discretion can and should be guided by conventions dictated by the design of government and prudence. "An executive officer . . . does not sit as a court of appeal from the Legislature. If he believes the law under which a prisoner is suffering to be unwise or unjust, still this opinion cannot incline him to grant a pardon, because the power which makes and unmakes laws is not in him, and officially he is required to look upon the law as just and wise, however his private opinion may revolt."[70]

Failure to abide by those conventions, the court suggests, could be deadly for the very law that authorizes executive clemency. "The granting of pardons is discretionary in its nature. . . . If it comes to be understood that a single man, entrusted with the high function of pardon, can open all the prisons of the country and let every guilty person go free, thus at a blow striking down the law itself . . . the most disastrous consequences to liberty and law will sooner or later follow. Such a conclusion is itself the annihilation of law and only upon law can liberty repose." Yet, as if conceding law's powerlessness to prevent its own annihilation, the court says that "this sort of executive abuse will not authorize the courts to decline giving effect to the executive pardon. . . . No court has the power to review the action of the executive in granting a pardon, for that would be the exercise of the pardoning power in part, and . . . would be a manifest usurpation of authority."[71]

Crump's defense of the dangerous, deadly powers of executive clemency is reiterated in a well-known case in which the U.S. Supreme Court turned down an actual innocence claim of a person condemned to death. This case, *Herrera v. Collins*,[72] is central to the Rehnquist Court's death penalty jurisprudence.[73] In explaining its refusal to allow a late-stage habeas to be based on such a claim, the Court took refuge in the availability of executive clemency. "This is not to say," Chief Justice Rehnquist wrote, "that petitioner is left without a forum to raise his actual innocence claim. For under Texas law, petitioner may file a request for executive clemency. Clemency is deeply rooted in our Anglo-American tradition of law, and is the historic remedy for preventing miscarriages of justice where judicial process has been exhausted."[74] In this description, Rehnquist transfers the ultimate responsibility for execution from the courts to state governors while at the same time juridifying clemency, treating it as the court of last resort. He concedes to governors a power to spare life that the Court's own arcane habeas doctrine prevents it from exercising. At the same time, he gives this court of last resort a limited jurisdiction and a public, not a private purpose, namely to remedy "miscarriages of justice,"[75] rather than a broad compass to mitigate deserved punishment on compassionate grounds.

Nonetheless, as if taking back what he just asserted, Rehnquist quotes Blackstone approvingly on the sovereign's "power to extend mercy, whenever he thinks it is deserved" and embraces Marshall's "pardon is an act of grace" conception of clemency. Mercy and grace may be dangerous because both are in principle not governable by law, but living with this "dangerous supplement" is necessary since executive clemency, in Rehnquist's view, provides the "'fail safe' in our criminal justice system."[76] "Fail safe" is the highly charged language of a nuclear nightmare. It marks the presence of the unthinkable that might destroy law itself, or at least expunge the sovereign prerogative to take life from the American system, in this case the prospect that an innocent man might be executed. To save us from that "disaster" law makes space for the very thing that must ultimately escape its control and, in so doing, endanger it. Rehnquist, like Agamben, Schmitt, and Derrida, acknowledges law's dependency on a legally sanctioned lawlessness, a lawless power that is in the last instance responsible for sparing life.

Rehnquist reiterates this acknowledgment in another death penalty case, decided five years after Herrera. In *Ohio Adult Parole Authority v. Woodard*,[77] the Court heard a challenge to the long-held view that clemency could not be subject to due process standards applicable to other executive and administrative acts. Ohio is one of a number of states that have endeavored to alleviate some of the anxiety about the executive's clemency power by elaborating an administrative framework that diffuses responsibility for all clemency decisions.[78] It requires that in death cases, the Ohio Adult Parole Authority hold hearings on any requests for clemency and make a recommendation to the governor prior to his decision. An inmate denied clemency sued, claiming that the Authority's procedures violated, among other things, the due process clause of the Fourteenth Amendment.

Justice Rehnquist responded by reaffirming a posture of judicial deference in respect to clemency.[79] He rejected the respondent's contention that the statutory establishment of the Authority's clemency procedures created a "life" interest any different from the interest "adjudicated at trial and sentencing."[80] But the core of his argument was his recognition that to subject clemency to due process would be to effectively extinguish it. In explaining the threat that Woodard's claim posed, Rehnquist expanded his conception of the jurisdiction of the executive in clemency cases beyond redress of erroneous convictions while also reaffirming his endorsement of Marshall's clemency as "grace" conception. "The process respondent seeks would be inconsistent with the heart of executive clemency, which is a grant of clemency as a matter of grace, thus allowing the executive to consider a wide range of factors not comprehensible by earlier judicial proceedings and sentencing determinations." Going further than in *Herrera*, Rehnquist asserted that clemency is not part of the "adjudicatory process," while anxiously reiterating his view of the danger legalization posed to executive prerogative. "Here the executive's authority would cease to be a matter of grace committed to the executive authority if it were constrained by the sort of procedural requirements that respondent urges."[81]

That Rehnquist's opinion garnered no majority gives further evidence of the legal indeterminacy that surrounds clemency.[82] Concurring with the holding that the respondent had no cognizable due process claim, Justice O'Connor nonetheless insisted that "some minimal procedural safeguards apply to clemency proceedings."[83] Yet she was not able to name what those procedures might be and could imagine judicial intervention only in cases of the most transparent and unreasoning arbitrariness, for example "a scheme where a state official flipped a coin to determine whether to grant clemency, or in a case where the State arbitrarily denied a prisoner any access to its clemency process."[84] Justice Stevens added to this list of barely imaginable horrors when he stated that "no one would contend that a governor could ignore the commands of the Equal Protection Clause and use race, religion, or political affiliation as a standard for granting or denying clemency."[85] O'Connor and Stevens looked executive prerogative in the eye and blinked, insisting that, at least in some barely speakable way, clemency be rescued from the conundrum of "responsiveness" and "determination."

Courts have generally read *Woodard* as requiring minimal due process.[86] Nonetheless, in most cases the same courts have found that whatever procedure was, or was not, provided passed constitutional muster. To take but one example, in *Bacon v. Lee*, the North Carolina Supreme Court held that the fact that the governor had previously served as attorney general and thus counsel of record during plaintiff 's appellate and postconviction proceedings created no due process issue in the governor's exercise of his clemency powers. Even *Woodard*, the court argued, recognized that clemency decisions are fundamentally different from adjudication within the judicial branch and that impartiality was not required of those in whose offices the clemency power was lodged.[87] It is precisely this difference that marks the borderland of law in which mercy and clemency are situated, a borderland in which law authorizes them, but cannot subject them to the governance of rules.

Conclusion

In January 2004, almost one year to the day after Governor Ryan announced his mass clemency, the Illinois Supreme Court handed down its decision in a case challenging his decision brought by Illinois attorney general Madigan. The Court chided Ryan for failing to exercise his clemency power for the purpose intended by the framers of the Illinois Constitution, namely to "prevent miscarriages of justice in individual cases" and for failing fully to tether clemency to mercy. At the same time the Court, following the long line of cases discussed in this chapter, noted that the power to pardon given the governor is "extremely broad" and can be controlled "only by his conscience and his sense of public duty."[88]

The *Madigan* court owned up to clemency's legally uncontrollable character and to its potential arbitrariness. It is exactly such seeming arbitrariness that generates doubt about clemency like Ryan's,[89] and that puts mercy on trial.

That doubt is intensified by our society's belief that the power of the government should, in all respects, be subject to the rule of law, and that no power, not even when enlisted on behalf of mercy, should be accountable solely to an official's conscience and sense of duty. It is today, of course, something of a truism to note that Americans frequently congratulate themselves on their commitment to the rule of law.[90] "The overwhelming majority of Americans," the prominent conservative thinker William F. Buckley proudly proclaims, "believe in the rule of law."[91] This commitment is deeply rooted, or so the story goes, in America's history and has been renewed from generation to generation. From Alexis de Tocqueville's early nineteenth-century observation that "[t]he spirit of the laws which is produced in the schools and courts of justice, gradually permeates . . . into the bosom of society"[92] to the present, numerous commentators have said about the United States that it has the "principled character . . . of a Nation of people who aspire to live according to the rule of law."[93]

These invocations of the rule of law serve as a constitutive boundary separating the United States from the rest of the world. Ronald Cass, former dean of the Boston University Law School, observes that the commitment to the rule of law is "central to our national self-definition. . . . For most of the world . . . the nation most immediately associated with the rule of law is the United States of America. The story of America . . . is *uniquely* the story of law"[94] (emphasis added). The philosopher Michael Oakeshott suggests that "the rule of law is the single greatest condition of our freedom, removing from us that great fear which has overshadowed so many communities, the fear of the power of our own government."[95] Similarly, former secretary of Housing and Urban Development Henry Cisneros argues that "the fundamental identity of the United States is not an identity based on how people look, what language they learnt first or over how many generations they absorbed Anglo-Protestant values. Rather it is based upon acceptance of the rule of law."[96]

Current controversies surrounding the war on terror and American intervention in Iraq have brought rule-of-law rhetoric to a fevered pitch, with public officials and others uncritically linking it to America's boundary-marking values, and arguments about America's distinctiveness. Typical was the statement of Jonathan

Lippman, chief administrative judge of the State of New York, who said, "[T]he rule of law is what separates us from those who seek to defeat our democratic institutions and way of life through violence and terror."[97] Commenting on the scandal at Abu Ghraib, former defense secretary William Cohen argued, "The strength of this country is its insistence that we adhere to the rule of law."[98] A particularly bellicose version of such arguments took the following form: "The rule of law separates civilized societies from despotic societies. Unlike Iraq, the United States is a nation of laws not men. . . . Yet if we blatantly violate the Constitution by pursuing an undeclared war, we violate the rule of law."[99]

Unchecked and uncheckable will, of the kind courts see in acts of mercy, neither sits easily with these rhetorical invocations of America's commitment to the rule of law nor fulfills the rule of law's promise to establish "a government of law not of men."[100] Indeed, if clemency has any resonance at all with the remainder of our constitutional scheme, that resonance is to be found in "the jurisprudence of emergency," which authorizes responses to grave threats to the nation.[101]

Lest there be any doubt about this resemblance, one need only reference Alexander Hamilton's defense of "vesting the power of pardoning in the President." There Hamilton discusses the need for executives to have the power to pardon in cases of treason, which he rightly describes as "a crime leveled at the immediate being of the society." As if to underline the connection between clemency and the jurisprudence of emergency, Hamilton reminds his readers that "treason will often be connected with seditions which embrace a large proportion of the community." And it is a "well-timed" offer of clemency, deriving neither from the "dilatory process of convening the legislature" nor its fractious deliberations, which in the "critical moments" of "seasons of insurrection or rebellion . . . may restore the tranquility of the commonwealth; and which, if suffered to pass unimproved, it may never be possible afterwards to recall."[102]

I suggest, however, that another context shaped the reception of Governor Ryan's clemency decision, throwing into disarray the political alignments of those who would, for example, approve of his blow to the death penalty system and yet remain suspicious of a large, discretionary executive power (and, indeed, those who would hold these positions vice versa). For Ryan's mass commutation may be a purely domestic issue and fit into familiar arguments about capital punishment, but there can be no doubt that the power he exercised springs from the same source that has recently seen the president of the United States seeking to install military tribunals and altogether remove subjects from the reach of the civil courts by declaring them "enemy combatants."[103] This resonance, this reminder of the affinity among mercy, clemency, and legally authorized, but unruleable, power, explains at least in part the trial of mercy in our times and the anxiety, uncertainty, and instability that marks the history of law's treatment of it and of the executive clemency in which it is embodied.

CHAPTER 4

Governing Clemency

FROM REDEMPTION TO RETRIBUTION

A genuine act of mercy is always unjustified."
—*H.R.T. Roberts*

The only good and sufficient reason for pardoning a felon is that justice is better served by pardoning than by punishing in that particular case.
—*Kathleen Dean Moore*

THROUGHOUT MOST of the twentieth century, the rehabilitative ideal dominated American thought about crime and punishment.[1] Supreme Court Justice Hugo Black, writing in 1949, called it the "prevalent modern philosophy of penology. . . . Reformation and rehabilitation of offenders have," he said, "become important goals of criminal jurisprudence." Black noted that rehabilitation's purpose was not to make the "lot of offenders harder. On the contrary, a strong motivating force . . . has been the belief that by careful study . . . convicted offenders could be less severely punished and restored sooner to complete freedom and useful citizenship."[2] Rehabilitative punishment was, in Black's mind, linked to mercy, and mercy in turn to a social project that criminologist David Garland calls "penal welfarism."[3]

According to the 1976 Report of the Committee for the Study of Incarceration, rehabilitation emerged from "a humanistic tradition which, in pressing for ever more individualization of justice . . . demanded that we treat the criminal, not the crime." It relies, the report continued, "upon a medical and educative model, defining the criminal as, if not sick, less than evil. . . . As a social malfunctioner, the criminal needs to be 'treated' or to be reeducated, reformed, or rehabilitated."[4] With this attention to the criminal and his or her humanity, rehabilitation seems compatible with, if not directly nurturing of, a merciful disposition.

Rehabilitative theories were embodied in indeterminate sentencing schemes in which judges would sentence those convicted of crimes to a range of prison time, leaving determination of the exact amount of time served to parole boards whose job it would be to carefully monitor the inmates' progress on the road to reform.[5] In addition, they were reflected in the internal organization of prisons, where education, work, and therapy provided much of the day-to-day activity of the convict population.[6] Finally, they shaped a widespread belief in what law professor Elizabeth Rapaport has called a "redemptive theory of clemency."[7]

That theory unapologetically rejects an act- and desert-based conception of justice as the supreme value served by a system of criminal punishment, and looks for reasons to do mercy's work.[8] It completely and wholeheartedly embraces leniency rooted in compassion. As a result, it advocates using commutations and/or pardons to reduce punishment below what justice, strictly construed, demands. The merciful disposition says, in effect, "This is what you deserve, but I will nonetheless reduce your punishment."[9] Clemency, Rapaport argues, like "'mercy,' characterizes a judgment or action when a person with the power to exact punishment or payment declines to exact all or some of what he or she is entitled to exact. No wrongdoer or debtor has a right to such leniency—where a right to demand relief exists, clemency or mercy is neither asked nor can be granted."[10]

A redemptive approach to clemency treats "punishment . . . as part of a dynamic process, at least potentially of transformation," and links the use of executive clemency with rehabilitative goals. Like rehabilitation, it focuses on the postconviction lives of criminals. When chief executives consider clemency, they must take an interest in who prisoners become and what they do once their punishment has begun. "Redemptive clemency," Rapaport argues, "may be deserved in the sense that it is earned but not owed. . . . There are," she continues, again making the tie between a rehabilitative theory of punishment and clemency as redemption explicit, "at least two types of cases that exemplify post-conviction merit, rehabilitation and heroic service."[11] Prisoners who experience a moral transformation, acknowledge their wrongdoing, and give evidence of a desire to serve the community and reconcile with those they have harmed have a stronger case for clemency than those who do not, regardless of the justness of their original conviction and sentence.[12] Clemency as redemption "rejects the Manichean division of people into good and evil. . . . From the redemptive perspective, free citizens are also mean, weak, selfish, and takers of bad risks. And transgressors, like the rest of us, have the potential for morally adequate lives and lives of high moral achievement." Finally, Rapaport notes that "[h]ope is also a redemptive criminal justice value: the example of clemency . . . would foster hope for release and reconciliation among those willing to take on the rigors of self-transformation."[13]

If the rehabilitative ideal and the redemptive theory of clemency were indeed important throughout a large part of the twentieth century, by the late 1960s both were on the verge of a dramatic and massive repudiation. Fueled by philosophical criticisms from both conservatives and liberals, and the mobilization of crime and punishment as national political issues during presidential elections from 1968 through the end of the century, leniency, mercy, rehabilitation, and redemption were discredited and largely abandoned in a massive reorientation of the American penal system.

Thus, while at the start of the 1970s every state as well as the federal system had an indeterminate sentencing scheme, today every state has some version of mandatory minimum sentences that typically require long-term incarceration for a variety of crimes. Many states and the federal government went further and enacted sentencing guidelines that require judges to sentence within narrow ranges. The result of these changes has been to severely limit judicial discretion and the judicial role in sentencing.[14] Additionally, most states have abolished, or severely restricted, parole boards, ensuring that inmates serve virtually all of their sentence, regardless of how well they behave behind bars. Finally, in state after state, prison programs necessary for rehabilitation have been eliminated.

The stark results of the reorientation of our governing philosophies of punishment have been chronicled in many places, but one result is captured in the following news story from the July 26, 2004, *New York Times,*

> The number of Americans under the control of the criminal justice system grew by 130,700 last year to reach a new high of nearly 6.9 million, according to a Justice Department report released today. The total includes people in jail and prison as well as those on probation and parole. This is about 3.2 percent of the adult population in the United States, the report said. The growth in what the report termed the "correctional population" comes at a time when the crime rate nationwide has been relatively stable for several years. It also comes when many states, faced with budget deficits, have passed new, less strict sentencing laws in an attempt to reduce the number of inmates. The report does not address why the number of men and women in jail and prison and on probation and parole has continued to increase. But experts say the most likely reason is the cumulative effect of the tougher sentencing laws passed in the 1990's, which led to more people being sent to prison and being required to serve longer terms."[15]

Tougher sentencing laws in the form of mandatory minimums for a variety of crimes, increased severity of punishments across the board, more draconian conditions in prisons, increased use of the death penalty: these are all symptoms of a society "governed through crime."[16] By the late 1960s, against a background of urban disorder and rising crime rates, "law and order" had become the watchword of the day for politicians seeking to turn the stark sociological facts about crime to partisan advantage. While in other nations the question of who should be punished, how, and for what offenses, has long been regarded as technical matters best left to experts, politicians in the United States seized the initiative, stirring up popular anger and indignation, making political capital by claiming to speak cultural common sense against expert knowledge. As law professor James Whitman argues,

> American punishment practices are largely driven by a kind of mass politics that has not succeeded in capturing Western European state practices. We have . . . "popular justice" and indeed populist justice. The harshness of American punishment is made in the volatile and often vicious currents of American democratic electioneering. Calling one's opponent "soft on crime" has become a staple of American campaigning and . . . this has had a powerful, often a spectacular, impact on the making of harsh criminal legislation in the United States.[17]

The "Myth of Crime and Punishment" and The Decline of Rehabilitative Punishment and Redemptive Clemency*

Since the mid-1960s, criminal justice populism has stirred uneasiness about social disorder generally, and about criminal behavior in particular, and given rise to what political scientist Stuart Scheingold calls the "myth of crime and punishment."[18] According to Scheingold, this myth provides a simplistic understanding of criminal behavior and stresses punitiveness as the only appropriate and effective response to crime, in contrast to now out-of-vogue alternative scenarios he identifies as the "myth of redemption" and the "myth of rehabilitation."[19] The myth of

* The next several pages are a slightly revised version of text that originally appeared in Benjamin Steiner, William Bowers, and Austin Sarat, "Folk Knowledge as Legal Action: Death Penalty Judgments and the Tenet of Early Release in a Culture of Mistrust and Permissiveness" 33 *Law and Society Review* (1999), 461, 464–71.

crime and punishment, Scheingold says, "portrays criminals as predatory strangers awaiting opportunities to attack persons and property, as persons fundamentally different in character (and appearance) from law-abiding members of society."[20]

Today the prevailing cultural common sense holds that we need to punish severely in order for punishment to be effective and that mercy should be severely limited in order to ensure criminals are not released from prison "far too soon."[21] At the heart of these beliefs is the view that the criminal justice system in the past was overly solicitous of defendants' rights and too lenient in responding to crime. And no amount of increased severity in punishment can, so it seems, penetrate, satisfy, or alter this folk understanding. So our prisons fill up, our death rows expand, the rate at which clemency is granted declines, and our understanding of what we are doing with those we punish shifts from rehabilitation and redemption to other harsher theorizations of punishment.

Fuel for criminal justice populism is supplied by periodic news accounts of the recidivism of ex-convicts or persons on probation, parole, or furlough from prison—in the worst case, by the narrative nightmare of the murderer released to murder again.[22] High-profile news accounts of the abduction and murder of children comport with, if they do not help to create, public consciousness of crime and punishment. They contribute to the belief that leniency exemplified by early release is a widespread infirmity of the American criminal justice system.[23] Moreover, folk knowledge about crime and punishment invites politicians to assume a "get tough" posture in their political campaigns, and to use stories of early release and what they will do about it as a way of garnering support from a public ever wary of crime.[24]

Perhaps the single most vivid example of the politicization of crime and punishment and the attack on mercy occurred almost twenty years ago in the 1988 presidential contest between then–vice president George Herbert Walker Bush and Massachusetts governor Michael Dukakis. During that campaign, one that to this day haunts the Democratic Party, Bush ran a series of advertisements, the so-called Willie Horton ads. They proved to be ideal fodder for an election-year media rampage that turned the tide for Bush.[25] They created a nightmare of escape from punishment that resonated with public fears of criminal violence and have provided the bedrock both for political rhetoric and the consciousness of crime and punishment ever since. The Horton narrative did so by making a black man who senselessly brutalized a white couple the symbolic representation of Dukakis's alleged criminal justice policy failure—a racial theme apparently also echoed in media crime coverage.[26]

The Horton advertisements blamed Dukakis for the occurrence of senseless, brutal crimes and pinned it all on his soft-on-crime embrace of mercy. Specifically, the advertisements "George Bush and Michael Dukakis on Crime" and "Governor Dukakis's Liberal Furlough Program Failed" attacked Dukakis' "liberal" punishment policy, a policy quite out of step with folk knowledge and cultural common sense. The first ad showed a turnstile with running text that claimed that 268 convicts escaped while on furlough in Massachusetts, and a voice-over stating that many leave prison early only to commit crimes again.[28] The second ad, narrated by the sister of the teenager killed by Horton, provided emotional testimony about Dukakis's record of leniency, failed furloughs, and vetoes of capital punishment.

University of Pennsylvania professor of communication Kathleen Hall Jamieson has demonstrated the substantial effect of these ads on the public's consciousness of crime and punishment, a consciousness that put mercy on trial and held it to account for society's inadequate responses to the crime problem. In her analysis of that effect, she describes, for example, how a nine-member Dallas focus group that favored Dukakis, five to four, in early September 1988 shifted to Bush, seven to two, shortly after the airing of the Horton ads. More important, by early November 1988, there was a hardening of attitudes in favor of "get tough" crime policy and the death penalty. The principal elements of the Horton narrative that focus-group members identified as key to their thinking were the fear of such crime, the need to keep criminals in prison or execute them, and the complicity of Dukakis in letting Horton out of prison.[29]

Specifically, Jamieson asked respondents to write a description of the Horton incident and to indicate the source of their information for each sentence with a "PN" for print news, "BN" for televised broadcast news, "RN" for radio news, "A" for advertising, "H" if they had heard it in conversation, and "NS" to indicate that they weren't sure where they had heard/read/seen it. As an example, one member of the focus group wrote:

> Willy Horton was a killer and wasn't electrocuted (H/PN). . . . He kept raping the wife (BN). He [Horton] was black and the wife [*sic*] was white. . . . Her husband went crazy. . . . He [husband] still can't forgive himself. That's why he is against Dukakis (BN). Her husband says that she is afraid that he will come back (BN/NS). He [Horton] killed a boy in a supermarket in Maryland (H). . . . I believe in the death penalty for people like that. . . . George Bush opposes gun control and favors executing Hortons (Radio—I think it was an ad). I would guess Willy Horton doesn't."[30]

Analyzing this response, Jamieson notes that "the cues in the media . . . triggered a broad chain of associations." While some of the details were garbled or confused, the main theme is clearly evident. She observes that the Horton narrative—"murderer released to murder again"—resonated with the public's fear of violent crime and desire for a commonsense explanation for why it occurs. In her words the Horton ad "completes in a satisfying manner a narrative that is already cast with a menacing murderer in a mug shot; anguished, outraged victims; and an unrepentant, soft-on-crime liberal. In such narrative construction, the governor will be unmasked for what he is because the *murderer will murder again* [emphasis added]. Horton is incapable of redemption. Prison has accomplished nothing. He deserved the death penalty Bush is touting."[31]

"Incapable of redemption"—this is a key to the public's increasing suspicion of mercy and its rejection of rehabilitation and a redemptive theory of clemency. This suspicion and rejection was, by 1988, so deep that citizens had become quite resistant to the kind of evidence that might have debunked the accusations against Dukakis. Statistics documenting the overall success of the Massachusetts furlough program, as well as statistics from the federal government showing higher rates of early release and recidivism in California during the gubernatorial term of Ronald Reagan, provoked one person to say: "You can't change my mind with all of that. . . . When you support the death penalty, the really bad ones get killed. That's, the liberal, the problem with [*sic*], about liberals." Another citizen dismissed statistical evidence: "We should ship all our criminals to the college liberals in College Station . . . or Austin. Crime's not statistics, honey."[32] These responses indicate the depth of suspicion that attaches to mercy, and the resistance to change of postrehabilitation assumptions about the right way of dealing with criminals.[33] This suspicion and resistance has, if anything, only deepened since 1988.

Whatever the reason for its profound and lasting impact, the early-release narrative conveyed in the Willie Horton incident, and many media sensations since then, is one of a criminal justice system out of control, a system unable to keep even the worst offenders off of the streets. The message that comes across does not focus on the specific periods in which offenders, or in this case murderers, are being released, only on the fact that they are being released early. Or, in the words of Bush's 1988 campaign: "let . . . out on vacation." As Jamieson's focus-group data suggests, the Horton incident tapped into a broad "culture of mistrust" concerning crime and punishment policy, which did not depend on specific knowledge of what actually happened, or what policies Dukakis employed as governor. Instead it seized on the message that mercy was being granted promiscuously and that dangerous criminals were not being treated severely enough.

The post-1960s attack on mercy and the rehabilitative ideal that seemed too merciful not only originated in the media and in political campaigns, but was also seen in a flourishing industry of academic criticism. Since the late 1960s, academic critics on both the right and the left have voiced various worries about rehabilitation—that it depended on lodging discretionary authority in sentencing judges and that discretion was often associated with disparity and discrimination;[34] that it was too lenient and, as a result, ineffective in preventing recidivism;[35] and/or that it did not deal adequately with the underlying social causes of crime.[36] Critics called for reforms to cure one or another of these defects. Some advocated an end to rehabilitation in the hope that doing so would result in shorter prison sentences for fewer people.[37] Others pushed for approaches to punishment that would result in longer sentences for more offenders and a different attitude toward clemency.[38]

A Right to Be Punished

One of the most interesting and surprising academic critiques of rehabilitation is found in the work of Herbert Morris, an Oxford-educated philosopher and longtime professor of law in the United States.[39] While his work does not fit neatly with standard right or left responses to issues of crime and punishment, it is particularly instructive for what it can tell us about the trial of mercy and its consequences for clemency in capital cases. Moreover, it captures the flavor of the distinctly antimercy sentiment that would provide the backdrop for our national conversation for decades to come.

At the heart of Morris's critique of rehabilitation, and the apparently merciful attitude that rehabilitation embodied, was his belief that both are incompatible with the assumptions and requirements of a political order dedicated to maximizing individual freedom and respecting the choices made by free persons. Indeed so strong was Morris's conviction concerning the danger of rehabilitative approaches that he argued that each person possesses an inalienable "right" to be punished. Morris understood full well the deeply counterintuitive nature of the claim he was making, but was undeterred by its unnerving quality. "Reaction to the claim that there is . . . a right (to be punished) has been," he reports, "astonishment combined, perhaps, with a touch of contempt for the perversity of the suggestion. A strange right that no one would ever wish to claim! With that flourish the subject is buried and the right disposed of." Morris took it as his project to make sure that, as he put it, "the subject is resurrected."[40]

What did Morris mean when he advanced the claim that we have a right to be punished? What role does this idea play in his critique of rehabilitation? The foundation of his argument about the right to be punished is Morris's assumption that humans are free and moral agents, capable of knowing right from wrong and of making choices over a range of alternative courses of conduct. From this assumption, he goes on to argue that crime should be regarded "as if" it were a choice, freely made, decided on the basis of a rational calculation of the costs and benefits of following the law. "A voluntary agent," Morris argues, "diverging his conduct from what is expected or what the norms are, on general causal principles, is regarded as the cause of what results from his conduct." In this sense, Morris suggests, "a person chooses the punishment that is meted out to him."[41]

And if we are to respect the person making the choice to commit a crime, we must respect the choice itself. "We treat a human being as a person provided: first, we permit the person to make the choices that will determine what happens to him and second, when our responses to the person are responses respecting the person's choices." A person, Morris claims, has a "right to institutions that respect his choices. Our punishment system does that."[42] When we punish, Morris suggests, we express our respect for the choices individuals make in a way in which no other response can convey.

Unlike rehabilitation, which takes what Andrew Von Hirsch calls a "non-moral approach" to crime,[43] punishment is in Morris's view "the imposition upon a person who is believed to be at fault of something commonly believed to be a deprivation where that deprivation is justified by the person's guilty behavior." In this definition of punishment, we see evidence of a retributive attitude, of Morris's insistence on thinking about punishment as something deserved in light of "guilty behavior." Indeed, as he sees it, the criminal wills his own punishment in the sense that he can be said to have "brought the punishment on himself."[44]

In Morris's view, the key problems of the rehabilitative approach to punishment begin with its view of crime, treating it as a "symptom of some pathological condition in the way a running nose is a symptom of a cold. Actions diverging from some conception of the normal are viewed as manifestations of a disease. . . . What a person does, then, is assimilated, on this conception, to what we believe . . . a person undergoes."[45]

Morris draws a stark contrast between punishment properly understood and rehabilitation, arguing that there are six relevant differences. First, while punishment focuses on the past, rehabilitation focuses on the present.[46] The latter, he says, is "normally associated with compassion for what one undergoes" rather than the justifiable "resentment" that guilty behavior properly evokes. Second, "with therapy . . . we do not seek to deprive the person of something acknowledged as a good, but rather seek to help and to benefit the individual who is suffering by ministering to his illness in the hope that the person can be cured."[47] Third, when we punish we focus on the "debt owed," while such ideas have no place in a rehabilitative system. Fourth, while punishment is associated with ideas of proportionality, namely that there should be some equivalence between the wrong done and the suffering inflicted,[48] in a rehabilitative system, Morris argues, "attempts at proportionality make no sense." Fifth, punishment depends on the occurrence of rule violations, yet in a rehabilitative system there is no reason "to wait until symptoms manifest themselves in socially harmful conduct." And, finally, rehabilitation, because of its commitment to providing persons the services they need, is incompatible with the "procedural safeguards we associate with punishment."[49]

Rehabilitation, as Morris saw it, was a kind of idealism gone bad, one that damaged those it intended to help and disserved a society it intended to serve. It fails the sternest and most important test by refusing to treat crime as if it were the product of individual choice. Acts become events, and choices become unrecognizable as choices. "The logic of sickness," Morris argued, "implies the logic of therapy."[50]

In the end, Morris's most profound worry was that rehabilitation invited a dramatic expansion of state power.[51] This, I think, explains his resort to the vocabulary of rights. For him, as for many philosophical liberals, rights provide trumps to state power—limits on it, ways of keeping it in its place. They provide a foundation that allows persons to go about the business of crafting a life for themselves.

If there indeed is a right to be punished, it would seem that clemency abridges that right and interferes with the duty that attaches to its recognition, the duty to punish offenders by altering the terms of our responses to their choices. Thus it should not be surprising that Morris criticized the impulse to forgive, to be merciful, to pardon. "[T]he practice of pardoning may," he says, "endanger . . . the practice of justice."[52] Thus punishment should turn away from what Von Hirsch calls "compromising considerations . . . [like] generosity and charity, compassion and love." We should, so the argument goes, shift "the emphasis from concern for the individual to devotion to the moral right." The result of such a shift "could lead to an abandonment of . . . [mercy] altogether."[53]

Moreover, without a commitment to retributive justice, clemency, in Morris's view, makes no sense at all. "A system of deprivations, or a practice of deprivations on the happening of certain actions, underlies the practice of pardoning and forgiving, for it is only where we possess the idea of a wrong to be made up or a debt owed to others . . . that we have the idea of pardoning for the wrong or forgiving the debt."[54] Pardoning, in Morris's view, always threatens the right to be punished unless it is inscribed within, and limited by, a principled commitment to retributive punishment. In this way he opens the door for the articulation of a similar approach to clemency, one that retributivists like Morris see as both respecting human dignity and limiting power by grounding it in a set of normative principles beyond law.

A Retributive Theory of Clemency: On The Search for Grounding Beyond Law

Some scholars have responded to Morris's worry about mercy as a threat to liberal values and to the indeterminacy of clemency described in chapter 3, by offering what they see as a set of stabilizing prescriptions, philosophies, and guidelines to govern clemency. Taking off from Justice Rehnquist's idea that clemency only should be used to remedy "miscarriages of justice,"[55] they have elaborated a retributive theory of clemency or, perhaps more accurately, tried to harmonize clemency with a retributive theory of punishment. Rejecting redemption as a legitimate basis for clemency, they argue that in clemency, "like the imposition of punishment, the remission of punishment must be administered in a principled, consistent fashion."[56]

The most extended example of this search for principle and consistency has been offered by Kathleen Dean Moore. Moore begins from the proposition that clemency as it is currently understood is an archaic idea that needs to be refurbished to comport with constitutional democracy in the modern state. She insists on the necessity of stripping away "all of the concepts left over from the seventeenth century—all the 'acts of grace' and 'divine forgiveness'—and look at pardons operationally." When we do so, she contends, what she calls the "close relationship" of pardons and punishment will be apparent.[57]

While this equation seems inconsistent with the basis of sovereign power in a constitutional democracy, which splits punishments and pardons, that division must be repaired, at least at the conceptual level, if we are to produce a coherent, and stabilizing, account of pardons. When looked at operationally, Moore argues, executives may not have the direct right to assign punishments, but their uses or refusals to use clemency are punitive. They determine "who will be punished and who will not, and how much and how little."[58] This is true in one sense since a decision not to pardon or commute sentence is, in effect, a ratification of the previously imposed sentence. But it is hardly what "determines" punishment, since in the overwhelming proportion of cases, clemency is neither asked for nor granted.

If we grant the equivalence between pardon and punishment, Moore notes, we will accept that pardons, like punishment, need to be "justified by reasons having to do with what is just." While Moore concedes that pardons sometimes "make exceptions to rules . . . when general presumptions are defeated by exceptional circumstances," she insists they can and should be disciplined. "In the American democracy," Moore argues, "the pardon is not a gift from the sovereign and cannot be exempt, on that ground, from the need for justification." In her view the simplest and best justification for punishment is that it is "deserved."[59] While there are other justifications, none is, as she sees it, as powerful as retribution.

A retributive theory of clemency has not only conceptual advantages, but the added benefit of harmonizing clemency with this era's prevailing theory of punishment. Even more important, it holds out the hope of bringing clemency to heel, of guiding and governing it in a way that allows courts and citizens to hold those who have the power to spare life accountable against a set of coherent standards.

Moore is a strict retributivist in the sense that she believes that helping to satisfy the demands of just desert is the *primary* basis on which modern clemency can be justified. As she says, "the only good and sufficient reason for pardoning a felon is that justice is better served by pardoning than by punishing in that particular case."[60] Pardons are correctives for legal mistakes that put the commands of justice at risk. They help the law adhere more closely than it otherwise could to those commands.

She lists several principles that justify pardons. Pardons are allowed in order to correct the punishment of the innocent (those who stand convicted of a crime they "may not have committed") and of those who are "guilty under the law but are not morally blameworthy."[61] They may be used when the punishment of a guilty and deserving offender is unduly severe or to prevent cruelty or relieve those whose suffering exceeds what they merit.[62] In our legal system, pardon is "a backup system that works outside the rules to correct mistakes, making sure that only those who deserve punishment are punished."[63]

Outside the rules, but not lawless, outside the rules but doing the work that a just system of rules requires, Moore seems, like the judges whose opinions I discussed in chapter 3, to want both to liberate and discipline clemency. She does so by continually distinguishing law from justice, reminding us that a punishment's validity does not ensure its desert. For her, there is no indeterminacy in the realm of just deserts. Justice can command. It can rescue law from the conundrum into which our timid judiciary has thrust it.

Moore is insightful in her efforts to distinguish law from justice. In these efforts her work instantiates a venerable philosophical tradition, showing its strength and reminding us of the limits of law. But at this point in the argument, a structural contradiction seems to emerge: If Moore concedes that no matter how exhaustive and detailed the extant law is it can never *fully ensure* a just punishment, why would the same problematic not apply to her set of prescriptions? That is, why is Moore confident that those prescriptions could be the antidote to every situation in which clemency is needed? And if it is conceded that they cannot, then are we not back to the need for *discretionary power* and executive clemency based in mercy? Undoubtedly, Moore would answer that her proposal is a set of principles not rules, but even such an answer leaves open the question of why then retain the institution of executive clemency at all.

Indeed, in a concluding paragraph, The Future of Pardon, Moore anticipates precisely such an objection, even as she offers her reasons for dismissing it.

> Every once in a while, someone will argue that the time has come to abolish the pardon system, since the legal system has finally reached a state close enough to perfection that pardon is no longer needed. . . . The argument cannot be accepted. Much of the progress in the legal system has been prompted by pardons. Pardons are being granted this very day that will have the cumulative effect of producing still further improvement in the legal system—perhaps some of those improvements suggested here. Pardon is indeed a "weapon" for reform, and its firepower has yet to be directed against the most basic structural economic and racial injustices.[64]

The idiom in which Moore articulates this anticipated criticism is, of course, the very idiom she uses to propel her project: utilizing the power of the sovereign prerogative of pardon in a reformist agenda for the improvement of the law. All of which leads to the question of what Moore thinks about the perfectibility of the law, whether the day of its perfectibility has not yet come or whether the day will *never* come. Nor is this a minor criticism, as it goes directly to the borderline cartography of executive clemency, its simultaneous outside-inside relation to a rule of law and procedural fixity. Even as Moore urges us to abandon the received theological and magisterial conceptions of the pardon power, to absorb clemency into a systemic operation of the law, one has to wonder if the "fire power" of executive clemency, which she hopes to harness for social justice, does not in fact depend on precisely the outside-inside status that I suggested in chapter 3 is constitutive of this power.

But, even more by tethering clemency to the principles of justice, retributivists like Moore believe that they can save it from its current malaise, namely the reluctance of executives to use their clemency power in capital cases. They make this claim on explicitly political grounds. They do so because they believe that "clemency practices overwhelmingly seem to be reflective of broader societal assumptions about punishment." Typical is law professor Daniel Kobil's argument that retributive justifications are the only game in town, that without them there is no hope of persuading presidents and governors to grant clemency. Retributive principles applied to clemency square with the "tough on crime" rhetoric that is so politically important today. "To put it bluntly," Kobil says, "[w]e have little chance of persuading those in authority to use clemency to further redemptive goals when, at the moment, most are reluctant to use clemency at all."[65]

Moore's effort to govern clemency with retributive principles has recently been subject to critique from *within* the retributivist camp. Daniel Markel's "Against Mercy" displays anxiety similar to Moore's about the ungovernability of mercy, but suggests that her argument concentrates too much on trying to assure a "tight connection between punishment and desert," and that as a result it does not "consider how the relationship between retributivism and liberal democracy affects dispensations of leniency."[66] Markel seeks to shift the grounds of the retributivist critique of mercy, yet, like Moore, believes that retributivism can and should discipline clemency.

Markel's indictment of mercy begins with the provocative suggestion that "mercy based on compassion is just as problematic as mercy motivated by bias or caprice."[67] Indeed it is Markel's point that mercy is always a kind of caprice, a dangerous blow to values central to liberal social order. Though he says he wants to identify grounds for leniency, the grounds he identifies turn it into something else. They do so by requiring that executives obtain specific authorization from legislative bodies to consider particular factors as making someone eligible for mercy. "[I]t would be consistent with retributivism for the *legislature* to authorize executive consideration of postconviction good behavior for a reduction in the severity of certain punishments. . . . [P]ostconviction actions," he contends, are, in fact, "susceptible to analysis of desert, and therefore are compatible with retributivism."[68]

The factors that legitimately may count in the calculus of desert must be prescribed in advance and thus brought within the reach of legal regulation. As Markel observes, "[I]f a state's executive extended leniency to the offender on account of postconviction conduct without specific imprimatur to consider that factor, then such leniency would be subject to a moral critique that such leniency is improper because it will lead to ad hoc and arbitrary disbursements of punishment discounts."[69] There is something a bit circular, but nonetheless revealing, in this argument. The circularity is found in the notion that taking account of a factor not prescribed in advance is ad hoc. While this seems true by definition, it is revealing of Markel's fear of clemency's ruleless quality. What separates Markel from Moore is not then his tolerance for clemency's lawful lawlessness, but rather the particulars of the theory he deploys in an effort to govern it. Thus he argues that

> prior retributivist critiques of mercy have failed to grapple with what I call the democratic difficulty of mercy, which is the difficulty presented to these critiques by mercy that is authorized by constitutional or democratic laws and institutions, such as the presidential pardon or grand jury nullification. It is difficult to speculate why these prior accounts have neglected the democratic difficulty: perhaps it is because theorists of retributivism often have the training and abstracting minds of philosophers rather than lawyers, and therefore are less sensitive to institutional perspectives. Regardless of the etiology of this problem, this article attempts to qualify the force of the critique against mercy from those critics who view their arguments as consonant with liberal democratic norms. Although I ultimately share prior retributivists' hostility toward mercy, I arrive at that conclusion for reasons not fully recognized before.[70]

One way to capture the disagreement between Markel and Moore is to say that for the former the proper bases of retributive punishments are not limited, as they are in Moore's account, to the claims of justice. Where justice is the exclusive focus of retributive critiques of clemency, theorists are led to conclude that "when mercy is separated from concerns about an offender's culpability, it should be enfeebled as much as possible." For Markel the problem of mercy is, as he puts it, less one of justice than of "equality under law."[71]

What does he mean by this claim? Markel argues that when an individual commits a crime he is displaying a kind of superiority over the victim of his offense.

> When I steal, rape, or murder, I am arrogating a license to act in ways that the polity has officially proscribed. I lord this license over my victim and those around me. It is a claim of superiority—namely, that I am a law unto myself, that society's laws do not bind me. . . . I am, [in essence] defecting from a legal order to which I have good reason to give my allegiance, and I am defecting in such a way that I am taking license to which others are not entitled. If no attempt is made to punish me, my claim to superiority over others commands greater plausibility than it would if I were made to experience some level of coercion that is not inflicted on nonoffending fellow citizens."[72]

Mercy does not, in Markel's estimation, advance the cause of equality under law. It cannot be granted to all similarly situated offenders without becoming something other than mercy.[73] As a result, mercy always contains an element of arbitrariness. "If everyone," he notes, "is entitled to the same package of liberties safeguarded by political and legal institutions, it is hard to see how granting mercy to some offenders but not to others effectuates this ideal."[74]

Finally, for Markel, mercy must be rejected, or severely regulated, because "it stands at odds with the nature of the modern liberal democratic regime under the rule of law."[75] Invoking this concern Markel speaks to something deep in American political culture, namely our commitment to, and yet anxieties about, the rule of law.

Conclusion

As I have argued in this chapter, worry about meaningful constraint, as much as substantive disagreements about the question of how severe punishment should be, is at the heart of the retributivist attack on mercy and the effort of scholars like Moore and Markel to find moral principles to do what law cannot do, but must be done if justice or equality under law is to be achieved, namely to bring mercy and clemency under a disciplining rubric. While rehabilitation and redemptive theories of clemency are attacked in the political arena as symptoms of our culture's allegedly corrosive leniency and permissiveness in responding to crime, retributive theories of clemency are moved by a commitment to minimizing as much as possible the risk of arbitrariness and abuse of power that attaches to clemency conceived of as a legally sanctioned, but not legally governed, power.

Critics have respond to these theories by rejecting their political premises and objecting to them as a sufficient basis for governing clemency. Some want to rehabilitate rehabilitation as a governing philosophy of punishment;[76] others articulate new ways of doing justice aimed to reintegrate offenders into society and promote reconciliation in the face of grievous injury.[77] Yet all of them agree that mercy, not justice, provides the conceptual key to clemency, with some emphasizing private[78] and others more public versions of that idea.[79] While retributivists seek to identify principles to govern clemency and, in so doing, tame it, their critics acknowledge that mercy and clemency are ungovernable, or at least unruly.[80]

Some of those critics revive respect for the history that Moore treats so contemptuously, cautioning that retributivists "devalue . . . [clemency's] historical association with compassion and redemption" and would turn executive clemency decisions into "judicial courts of last resort."[81] Instead of thinking of the executive making a clemency decision in a juridical posture, Margaret Love reminds us of the anxiety-generating association of clemency and emergency when she suggests that presidents should "use the pardon power like a good chief diplomat or military commander . . . [exercising] judgment in the face of the unexpected." She holds out for a different justification for clemency, one that would require no "major revisions in pardon's historical character"[82] and, at the same time, respect "[t]he inherent mystery of the pardon process."[83] She finds such a justification by treating clemency, à la Jeffrie Murphy, as a "collective exercise of mercy by the community as a whole through its chief executive."[84] Seeing mercy as public, Love hopefully notes, should allow us to live with the continuing and unresolvable tension between rules and exceptions, between the rule of law's insistence on subjecting power to rule and the confrontation with a power that cannot be subject to rule.[85]

Before taking up Love's invitation to embrace the mystery of clemency and its attendant risks, I return to George Ryan to see how his clemency responds to this opportunity and to the triumph of retribution over redemption. While at first glance Ryan's action might seem to mark the triumph of redemption and mystery, it was, as we will see, moved by neither redemptive purposes nor by an embrace of the inexorable mystery that sits just over the horizon of legality.

CHAPTER 5

Clemency without Mercy

GEORGE RYAN'S DILEMMA

Turning a terrible action into a story is a way to distance onself from it, at worst a form of self-deception, at best a way to pardon the self.
—*Natalie Zemon Davis*

WHEN ILLINOIS GOVERNOR GEORGE RYAN announced his decision to empty that state's death row, his speech shared many of the conventions of the standard genre of gubernatorial pardons. Yet it was in many ways a complex performance, a stitching together of different rhetorics, many borrowed from the world of judicial opinions.[1] His statement most closely resembles the justificatory act of a judge speaking through his opinion to the fact that, in a democracy, judges are often required by the structure of the judicial system to decide against majority opinion. Like a judge, Ryan presented his decision as "compelled," an act of duty not a personal choice. The language of compulsion is invoked from the outset in the very title of his speech, "I Must Act." This speech was, as law professor Robert Ferguson says of judicial rhetoric, "self-dramatizing,"[2] stressing in particular the importance of the fact that only Ryan could make the decision to grant clemency.

In addition, Ryan's statement worked "to appropriate all other voices into its own monologue," subsuming "difference into an act of explanation and moment of decision. . . . The monologic voice . . . can never presume to act on its own. It must appear as if forced to its inevitable conclusion by the logic of the situation and the duties of office, which together eliminate all thought of an unfettered hand."[3] Like an unelected judge, accountable only through the adequacy of his justifications, Ryan granted clemency as he was about to leave office, no longer subject to electoral accountability, with the imagined judgment of history as his target audience.

Ryan made his decision in a context established by capital clemency's dramatic but often troubled history, by law's ambivalent attitude toward mercy and clemency, and by the efforts of theorists to divorce clemency from mercy and root it solely in the requirements of justice. Moreover, he acted at a time when public support for the death penalty, while slightly off its historic highs, still ran around 70 percent,[4] when American society was said to be deeply in the throes of compassion fatigue,[5] and when political debate about crime and punishment was dominated by two powerful, but inconsistent forces, retributivism[6] and the victims rights movement.[7] While, at first glance, his clemency appeared to be an effort to revive redemptive approaches to clemency and an unusual moment of mercy,[8] appearances are deceptive. His rhetoric shows him to be less redemptive or compassionate than we might think, trying desperately to navigate within a legal, political, and cultural context pushed and pulled by retribution and victims rights.

As a rhetorical performance, Ryan's twenty-two-page, hour-long "I Must Act" was at times deeply personal and at other times flatly bureaucratic (see appendix A). In fact, Ryan's speech had two different registers and was riven along the important distinction between an individual grant of clemency and a mass commutation. If the first is more amenable to a language of compassion and largesse, then the second is inexorably systemic and speaks more in the discourse of institutions and the distribution of powers among them. The second of these registers was, I will argue, by far the most dominant in Ryan's decision.

In the course of the speech announcing the clemency decision, Ryan only mentioned mercy twice, and both times by quoting the words of others. This rhetorical gesture allowed him to appear to embrace mercy but to do so only tentatively, keeping it at what he hoped was a safe distance. Thus he told his listeners, without further elaboration or comment, that "[t]he Most

Reverend Desmond Tutu wrote to me this week stating that 'to take a life when a life has been lost is revenge, it is not justice. He says justice allows for mercy, clemency and compassion. These virtues are not weakness.' "[9] Second, reaching back into American history, Ryan quoted Abraham Lincoln's admonition that "mercy bears richer fruits than strict justice."

As the halfheartedness of these invocations of mercy suggests, Ryan's clemency did not represent a return to a redemptive view of clemency. Indeed how could his decision be merciful when it was directed not to particular individuals, but to everyone on death row? Mercy, after all, is not a wholesale virtue.[10] As the philosopher and critic Martha Nussbaum notes, mercy requires singularity and attention to particulars. It demands, she says, "flexible particularized judgment." To be merciful one must regard "each particular case as a complex narrative of human effort in a world full of obstacles."[11] Ryan's wholesale clemency was less an act of grace than a concession to the inadequacies of a death penalty system gone awry and to a political system unwilling or unable to address those inadequacies. Thus while his act produced mercy for those whose sentences were reduced, it was not given in a merciful spirit. Where the speech showed compassion, its compassion was directed mostly to the surviving families of murder victims or of offenders rather than to the murderers whose lives he spared.

While governors before him used their own wholesale clemency decisions to attack the death penalty per se, criticize it as immoral, and call for its abolition,[12] Ryan provided no such critique.[13] Instead Ryan's "I Must Act" explains his decision through two contradictory stories. The first is a story of victims and their suffering. Ryan's focus on victims gives further evidence that "We have become a nation of victims, where everyone is leapfrogging over each other, competing for the status of victim, where most people define themselves as some sort of survivor."[14] His second story focused on institutions and their failures, and fits well with a retributive theory of clemency.[15] In both, Ryan puts himself at the center. In one he seeks to authenticate his act by identifying himself as a suffering subject, able in his suffering to know the pain that families of murder victims suffer at the hands of the criminal and that they would suffer at his hands. In the other he describes himself as a reluctant actor seeking to ensure that justice is done in a failing justice system and a political system in paralysis.[16]

In the story of victims and their suffering, Ryan displays the fragility of democratic sovereignty, desperately seeking grounding in a shared conception of citizenship, in which what binds us is our common suffering and victimization.[17] In the story of institutional failure, he portrays himself as a committed retributivist using clemency to do the work that justice, not mercy, requires,[18] and he embraces a "fail safe" attitude toward clemency advocated by former president Clinton, by President George W. Bush and by Chief Justice Rehnquist.[19] If responsiveness to victims provided the point of departure for his clemency, retributive principles provided its disciplining core. Whereas compassion for the families of murder victims provided the rhetorical bedrock of his argument, his clemency was fashioned in such a way as to insulate Ryan against charges that it showed sympathy for those whose lives he spared.

Listening to Victims

Modern legality is founded on an effort to make reason triumph over emotion and due process over passion and to make punishments proportional in their severity to the crimes that occasion them.[20] As we saw in the last chapter, just deserts, not deterrence or rehabilitation, becomes the primary, if not the sole, norm governing punishment.[21] "Only the Law of retribution," Kant noted,

> can determine exactly the kind and degree of punishment; it must be well understood, however, that this determination must be made in the chambers of a court of justice and not in your private judgement. All other standards fluctuate back and forth and,

> because extraneous considerations are mixed with them, they cannot be compatible with the principle of pure and legal justice.[22]

Aladjem observes that,

> This inclination to make revenge over into a rational principle of justice has roots in democratic theory and in certain suppositions of natural law. It arose in claims about the founding of the state, where it was said that a process of consent converts the laws of nature into those of civil society and that the state acquires its right to punish from consenting individuals who thereby relinquish a natural right to avenge themselves. From the beginning, however, that reasoning presents a paradox: the state is supposed to arise from the inclinations of individuals as they might be found in nature, but it must rescue them from the very same inclinations. . . . [A] vengeful "natural man" turns to the state as a place of appeal from the injustices of nature *and* from the excesses of his own revenge.[23]

Victims and their pain must be kept at bay, so the argument goes, because they threaten to overwhelm us with an anger and passion that knows no limits.[24] As St. Augustine put it,

> We do not wish to have the sufferings of the servants of God avenged by the infliction of precisely similar injuries in the way of retaliation. . . . [O]ur desire is that justice be satisfied. . . . [W]ho does not see that when a restraint is put upon the boldness of savage violence, and the remedies fitted to produce repentance are not withdrawn, the discipline should be called a benefit rather than a vindictive punishment.[25]

Justice becomes public, and the voice of the victim is merged with the distanced state bureaucracy that speaks for "The People" against whom all offenses to the criminal law are said to be directed.[26] "It is sometimes the custom," Beccaria states,

> to release a man from the punishment of a slight crime when the injured pardons him: an act, indeed, which is in accordance with mercy and humanity but contrary to public policy; as if a private

> citizen could by his remission do away with the necessity of the example in the same way that he can excuse the reparation due for an offense. The right of punishing does not rest with an individual, but with the community as a whole, or the sovereign.[27]

Following Beccaria's maxim, the tendency of criminal justice systems in Western democracies has been to displace the direct victims of crime, to shut the door on those with the greatest interest in seeing justice done. In response, victims recently and insistently have demanded that their voices be heard throughout the criminal process.[28]

As a result, legal systems in the United States and Europe have been confronted by stern challenges in the name of victims rights. Here and elsewhere a tide of resentment is rising against a system of justice that traditionally tried to substitute public processes for private action and, in so doing, to justify the criminal sanction as a response to injuries to public order rather than to harms done to particular individuals. As President Bush put it when he announced his support for a victims rights amendment to the U.S. Constitution, "When our criminal justice systems treats victims as irrelevant bystanders, they are victimized for a second time. And because Americans are justifiably proud of our system and expect it to treat us fairly, the second violation of our rights can be traumatic. 'It's like a huge slap,' said one victim, 'because you think the system will protect you. It's maddening and frightening.'"[29] Over the last two decades the situation Bush described has been changing, and many of the demands of victims have been met.[30] But the victims rights movement wants more.[31] It seeks participation and power by making the victim the symbolic heart of modern legality. Moreover, it contests the attempted appropriation of the role of the victim by offenders and what it sees as the promiscuous use of the language of victimization throughout our culture.[32] The movement draws on standard stories and mobilizes around incidents that are "horrifying and aberrational,"[33] generating sentimental narratives of lives lost, families ruined, evil done. As

Ofer Zur puts it, "The victim stance is a powerful one. The victim is always morally right, neither responsible nor accountable, and forever entitled to sympathy."[34]

The victims rights movement contests the hegemony of the very normative constraints on which retributive justice insists[35] as well as what Professor Danielle Allen calls "the near-total erasure of the victim from the process of punishment."[36] It demands that the legal system respond to crime victims' grief and rage.[37] By turning punishment into a site for the rituals of grieving,[38] that movement would make private experiences part of public discourse. Yet in so doing, not only is a private colonization of public processes encouraged, public scrutiny also invades some of the most personal aspects of our lives—the ways we suffer and grieve. The victims rights movement highlights the difficulty of "reconciling grief and rage and vengefulness with practicable moral enforcements of civil association [and] of reconciling a cultural preoccupation with vengeance and . . . forms of legal punishment which deny it."[39] Retributive norms, so this argument goes, no longer, if they ever did, adequately express common moral commitments.

"I draw most of my strength from victims," former attorney general Reno once said, "for they represent America to me: people who will not be put down, people who will not be defeated, people who will rise again and stand again for what is right. . . . You are my heros and heroines. You are but little lower than the angels." So important has the image of the victim become in our political life that one scholar argues they have come to be "the most idealized form of political subjectivity. . . . It is as crime victims that Americans are most readily imagined as united by a threat that simultaneously downplays their differences and authorizes them to take dramatic political steps. . . . The innocent victim of violent crime becomes the paradigm example of the citizen who needs government."[40]

That Ryan's mass commutation is situated in the saga of an increasingly victim-centered political and legal environment and that compassion for crime victims was one of its dominant motifs is suggested by the great prominence that the language of victimization had in his speech.[41] "I have read, listened to and discussed the issue with the families of the victims as well as the families of the condemned," Ryan said, before sharing a story in which he identified himself as a crime victim twice removed. "I grew up in Kankakee which even today is still a small Midwestern town, a place where people tend to know each other," Ryan explained.

> Steve Small was a neighbor. I watched him grow up. He would babysit my young children which was not for the faint of heart since Lura Lynn and I had six children, 5 of them under the age of 3. He was a bright young man who helped run the family business. He got married and he and his wife had three children of their own. Lura Lynn was especially close to him and his family. We took comfort in knowing he was there for us and we for him. One September midnight he received a call at his home. There had been a break-in at the nearby house he was renovating. But as he left his house, he was seized at gunpoint by kidnappers. His captors buried him alive in a shallow hole. He suffocated to death before police could find him. His killer led investigators to where Steve's body was buried. The killer, Danny Edward was also from my hometown. He now sits on death row. I also know his family. I share this story with you so that you know I do not come to this as a neophyte without having experienced a small bit of the bitter pill the survivors of murder must swallow.

This is a ghostly as well as ghastly account, bringing before its listeners the specter of a dead man mercilessly slaughtered. That Ryan ties himself to this ghost is reminiscent of Fitzpatrick's account of the finitude that death imposes on law and the unfolding indeterminism of law's beyond. Clemency exercised to stave off death, confronting it, as it were, face-to-face and refusing its demand, helps to mark death as the horizon of law both as "supreme stasis" and "the opening to all possibility that is beyond affirmed order."[42] Moreover, metaphors of place, the small town, and the knowledge that Small was "there for us," contribute to the ghostliness of Ryan's account precisely by marking the placelessness of death and its irresistible ability to enter any place.[43]

But there is another specter in this story, this one of a life marked for its own untimely extinction.[44] By connecting himself to Danny Edwards, Ryan rhetorically invokes a kind of dual accountability that always governs clemency in capital cases, one side facing the already dead, the other those whose lives are in the balance. If Ryan's rhetoric is rightly thought of as juridical, then, like others who pass judgment in death penalty cases, he turns to "expressions of pain as others may once have turned to God, in trust that this 'sacred name' will make it possible for individuals to answer the question, 'In the name of what or whom do we judge?' "[45]

Moreover Ryan makes his persona, his private rather than his sovereign body, vividly present. In this story he is caught, almost literally torn, between the victim and the offender, reassuring his listeners that he has tasted murder's "bitter pill." This is hardly the language of a majestic, distant, undemocratic sovereignty, unresponsive to, or uninterested in, the pain of the victims. It is, instead, domesticated by that pain. For it is only by assuming the status of a victim of Danny Edwards's crime that he can be entitled to forgive it or to mitigate its punishment.[46] As Derrida says, pointing to the condition that creates Ryan's dilemma, "Who would have the right of forgiving in the name of the vanished victims? They are always absent, in a certain manner. Missing in essence, they are never themselves absolutely present, at the moment pardon is asked for, as the same they were the moment of the crime; and they are sometimes absent in body, which is to say dead."[47]

As victim and as someone in contact with the experience of victimization, Ryan treated his listeners as particular kinds of political subjects, earning their attention, as it were, through his own earnest attention to their claims as victims, even as he both broadens and blurs the referent of the term.[48] "I was struck," Ryan said, "by the anger of the families of murder victims." This anger, in Ryan's view, led them to demand the death penalty. "They pleaded with me to allow the state to kill." In the face of this anger and its demand, Ryan conceded the inadequacy of his own understanding, adding a respectful acknowledgment of his inability to walk in the shoes of the surviving families of murder victims to his earlier efforts at identification. "I cannot imagine losing a family member to murder. Nor can I imagine spending every waking day for 20 years with a single minded focus to execute the killer."

Confronting this anger and this acknowledgment, he brought the commutation decision back to a more domestic register, as if to reauthorize himself through his own experience as a victim. "As I came closer to my decision, I knew that I was going to have to face the question of whether I believed so completely in the choice I wanted to make that I could face the prospect of even commuting the death sentence of Danny Edwards the man who had killed a close family friend of mine. I discussed it with my wife, Lura Lynn, who has stood by me all these years. She was angry and disappointed at my decision like many of the families of other victims will be."

His listeners are again reminded of Ryan's own "suffering." And anger again enters the scene, an anger now directed not at those who kill but at Ryan himself, an anger strong and insistent enough to issue from someone who had otherwise shown her steadfastness as his wife. In addition, there is an interesting use of verb tenses here with Ryan again describing himself as caught, this time between the past with its own imagined future—"was going"—and the present with its imagining of the coming anger and disappointment of the community with which he is rhetorically allied. Danny Edwards returns to the story, this time as the touchstone of Ryan's accountability to his dead "close family friend." The measure of his commitment to clemency would be found in the answer to the question of whether his beliefs and convictions could pass the Danny Edwards test. Were the reasons to commute every death sentence sufficiently persuasive to move him to spare even Edwards's life? This is a stern test indeed, converting clemency into a measure of personal conviction and strength for Ryan himself.

As if not able to say it enough times, Ryan repeatedly tried to assure his listeners that he had indeed heard the voice of victims. "I have conducted private group meetings, one in Springfield and one in Chicago, with the surviving family members of homicide victims. Everyone in the room who wanted to speak had the opportunity to do so. Some wanted to express their grief, others wanted to express their anger. I took it all in. . . . I redoubled my effort to review each case personally in order to respond to the concerns of prosecutors and victims' families." Unlike the minimal due process that some justices of the U.S. Supreme Court believe must be provided for those seeking clemency,[49] Ryan accords to victims a deep and respectful attentiveness. He takes into himself their grief and anger, again rhetorically refiguring himself into a victim. In Ryan's account there is a responsiveness to pain and a grounding not in sovereign grace, but in the need to pay homage to suffering.[50]

Just as Ryan's rhetoric positions him between victim and offender and through him establishes connections between them, in his expansive use of the category of victim he attempts to establish connections between the relatives of those who have died and those who are sentenced to death. Everyone, it turns out, is in pain; the political community is imagined as constituted by shared suffering.[51]

> I also had a meeting with a group of people who are less often heard from, and who are not as popular with the media. The family members of death row inmates have a special challenge to face. I spent an afternoon with those family members at a Catholic Church here in Chicago. At that meeting, I heard a different kind of pain expressed. Many of these families live with the twin pain of knowing not only that, in some cases, their family member may have been responsible for inflicting a terrible trauma on another family, but also the pain of knowing that society

> has called for another killing. These parents, siblings and children are not to blame for the crime committed, yet these innocent stand to have their loved ones killed by the state. . . . They are also branded and scarred for life because of the awful crime committed by their family member. Others were even more tormented by the fact that their loved one was another victim, that they were truly innocent of the crime for which they were sentenced to die.

Again Ryan deploys his own kind of due process. He is the sovereign holding court to receive the petitions of his subjects, in a church not in a castle. He is a sovereign listening, hearing, heeding the voice of another group figuratively silenced by their connection to death, the death of those whose time of death has been made calculable by society's choice. And it is pain that provides the connective tissue between speakers and listeners.

He registers this pain by once more returning to the familiar, telling his listeners another story in which he puts himself at the center:

> It was at this meeting that I looked into the face of Claude Lee, the father of Eric Lee, who was convicted of killing Kankakee police officer Anthony Samfay a few years ago. It was a traumatic moment, once again, for my hometown. A brave officer, part of that thin blue line that protects each of us, was struck down by wanton violence. If you will kill a police officer, you have absolutely no respect for the laws of man or God. I've know the Lee family for a number of years. There does not appear to be much question that Eric was guilty of killing the officer. However, I can say now after our review, there is also not much question that Eric is seriously ill, with a history of treatment for mental illness going back a number of years. The crime he committed was a terrible one—killing a police officer. Society demands that the highest penalty be paid. But I had to ask myself—could I send another man's son to death under the deeply flawed system of capital punishment we have in Illinois? A troubled young man, with

> a history of mental illness? Could I rely on the system of justice we have in Illinois not to make another horrible mistake? Could I rely on a fair sentencing?

Ryan holds himself out as someone who would hear, even if he could not fully understand, the pain that was all around him; he would hear, if he could not fully feel, the anguish of the families of murderers as well as the anger of their victims' families. But he suggested that it was his duty to do more than provide a vehicle through which pain and anger could find its desired target. "But is that the purpose of capital punishment?" Ryan asked. "Is it to soothe the families?" He saw it as his role not to give in to pain and anger and linked his task with the work of Abraham Lincoln. "President Lincoln," he said, "often talked of binding up wounds as he sought to preserve the Union. We are not enemies, but friends. We must not be enemies. Though passion may have strained, it must not break our bonds of affection."[52]

Yet, however they are portrayed, and however he portrays his own task, it is striking how much of Ryan's rhetoric is addressed to victims. Comparing his announcement to a similar statement given seventeen years earlier by New Mexico's governor Tony Anaya, when he commuted five death sentences, I am struck by how little attention Anaya gives to victims. Holding himself out as a reformer, someone for whom clemency was part of an effort to end capital punishment, the most that Anaya said about victims was that he hoped that he could "assist the victims of crime in a compassionate and practical manner." Perhaps the difference between Anaya's and Ryan's rhetoric marks the difference between the mid-1980s, a time when the community of victims was still largely ignored in the criminal justice process and was barely beginning to mobilize itself politically, and today's victim-centered political culture.

Thus, it should not be surprising that throughout Ryan's statement he spoke to victims and their concerns. He spoke to them, even as he refused to do their bidding. He identified with them in their anger and their pain, even as he talked of the need to get beyond anger and pain.

But in spite of this attention and identification one might ask what victims can provide for those with the power to grant clemency. While they are present in every clemency decision, whether it is granted or refused, the judgment, and responsibility for that decision, could only be his. Despite his rhetorical identification with victims, he could not, as the reactions of Cathy Drobney and John Woodhouse described in chapter 1 suggest, dispense forgiveness in their name. Despite the connections he tried to forge in a community with many different kinds of victims, stable grounds for his act could not be established in its shared pain. So he turned from responsiveness to suffering in a community of victims to a critique of the institutions of the legal and political system for being insufficiently attentive to the claims of retributive justice.

Clemency and the Requirements of Justice

Even as Ryan changed the subject, the pull of victims and their concerns continued to exert itself. As a result he used victims and their needs as a bridge to his broad indictment of Illinois's death penalty system. Victims, it turns out, are also victimized by that system. Speaking of the relative rarity of capital punishment, he says, "There were more than 1000 murders last year in Illinois. There is no doubt that all murders are horrific and cruel. Yet, less than 2 percent of those murder defendants will receive the death penalty. That means more than 98% of victims families do not get, and will not receive whatever satisfaction can be derived from the execution of the murderer."

"Whatever satisfaction" registers Ryan's doubt about what executions do for victims' families, his doubt that they provide their much-advertized virtue of "closure."[53] "To a family they talked about closure," Ryan says, "They pleaded with me to allow the state to kill an inmate in its name to provide the families with closure. But . . . is that truly what the families experience?" Imagining the crime victim's family as the paradigmatic needy citizen, Ryan asks, "What kind of victims services are we providing? Are all of our resources geared toward providing this notion of closure by execution instead of tending to the physical and social service needs of victim families?"

He worried that the families of murder victims are badly served by a legal system that takes as long as ours does to move someone from a death sentence to an execution. "It is cruel and unusual punishment," Ryan noted, "for family members to go through this pain, this legal limbo for 20 years. Perhaps it would be less cruel if we sentenced the killers to . . . life, and used our resources to better serve victims."

But Ryan's rhetorical identification with victims is overridden in his "I Must Act" statement by a commitment to ensuring that offenders get what they deserve. Retribution provides a disciplining presence in his exercise of clemency,[54] an anchor of lawfulness in the presence of his potentially uncheckable power.[55]

Ryan's commitment to a just-deserts theory of punishment moved him from individual cases, on which clemency typically focuses, to the systemic level. "The facts I have seen in reviewing each and every one of these cases," Ryan observed, "raised questions not only about the innocence of people on death row, but about the fairness of the death penalty system as a whole. If the system was making so many errors in determining whether someone was guilty in the first place, how fairly and accurately was it determining which guilty defendants deserved to live and which deserved to die? What effect was race having? What effect was poverty having?"

In this rhetorical movement from the individual to the system and in his reference to the effect of race in the system of state killing, Ryan inverts the logic of the Supreme Court's decision in *McCleskey v. Kemp*. Presented with a wholesale challenge to Georgia's death penalty system the Court refused to inquire into systemic problems that might undermine confidence in decisions at the "heart of the criminal justice system."[56] While the Court refused to move from the particular to the general,[57] this is exactly what Ryan's commutation statement insisted be done.

Ryan's "I Must Act" unfolds as a journey narrative, a story of his own gradual education about the retributive flaws in the death penalty system.[58] "Four years ago I was sworn in as the 39th Governor of Illinois. That was just four short years ago; that's when I was a firm believer in the American System of Justice and the death penalty. I believed that the ultimate penalty for the taking of a life was administrated in a just and fair manner. Today, 3 days before I end my term as Governor, I stand before you to explain my frustrations and deep concerns about both the administration and the penalty of death."

In this journey he notes two events that played singular roles in his education about the inability of the Illinois death penalty system to deliver retributive justice. First was the case of Anthony Porter that I discussed in chapter 1. Saying "I never intended to be an activist on this issue," Ryan noted that he "watched in surprise as freed death row inmate Anthony Porter was released from jail. A free man, he ran into the arms of Northwestern University Professor Dave Protess, who had poured his heart and soul into proving Porter's innocence with his journalism students. He was 48 hours away from being wheeled into the execution chamber where the state would kill him. It would all be so antiseptic and most of us would not have even paused, except that Anthony Porter was innocent of the double murder for which he had been condemned to die."

The second milestone on Ryan's journey was the report by *Chicago Tribune* reporters Steve Mills and Ken Armstrong documenting the systemic failures of our capital punishment system. Ryan reminded his listeners that Mills and Armstrong reported that

> Half of the nearly 300 capital cases in Illinois had been reversed for a new trial or resentencing. 33 of the death row inmates were represented at trial by an attorney who had later been disbarred

> or at some point suspended from practicing law. Of the more than 160 death row inmates, 35 were African American defendants who had been convicted or condemned to die by all-white juries. More than two-thirds of the inmates on death row were African American. 46 inmates were convicted on the basis of testimony from jailhouse informants.

Ryan reports his incredulity as he read those figures. "How does that happen? How in God's name does that happen? I'm not a lawyer, so somebody explain it to me. But no one could. Not to this day."

But these were not the only unanswered questions about the death penalty system that emerged on Ryan's personal odyssey. "The death penalty has been abolished in 12 states," Ryan said.

> In none of these states has the homicide rate increased. In Illinois last year we had about 1000 murders, only 2 percent of that 1000 were sentenced to death. Where is the fairness and equality in that? The death penalty in Illinois is not imposed fairly or uniformly because of the absence of standards for the 102 Illinois State Attorneys, who must decide whether to request the death sentence. Should geography be a factor in determining who gets the death sentence? I don't think so but in Illinois it makes a difference. You are 5 times more likely to get a death sentence for first degree murder in the rural area of Illinois than you are in Cook County. Where is the justice and fairness in that? Where is the proportionality?"

Instead of a system finely geared to assigning punishment on the basis of a careful assessment of the nature of the crime and the blameworthiness of the offender, Ryan, quoting Justice Blackmun, concluded that "the death penalty remains fraught with arbitrariness, discrimination, caprice and mistake." In all this, the most powerful retributivist indictments of the death penalty system were the all-too-frequent erroneous convictions and death sentences imposed on innocent people—what Ryan labeled

> an absolute embarrassment. 17 exonerated death row inmates is nothing short of a catastrophic failure. But the 13, now 17 men, is just the beginning of our sad arithmetic in prosecuting murder cases. During the time we have had capital punishment in Illinois, there were at least 33 other people wrongly convicted on murder charges and exonerated. Since we reinstated the death penalty there are also 93 people, 93, where our criminal justice system imposed the most severe sanction and later rescinded the sentence or even released them from custody because they were innocent. How many more cases of wrongful conviction have to occur before we can all agree that the system is broken?

Asking this question, Ryan assumes, as I noted in chapter 1, the posture of a new abolitionist,[59] of someone interested less in the morality of state killing than in the way it is administered. Thus Ryan noted that

> prosecutors in Illinois have the ultimate commutation power, a power that is exercised every day. They decide who will be subject to the death penalty, who will get a plea deal or even who may get a complete pass on prosecution. By what objective standards do they make these decisions? We do not know, they are not public. . . . [I]f you look at the cases, as I have done both individually and collectively—a killing with the same circumstances might get 40 years in one county and death in another county. I have also seen where co-defendants who are equally or even more culpable get sentenced to a term of years, while another less culpable defendant ends up on death row. . . . Our capital system is haunted by the demon of error, error in determining guilt, and error in determining who among the guilty deserves to die.

Ryan issues a stunning, though by now widely shared, indictment of a system in which decisions about who gets the death penalty and who does not are made without reference to "objective standards." He draws attention to the contrast between his own publicly delivered justification and the daily "commutation" decisions of prosecutors, made without explanation, privately, outside of the public eye. Ryan finds arbitrariness deeply enfolded in the operations of the death penalty system, pointing to the influence of irrelevant factors like geography and the fact that offenders committing the same acts end up with radically different sentences. In a system marked by such arbitrariness, perhaps only the arbitrary power of clemency provides a route to justice.

Ryan invoked yet another calculus of desert to justify his commutation, returning Danny Edwards to the center of the story, and in so doing reassuring his listeners that his clemency would not be experienced by all to whom it was granted as an act of mercy.

> Some inmates on death row don't want a sentence of life without parole. Danny Edwards wrote me and told me not to do him any favors because he didn't want to face a prospect of a life in prison without parole. They will be confined in a cell that is about 5-feet-by-12 feet, usually double-bunked. Our prisons have no air conditioning, except at our supermax facility where inmates are kept in their cell 23 hours a day. In summer months, temperatures in these prisons exceed one hundred degrees. It is a stark and dreary existence. They can think about their crimes. Life without parole has even, at times, been described by prosecutors as a fate worse than death.

Ryan tells his listeners of Edwards's preference not to be spared. He does so in order to assure them that his commutation decision actually satisfies the requirements of justice better than would capital punishment and that he feels no sympathy for those whose sentences he commuted. He describes a future spent in thinking about one's worst deed, a kind of living self-torture, a "fate worse than death," and in doing so again calls attention to his own future suffering. "I realize it will draw ridicule, scorn and anger from many who oppose this decision. They will say I am usurping the decisions of judges and juries and state legislators. . . . I may never be comfortable with my final decision, but I will know in my heart, that I did my very best to do the right thing."

Indeed, it is worth noting here how the idiom of Ryan's statement shifts: While his speech opened with an elaborate acknowledgment of people in the audience "who spared the lives and secured the freedoms" of the falsely accused—a task of the "highest calling"—toward the end this vocabulary seems to be disavowed. If for most inmates Ryan is the source of equity beyond all courts, for those like Danny Edwards for whom commutation is a "fate worse than death," the only relief is to *kill themselves*. Indeed, Ryan goes out of this way to emphasize that such an action would be possible and permissible. "Yesterday," Ryan notes, "I mentioned a lawsuit in Livingston County where a judge ruled the state corrections department cannot force feed two corrections inmates who are on hunger strike. The judge ruled that suicide by hunger strike was not an irrational action by the inmates, given what their future holds."

Some of this rhetoric is, of course, familiar: the verbiage of anti-death-penalty politicians who must nonetheless remind us that they are still tough on crime and criminals. Nevertheless, there is something quite odd, if not outright incoherent, about a grant of clemency that ends by offering the possibility of suicide as a source of relief. Some of this oddity stems from the fact—and Ryan knows it—that while mercy is an act that is not amenable to a notion of predictive rules precisely because of its individual nature, a mass commutation that does not take individual conditions into account is not fully amenable to a language of mercy.

Thus Ryan seeks grounding in the determinism of a retributive calculus. As Kobil says, in an effort to support his own commitment to a retributive theory of clemency:

> Although there has been substantial public outcry against Ryan's actions and even legal challenges to some of his commutations, it appears that for now retributive justifications have carried the day. . . . Ultimately Governor George Ryan was persuaded to grant clemency to every person on Death Row not as a grand gesture of forgiveness, but because his faith in the ability of the Illi-

nois system to give only deserving defendants a sentence of death had been destroyed by a series of blatant errors and mistakes.[60]

Nonetheless, as Ryan's discussion of Danny Edwards's views on life without parole highlights, retributivism could provide no more stable grounds for determinant judgment than could the imagining of the victim ensure responsiveness. Whether life without parole is worse than death for the crime of murder cannot be subject to a calculus that eliminates or grounds decision in a certitude beyond contest and, thus alleviates the need to take responsibility for that decision. It is that decision, along with the power to actualize it, that defines the essence of clemency whether in monarchical or democratic governments.

Political Paralysis

The last element of Ryan's rhetorical strategy was, in fact, to emphasize the responsibility and the power that his position accorded him. "My responsibilities and obligations are more than my neighbors and my family. I represent all the people of Illinois, like it or not. The people of our state have vested in me the power to act in the interest of justice. Even if the exercise of my power becomes my burden I will bear it. . . . I know," he said, "that my decision will be just that—my decision."

But why was it necessary for him to make that decision and exercise that power? Here Ryan's critique is not directed at the system through which the death penalty is administered. His critique moves from a retributivist's indictment of the flaws in that system to a criticism of the failures of the political system, failures, in the absence of which, clemency would have been unnecessary.

Turning first to the Illinois State Supreme Court, Ryan portrays it as "divided" on issues that he sees as clear-cut, and as lacking courage in failing to address the ultimate question of the constitutionality of capital punishment itself. "We have come very close," Ryan reports,

> to having our state Supreme Court rule our death penalty statute—the one that I helped enact in 1977—unconstitutional. Former State Supreme Court Justice Seymour Simon wrote to me that it was only happenstance that our statute was not struck down by the state's high court. When he joined the bench in 1980, three other justices had already said Illinois' death penalty was unconstitutional. But they got cold feet when a case came along to revisit the question. One judge wrote that he wanted to wait and see if the Supreme Court of the United States would rule on the constitutionality of the new Illinois law. Another said precedent required him to follow the old state Supreme Court ruling with which he disagreed. Even a pharmacist knows that doesn't make sense. We wouldn't have a death penalty today, and we all wouldn't be struggling with this issue, if those votes had been different. How arbitrary.

Judges with "cold feet," hiding behind precedent, waiting for a higher court to rule, provide a perfect foil for a governor who wants to present himself as acting courageously to prevent injustice. As if to reinforce this criticism of the Illinois Supreme Court, Ryan recounted an episode in which the "great minds" on the court were unable to agree to do what, in Ryan's view, simple, common sense required:

> After the flaws in our system were exposed, the Supreme Court of Illinois took it upon itself to begin to reform its' rules and improve the trial of capital cases. It changed the rule to require that State's Attorneys give advance notice to defendants that they plan to seek the death penalty to require notice before trial instead of after conviction. The Supreme Court also enacted new discovery rules designed to prevent trials by ambush and to allow for better investigation of cases from the beginning. But shouldn't that mean if you were tried or sentenced before the rules changed, you ought to get a new trial or sentencing with the new safeguards of the

> rules? This issue has divided our Supreme Court, some saying yes, a majority saying no. These justices have a lifetime of experience with the criminal justice system and it concerns me that these great minds so strenuously differ on an issue of such importance, especially where life or death hangs in the balance.

But his strongest criticism was directed toward the state legislature of which he was once a member.

> I have also had to watch in frustration as members of the Illinois General Assembly failed to pass even one substantive death penalty reform. Not one. They couldn't even agree on ONE. How much more evidence is needed before the General Assembly will take its responsibility in this area seriously? . . . I don't know why legislators could not heed the rising voices of reform. I don't know how many more systemic flaws we needed to uncover before they would be spurred to action. Three times I proposed reforming the system with a package that would restrict the use of jailhouse snitches, create a statewide panel to determine death eligible cases, and reduce the number of crimes eligible for death. These reforms would not have created a perfect system, but they would have dramatically reduced the chance for error in the administration of the ultimate penalty.

Juxtaposed to his earlier emphasis on hearing, listening, and attending as one of the attributes of a responsible public official, his discussion of the legislature's failure to "heed the rising voices of reform" is particularly striking. Doing his duty as chief executive, he proposed reforms to fix the system that he had earlier criticized as "arbitrary" so that it could better meet the requirements of a retributive theory. However, almost inexplicably, the legislature, like the Supreme Court, did not, would not, act responsibly.

The legislature's failure to take responsibility and act responsibly is not its failure alone. It is, on Ryan's account, "a symptom of the larger problem" in the domain of state killing. "Many people express the desire to have capital punishment. Few, however, seem prepared to address the tough questions that arise when the system fails. It is easier and more comfortable for politicians to be tough on crime and support the death penalty. It wins votes. But when it comes to admitting that we have a problem, most run for cover."

Saying that he "never intended to be an activist" on the death penalty, Ryan portrays himself as someone who is propelled against his own inclination to do a painful and costly duty that others refused to do. "We are a rudderless ship because they failed to act." Seizing that rudder is today, as it long has been, one of the imperatives of executive leadership in times of crisis. Saying "The legislature couldn't reform it. Lawmakers won't repeal it. But I will not stand for it. I must act," Ryan granted clemency without compassion toward those who were its beneficiaries and plunged into that lawful lawlessness that today, as it always has, marks the exercise of sovereign prerogative.[61]

Conclusion

George Ryan's commutation is symptomatic of the status of clemency in a constitutional democracy and of the condition of mercy in our time. Despite its unusual sweep and the controversy that it generated, Ryan's clemency was within the bounds of traditional understandings and was responsive to major forces in contemporary society for which mercy is anathema, those who seek to advance victims rights and those who seek to ground punishment in retributivist claims. While seeming to be a grand gesture of sovereign grace, it fit well within the anti-mercy conceptions of clemency embraced by Bill Clinton, George W. Bush, and William Rehnquist. Far from disrupting the essential rhythms of American politics by revivifying mercy and compassion in our criminal justice system, Ryan's clemency gave new voice to ongoing trends in our political and cultural lives in its emphasis on suffering and victimization, in its embrace of retributive principles, and in its demonstration of "energy in the executive."[62]

And yet, George Ryan's statement is so deeply symptomatic because, even as it inhabits these paradigms, it pushes their logic (or perhaps pulls them in) to the unchartable border of a legal alegality that clemency inhabits. Thus, for example, while I agree with Kobil that Ryan's argument proceeds along a retributivist line,[63] it exposes the limits of that position: Ryan's mass commutation certainly prevents people from receiving an undeserved punishment (and the reasons Ryan gives for that undesert range from individual innocence to systemic vagaries by which the death penalty is sought or not for even similar cases), but not because Ryan believes that no one deserves death—indeed, he thinks some people very much deserve to die—but rather because he admits that he does not and may never know what justice demands in each case. This, it seems, is a significant concession to a certain incalculability of justice that retributivist theorists would be loath to concede. It is this very incalculability that points to the need for the discretionary quality of mercy even as it makes us uncomfortable, forcing us to admit and live with our constitutive fallibility.

George Ryan's commutation was, as I have suggested, pulled in two incompatible directions. That he found himself in this situation is attributable, in part, to the importance of the victims rights movement in the United States. While he did not do what the victims community wanted, his justificatory rhetoric paid homage, perhaps undue homage, to the victims. While he broadened and complicated the category of victim, he sought to use his clemency decision to identify with and express respect for them. If there was a failure in its justification, it is to be found in trying to reconcile the irreconcilable by combining fidelity to victims and their suffering with commitment to retributive justice and by trying to be responsive both to private pain and the strict dictates of public justice. He could not feel the pain of the victims and then seem to ignore it without enraging them and leaving them feeling, as noted above, like they had suffered another undeserved injury.

These tensions are illustrated in Robert Nozick's discussion of the demands of retributive justice.[64] Nozick identifies five attributes of retribution and five ways that it distances itself from the claims of private victims. First, retribution, according to Nozick, is only done for a "wrong" while victims may seek punishment "for an injury or harm or slight and need not be for a wrong."[65] What counts in the realm of injury, harm, or slight is the private pain of the victim and not the intent of the person whose action caused that pain.

Next, while retribution "sets an internal limit to the amount of punishment, according to the seriousness of the wrong," victims often recognize no such limit.[66] What Nozick means is that retributive punishment must be proportional to the wrong committed.[67] In addition, "The agent of retribution," Nozick tells us, "need have no special or personal tie to the victim."[68] It is, of course, just this element of impersonality in retributive justice that causes discomfort and concern in the victims rights movement. The goal of victims and those who take up their cause is to repersonalize criminal justice so that the sentencer has to declare an alliance—with either the victim or the offender. Criminal sentencing thus becomes a test of loyalty.

As Nozick sees it, retributive justice involves no "emotional tone."[69] The desire to experience a direct, immediate, passionate connection to the suffering of the criminal fuels the victims rights movement. Only when victims become agents in the suffering of the people responsible for their own suffering is a kind of social equilibrium reached. "The notion of paying back," Miller argues, "makes no sense unless the victim or his representative is there to hit back. Under this paradigm . . . the focus is . . . on the obligation to repay the wrong done to him by retaliating against either the wrongdoer or someone closely connected to him."[70] When punishment is guided by retributive principles, the victim's right/need to pay back remains unsatisfied.

Finally, retribution is based on "general principles . . . mandating punishment in other similar circumstances."[71] This means that if a concern for systemic failure provides the grounds for clemency, it must be given even to Danny Edwards. Victims, in contrast, care most, by definition, about their injuries and the punishment inflicted for them.[72]

If philosophers like Nozick cannot reconcile retributive justice and the desires of victims, it should not be surprising that George Ryan did not succeed in this same endeavor. Despite Ryan's gallant efforts to ground and authorize his acts in the suffering of victims, the systemic flaws of the capital punishment system, or the failures of political institutions, he could neither resolve the contradictory forces that mark our contemporary political condition nor satisfy our need for, and yet discomfort with, the sovereign prerogative of mercy and power to spare life.

CHAPTER 6

Conclusion

ON MERCY AND ITS RISKS

By executive powers we mean no reference to those powers exercised under our former government by the crown as its prerogative. . . . We give him those powers only which are necessary to execute the laws.
—*Thomas Jefferson*

From pardon power unrestricted, comes impunity to delinquency in all shapes: from impunity to delinquency in all shapes, impunity to maleficence in all shapes; from impunity to maleficence in all shapes, dissolution of government; from dissolution of government, dissolution of political society.
—*Jeremy Bentham*

There have always been doubts and fears surrounding the pardoning power in America.
—*James Whitman*

AT THE DAWN OF the twenty-first century, the killing state is alive in the United States. Under pressure from external forces (globalization) and internal forces (governmentality), and backed by the public, the state's attachment to capital punishment hangs on. Fueled by the politicization of crime and punishment and the attack on rehabilitation and redemption, the death penalty helps the state to

> occlude its ineptitude on the home front, and tame . . . "the globalization of contingency." . . . Executed bodies perform their political mission well when their utter impotence, their absolute lack of vitality, testifies to the robust agency of the state. . . . On this reading . . . executions are . . . not manifestations of an

> already-realized sovereign authority. . . . Instead capital punishment is . . . a means by which the late liberal state seeks to manufacture that authority.[1]

And in today's America, capital punishment remains a major front in the culture war. As Connolly rightly notes, state killing

> mobilizes political divisions between one set of partisans, who seek to return to a fictive world in which the responsible individual, retributive punishment, the market economy, the sovereign state, and the nation coalesced, and another set, who seek to respond in more generous ways to new experiences of the cultural contingency of identity, the pluralization of culture, the problematical character of traditional conceptions of agency and responsibility, and the role of the state in a new world order.[2]

In this state, mercy has been put on trial in the court of public opinion as well as in the courts of law. It has been found wanting in the domain of capital clemency and exiled from the legal and political arena. The movements for victims rights and retributive punishment, those two contradictory forces that today battle for supremacy and dominate contemporary thinking about criminal justice in general and the death penalty in particular, have combined to overwhelm mercy and give it a bad name. Thus even when the right to impose a particular punishment is forgone, as it was in George Ryan's clemency, mercy is denied, disguised, and dressed up in other language. And if compassion is shown, it is not directed toward those to whom clemency is given. Ryan did the right thing when he used his prerogative power to prevent state killing. But he did it for the wrong reasons, playing to victims, embracing retributivism, trying to prove that he was tough on crime. Yet he was not solely at fault. Only if American society develops a fuller tolerance for humanity and its weaknesses and a more complete understanding of humanity and the forces that propel us toward evil, will it be possible to offer clemency without all the strained qualifications that our age forces on those granted this power. Until then capital clemency will rarely be exercised and, when exercised, will continue to be stripped of compassion.

The association of clemency and mercy that is so foreign to us has roots that extend as far back as the Roman Empire. There, Seneca, in one of the great essays on clemency, praises it, saying that "of all men . . . mercy becomes no one more than a king or a prince." Mercy, as Seneca defined it, "means 'self-control by the mind when it has the power to take vengeance' or 'leniency on the part of a superior towards an inferior in imposing punishments.' . . . We might speak," he continues, "of mercy as moderation that remits something of a deserved and due punishment."[3]

In this country Alexander Hamilton, writing in 1788, set out to explain and defend what seemed to his contemporaries something of an anomaly in America's new constitutional scheme, namely lodging the power to grant "reprieves and pardons for offenses against the United States" solely in the president of the United States.[4] Although the original versions of the New York and Virginia Plans that provided the frameworks for debate at the Constitutional Convention included no provisions for pardon, revisions to both plans eventually did. The power that emerged from the convention was regarded by Hamilton as one of the great prerogatives of sovereignty, necessary in times of emergency.

But this prerogative was also, in his view, to be used mercifully and, in its merciful use, to be seen as a moment in which awesome power would ennoble those who wielded it. Thus Hamilton noted that without mercy, "justice would wear a countenance too sanguinary and cruel." This is what Hamilton had in mind when, in Federalist 74, he mentioned "necessary severity" and "unfortunate guilt." Moreover, he suggested that lodging such awesome power in one person would inspire in the chief executive "scrupulousness and caution."[5]

Yet Hamilton recognized that, notwithstanding its advantages, granting such a power to the chief executive breached the boundary between the rule of law and monarchical privilege. Traditional ideas of sovereignty would be imported into a document dedicated to constructing a government of limited powers. Like the king acting "in a superior sphere," lodging the power to pardon exclusively in the president meant that the fate of persons convicted of crimes would be dependent ultimately on the *"sole fiat"* of a single person. This was hardly the image of a government of laws and not of persons that Hamilton sought to defend. This is why, unlike the president's power as commander in chief of the army and navy, a constitutional provision the propriety of which, in Hamilton's view, was "so evident in itself . . . that little need be said to explain or enforce it," the president's power to pardon seemed to him neither self-evident nor self-explanatory. Yet explain and defend it he did, while also claiming that what he called "the benign prerogative of pardoning . . . (unlike almost every other government power in the new constitution) should be as little as possible fettered."[6]

Accounting for Clemency/ Domesticating Sovereignty

To a twenty-first century audience, Hamilton's faith in the ennobling effect of the grant of the clemency power as well as in its crucial role as a vehicle for mercy, may sound odd at best and dangerous at worst. His defense of this power seems, in some ways, inadequate or incomplete for failing to acknowledge and document mercy's risks. This suggests that the need to explain and defend executive clemency is as pressing today as it was in Hamilton's time. In one or another form, those who exercise this power regularly respond to a compulsion to speak, to narrate, to give what the sociologists Marvin Scott and Stanford Lyman call "accounts."[7]

These accounts, like the one provided by George Ryan on the day he announced his clemency, speak to the risks of mercy in a constitutional democracy, and seek to domesticate the exercise of sovereign power and thus establishing its compatibility with democratic politics. Those who wield undemocratic power want to legitimate it by addressing the background expectations of the political and legal culture. Using familiar tropes and comforting rhetorical appeals to commonsense values, conscientious decision making, the priority of conscience, and the burden of decision, contemporary "pardon tales" are addressed to an audience imagined to be reluctant to take the mercy's risks and made anxious by the use of the sovereign's power to spare life.

Each exercise of clemency in capital cases speaks to the spirit of its age. Just as appeals for mercy were, the historian Natalie Zemon Davis argues, particularly good sources for understanding "contemporary habits of explanation, description, and evaluation" in sixteenth-century France,[8] so are responses to those appeals in our time. Those responses seek to soothe anxiety and quiet doubt, to suture the breach between law and sovereign prerogative, between our culture's desire for rule-governed conduct and the ungovernability of mercy. Below I examine two such pardon tales as they address mercy's risks. These stories, though they are different from the one provided by Ryan, share a similar attitude toward mercy in the killing state and deploy similar strategies for soothing the anxiety aroused by its exercise.

Edmund G. (Pat) Brown: Public Justice, Private Mercy

That George Ryan spoke to, and through, a genre of contemporary pardon tales was marked by his invocation of the name of Edmund G. (Pat) Brown, former governor of California who, during his eight-year term of office (1959–67), commuted almost two dozen death sentences and whose 1989 book, *Public Justice, Private Mercy*, is a widely recognized classic among contemporary pardon tales.[9] Ryan came into possession of that book by coincidence; it was sent to him by Governor Brown's daughter a few weeks before he announced his decision. In his speech, Ryan took heed of Brown's warning that "'no matter how efficient and fair the death penalty may seem in theory, in actual practice it is primarily inflicted upon the weak, the poor, the ignorant and against racial minorities,'" and that the death penalty "'has neither protected the innocent nor deterred the killers. Publicly sanctioned killing has cheapened human life and dignity without the redeeming grace which comes from justice meted out swiftly, evenly, humanely.'"[10]

Yet Brown was by no means a consistent opponent of capital punishment. Before his service as governor of California, he was a district attorney who strongly supported the death penalty. While he continued to do so as attorney general of California and when he was first elected governor, he ultimately turned against it.

As the quotations used by Ryan suggest, *Public Justice: Private Mercy* chronicles the evolution of Brown's views on capital punishment. At the same time, it offers a narrative account of the clemency decisions he made during his time in office that is rich and engaging in its detail, even if a bit repetitive. Each chapter tells the story of a different case in which Brown decided whether or not to commute a death sentence. Each details the principles and individual circumstances that moved him one way or the other and, in so doing, draws attention to the uniquely individualized nature of Brown's clemency considerations.

Throughout the book Brown portrays himself as deeply engaged in the clemency process and conscientious in the discharge of his clemency powers. Indeed he writes as if these attributes would reassure his readers that his clemency decisions were, even if lawless, nonetheless responsible and responsive to democratic expectations. He writes as if seeking forgiveness for decisions with which his readers might strongly disagree and as if he could obtain forgiveness if only he could convince them of the care he took in making his clemency decisions. Thus, early on in the book, he says, "I inaugurated the practice of personally conducting executive clemency hearings in every death case," and "I insisted on conducting every clemency hearing myself, often sending out investigators to collect more information if I thought some area still needed clearing up."[11]

To drive home the point about his engagement and conscientiousness, he draws an explicit contrast between his careful consideration of each case and the blanket clemency issued by Toney Anaya three years before the publication of his book. "[U]nlike the recent governor of New Mexico," Brown writes, "who was so opposed to the death penalty that he refused to let *anyone* be executed. . . . I refused the clemency requests of thirty-six condemned prisoners during my eight years in office. . . . For each of them, no matter how hard I searched, I couldn't find a compelling reason to go against the judgment of the court and the law of the state."[12]

Brown's emphasis on an individualized approach to clemency also serves as a kind of anticipatory criticism of Ryan. Here little is left to the imagination. Writing about his last days in office, Brown says, "[T]he pressure on me to make some parting gesture against capital punishment was great pressure from church groups and other opponents and also from inside that part of me which felt that whatever I'd done over the years really hadn't changed anything. . . . But it's also true that I never seriously considered giving blanket reprieves or commutations to all sixty-four on Death Row."[13]

Explaining why he refused these entreaties, Brown seems very aware of the conundrum of clemency's lawful lawlessness, and, as if refuting the charge that his clemency decisions disrespected and/or damaged the law, he goes out of his way to emphasize his commitment and fidelity to law. "I had been elected twice," he says, "by a majority of the people of California in a pact or trust to uphold their constitution and their laws, and I wasn't about to break that pact or violate that trust now that a few hundred thousand votes had shifted the other way." Or, as he put it earlier in the book, "[T]he death penalty was the law of the state, one of the laws I was sworn to uphold. If I disagreed with a law, it was my job to try to change it through the legislative process, not by evading my responsibility and refusing to enforce it."[14]

Brown reassures his readers worried about mercy's risks that he understood that clemency is "an extraordinary power" in a constitutional democracy and that he set a very high burden of proof for its use. It is, he wrote, "to be exercised only when justified by *compelling* circumstances." Elsewhere he says that in order to grant clemency, "I as governor had to look for some *extraordinary* reason why the defendant should not be executed"[15] (emphasis added).

As he describes his reasons for commuting death sentences, several things stand out. First, he takes every chance to acknowledge the special nature and limited focus of his clemency decisions, as if he were acting in a posture of deference to other branches of government. "[T]he section of the Constitution that granted the governor the power of clemency," Brown writes, "had little to do with guilt or innocence or even with the finer points of the law."[16]

While admitting that he "was trying to move beyond legal limits as I looked for reasons to commute," mercy plays little role in Brown's story. Indeed most of the reasons he gives for commutation sound vaguely retributivist, for instance, addressing new evidence, an inability to resolve questions about actual innocence, redressing unequal penalties. "As the last stop on the road to the gas chamber," he wrote, "it was up to me to make sure that the law—even if I disagreed with it—was being fairly applied." In addition, Brown notes that he frequently found "examples of unfairness and injustice that even the hardest heart couldn't ignore."[17] Like Ryan, Brown's story repeatedly distances him from compassion and forgiveness, assuring us time and again of his disgust at the crimes that put people on death row.

Yet in each of these moments he is also the hero of the piece battling against those feelings to do what his office required of him. "Some crimes," he says, "were so terrible that I could fully understand and sympathize with the judges and juries who sentenced those who committed them to death. But during the clemency process I had a different kind of decision to make." In another place, he notes that "[r]eading those case reports filled me with as much anger at the killers as any man alive, but anger is a luxury that a governor can't afford."[18]

Here the story reverts to what in contemporary pardon tales is the familiar portrait of the solitary man wrestling with his conscience, seeking to do the right thing under very trying circumstances.[19] Thus Brown says of his clemency decisions, "They didn't make me feel godlike . . . far from it; I felt just the opposite." Referring to the power over life and death that supplies sovereignty's very definition, Brown writes, "It was an awesome power that no person or government should have."[20] Rather than enjoying his exercise of sovereign prerogative, Brown argues that removing the clemency power would be "more humane and compassionate than forcing (any governor) constantly to decide on the life or death of an individual." And, in this invocation of compassion, not for the condemned, but for those with the power to spare life, Brown joins Ryan in presenting himself as a kind of victim. "[E]ach decision," he says, "took something out of me that nothing—not family or work or hope for the future—has ever been able to replace."[21]

Public Justice, Private Mercy, written when Brown was eighty-three years old and more than twenty years removed from office, reads like the dying declaration of a man unable to put to rest decisions made decades before. It is as if it were written less to convince his readers of the grounding and purpose of his clemency decisions than to convince, and pardon, himself. "I am eighty-three years old as I write these words. I've done many things during my life that have given me a great deal of pleasure and pride and a few things that I'd either like to forget or to have another chance at. But the longer I live, the larger loom those fifty-nine decisions about justice and mercy that I had to make as governor."[22]

Ultimately, Brown's book poses what he calls a "selfish question," namely, "Have my decisions on Death Row really made any difference?"[23] This unanswered, perhaps unanswerable question, haunts the text, leaving its readers to ask whether any account of clemency can help us rest easier with its lawful lawlessness and its association with ungovernable mercy.

CHAPTER 6

Michael DiSalle: The Power of Life or Death

From Ryan's recent speech and Pat Brown's 1989 book, we look back several decades to another governor, Michael DiSalle and his pardon tale. DiSalle, who served as governor of Ohio from 1959 to 1963, was the oldest of seven children. He was born in New York City on January 6, 1908, and was three years of age when his family moved to Toledo, Ohio, where the future governor attended public and parochial schools and served uneventfully as mayor. His subsequent term as governor was, however, anything but quiet, leading one reporter to observe that DiSalle "did not know how to pick his fights, and warred unproductively with everyone from newspaper editorial boards to the legislature. He did not know how to capitalize on his successes or avoid blame for public relations failures on his watch."[24]

In contrast to Ryan and Brown, DiSalle was a lifelong opponent of capital punishment. "I have long felt," he reports, "that only the Giver of Life has the right to take away life. I do not believe we achieve justice by practicing retribution, but I had sworn to uphold the laws of Ohio."[25] He believed that "punishing and even killing criminals may yield a grim kind of satisfaction. . . . But playing God in this way has no conceivable moral or scientific justification." Thus during his term as governor he commuted six death sentences. Yet, somewhat surprisingly, he also allowed six others to be carried out.[26]

Two years after he left office, in 1965, DiSalle turned clemency into literature, publishing an account of the decisions he made in each of the twelve capital cases that came to his desk. *The Power of Life and Death* is in many ways a remarkable book, straightforward in its exposition, lucid in its prose, revealing in its rhetoric.[27] DiSalle's deploys language, detail, and order to tell a story of conflict between his conscience and his duty, his moral principles and the oath of office that binds chief executives to faithfully execute the law of the land even when they find it morally abhorrent.

Like Ryan's and Brown's pardon tales, it relies on the trope of anguish, the agony of the person forced by circumstance to exercise godlike power on the basis of fallible human judgment. And like Brown's *Public Justice, Private Mercy*, one of the most remarkable and revealing aspects of this book is its primary narrative device, a series of detailed accounts of the twelve instances in which DiSalle considered clemency in a capital case.

On page after page he recounts the details of the crime, of the life and circumstances of the criminal, of the legal processing of the case, and of his own efforts to get at the truth and reach a judgment that would heal the rift between his moral objection to capital punishment and Ohio's embrace of it. Each of the cases is introduced by a hackneyed headline or transparent play on words—"The Lovesick Den Mother," "The Equality of Justice Is Not Strained," "The Four-Angled Triangle," "The Bookie and the Wise Guy," and so on. As he moves through each case, DiSalle is didactic and at the same time defensive, trying both to encourage more informed and rational responses to crime and criminals and also to provide a convincing account of each of the decisions he made.

By presenting the stories of the cases in which he considered or granted clemency, he offers evidence against which his decisions can be judged. Unlike Brown, whose pardon tale seems to be a self-referential look back through time at the meaning and impact of his clemency decisions, DiSalle writes as if he were putting himself on trial in the here and now. He calls himself before the bar of public opinion to defend himself against an accusation frequently made during his term as governor, namely that in his use of the clemency power he set himself above and outside the law, arrogantly and irresponsibly deploying a power that should be used more sparingly than he used it—if it should be used at all.

Indeed, over and over again DiSalle reminds his readers of charges leveled against him in newspaper stories and letters addressed to him. He enfolds the voices of his critics in his story, often characterizing them in sweeping terms, for instance: "Most

Ohio newspapers cried out in editorial horror and indignation each time I exercised clemency; they spoke in whispers each time I allowed a man to die." Or, as he puts it in response to his first commutation, editorial writers "excoriated me for having set myself above the conclusions of the courts and jurors."[28]

In other places he quotes particular criticisms communicated directly to him. For example, "We no longer need police, courts, juries or judges. The great DiSalle will see that justice is served." Or, as another outraged citizen wrote, "It is difficult for an ordinary Ohio voter to understand how an elected Chief Executive can allow his beliefs to cause him to overrule the judiciary."[29]

As to its avowed purpose, DiSalle says that his book was "written in the hope that judges prosecutors, criminologists, law enforcement officers, and the ordinary citizen . . . will make a sober, disinterested judgment, when passions are not raised to a fever heat by inflammatory headlines blazing the news of some monstrous crime."[30] A sober, disinterested judgment of what? Or, of whom?

At first glance one might think that the object of this admonition is crime and punishment policy, but as the book unfolds it is clear that it is written as a reply brief to the charges he has so scrupulously documented. Explaining his use of "case histories," he exclaims, "Let the reader judge."[31] The reader's sovereignty substitutes for popular sovereignty, placing the once powerful governor within the frame of a kind of democratic community. The reader's imagined judgment is a stand-in for the verdict of history itself.

In the course of his pardon tale, DiSalle, like Ryan, attempts to reassure his readers that though his exercise of clemency, like all such exercises, was a kind of lawful alegality authorized but not governed by law, it was in every case grounded in values and beliefs he shared with the citizens of Ohio. And like Brown, he writes as if trying to persuade his readers that his use of clemency was less a majestic moment of sovereign prerogative, than just the kind of thing they too would have done had they been in his shoes.

In this way his pardon tale speaks to mercy's risks by domesticating and diminishing prerogative even as it details its exercise. To do so, it tells two different stories, one substantive, the other procedural.

First, DiSalle seeks to convey to his readers that while they might disagree about particular judgments, his exercise of power was disciplined by principles deeply rooted in the legal and political culture. The first of these is that clemency is appropriate when "the inflexibility of legal procedure prevented the entire truth from reaching the jury." Second, DiSalle explained that clemency should be used to assure equal treatment under the law as in instances when "there was an obvious inequity of justice in administering punishment." Third, clemency is appropriate when particular factors, such as youth or mental incapacity, "mitigate guilt."[32]

These principles seem again to be retributivist. They position clemency as merely a corrective for some deficiency in the legal process. However, the third does leave space for mercy, albeit on limited grounds. Nonetheless DiSalle, like Ryan and Brown, offers a pardon tale in which clemency does not forgive. It as if DiSalle, like Richard Celeste, another governor of Ohio, wanted to say about his commutation of death sentences, "I didn't forgive them [criminals]. I did not forgive them."

DiSalle's principles supply, in his view, the only "legitimate reasons" for granting clemency. Where one or more were present, clemency would be granted; where none were present, clemency would be denied. As DiSalle informs his readers, "[F]or the six who died I could find no extenuating circumstances, no unequal justice, no questionable legal procedure, no reasonable doubt, to justify my reversing the sentences of the courts."[33]

It is worth noting that in these principles there is little of the kind of concern for victims that played such a large role in Ryan's pardon tale.[34] This difference registers a profound change in the background assumptions to which pardon tales must speak if they are to do their justificatory work. It registers change from a time when criminal justice was thought to be public justice to today when victims have succeeded in transforming the discourse of our political and legal culture.

In addition to the substantive grounds on which DiSalle's pardon tale seeks to reassure its reader-judges, it repeatedly details the process he employed in reaching his clemency decisions. DiSalle suggests that his decisions were made with great care and that there were great personal costs associated with each and every instance of clemency. While Ryan's narrative task was to account for a use of clemency that refused to draw distinctions and make individual judgments, DiSalle's book is filled with stories of uniquely, almost obsessively, individualized judgment.

In each of these stories DiSalle presents himself as an engaged and active participant, reviewing extensive case files, reading pleadings, asking questions, and in several instances going to death row himself to interview the person whose fate he would ultimately decide. As he notes in regard to one of the cases in which he granted clemency:

> In due course I received an application for executive clemency, and gave it long and serious consideration. . . . I was left with no alternative but to conduct my own investigation. I spent weeks researching the legal and philosophical basis for executive clemency. I spent more weeks digging into the archives for the result of clemency appeals in cases, particularly in the state of Ohio, in which people found guilty in the same crime received different sentences. I went to the gray stone fortress that is the state penitentiary to talk to the principals in the case."[35]

In another case he writes that he went "to see the physical layout of the scene of the crime so that I could understand what really took place." In still another he says, "I pursued my own investigation into the question of responsibility. The day before Nelson was to die, I drove to the penitentiary to talk to the condemned youth."[36]

Like Brown, DiSalle recounts the substantial personal pain that acting beyond rules imposes on those who wield life or death power. He writes of the "harrowing days" on which he had to "go into a long executive session with his conscience" while he decided on clemency petitions in capital cases. In so doing he turns clemency into melodrama, reminding his readers at the outset that his story comes from "someone who . . . had the final word on whether or not a fellow man was to die."

The Power of Life or Death describes DiSalle as an agonizing and agonized decision-maker, as if by recounting his pain he could convince his readers that his use of sovereign prerogative was reluctant and responsible. Describing each of the days on which an execution was carried out as "a waking nightmare," he said that "I could never get used to the idea that a man would die—even a man guilty of the most incredibly inhuman behavior—because I had not exercised the power that was mine as long as I was governor, the power to keep him alive." In another place DiSalle writes, "Even when I was convinced of the man's guilt, doubt haunted my unconscious long after the warden had notified me that the prisoner was dead." He says that when he refused clemency, he "owed the whole human race an apology" and that he "could not bear to see the imagined reproach in anyone's eyes."[38]

In the end, despite his efforts to bridge the gap between himself and his readers through an appeal to common principles, a demonstration of the care he took in making his decisions and of the agony associated with them, he doubts that narrative can supply the materials for truly empathetic judgment. He warns his reader-judges, and reminds himself, that inevitably they must judge him from a distance that no set of stories, or narrative conventions, can close. Finally, admitting the impossibility of the task he set for his pardon tale, DiSalle concedes that "[n]o one who has never watched the hands of a clock marking the last minutes of a condemned man's existence, knowing that he alone has the temporary God-like power to stop the clock, can realize the agony of deciding an appeal for executive clemency."[39]

Confronting Mercy's Risks

In the face of clemency's lawful lawlessness, and its seemingly anomalous place in a constitutional democracy, contemporary pardon tales address mercy's risks and provide some semblance of order by connecting sovereign prerogative and the lived experience of readers in a democratic culture. Those stories are produced to provide closure, if not for their listeners or readers then for their authors. They console those who exercise sovereign power in a world of violence and pain.

Yet, as DiSalle worries, they may be unable to bridge the gap between sovereign and citizen and provide comforting assurance about clemency and its use in capital cases. Because clemency exists in a domain beyond rule, lawfully authorized but lawless nonetheless, it forces citizens to confront another gap, an indeterminacy, a risk. Sanctioning the exercise of mercy, it turns out, always involves risk. This risk, as we have seen throughout this book, has been variously described—recall Blackstone's recognition of the "danger" associated with mercy, Margaret Love's description of mercy as a "mystery," or Justice O'Connor's dreaded image of a governor deciding whose life to spare and whose to end by flipping a coin. However they are described the risks are that this unruly power will be abused, that it will defeat, not advance, the moral purposes for which it was granted to chief executives and become a vehicle for unchecked favoritism or discriminatory treatment.[40]

The risk that clemency or mercy will turn into favoritism or bias attaches, I would argue, wherever unreviewable, unaccountable power lies, whether in a governor's decision to commute or pardon, a prosecutor's decision not to charge someone with a crime, or a jury's decision to acquit. Indeed, these risks came into focus quite clearly in the 1972 Supreme Court case of *Furman v. Georgia*, which brought a temporary halt to executions in the United States.[41] At issue in *Furman* was a statute that granted broad discretionary power to juries to decide whom to sentence to death and whom to spare.

Writing about that statute, Justice William O. Douglas said, "We deal with a system of law and of justice that leaves to the uncontrolled discretion of judges or juries the determination whether defendants committing these crimes should die or be imprisoned. Under these laws no standards govern the selection of the penalty. People live or die, dependent on the whim of one man or of 12." Moreover, as if to further emphasize the risk necessarily attached to such discretion, he noted that it is "pregnant with discrimination." Finally, echoing James Whitman's argument about America's continuing anxieties about mercy, Douglas wrote, "We know that the discretion of judges and juries in imposing the death penalty enables the penalty to be selectively applied, feeding prejudices against the accused if he is poor and despised, and lacking political clout, or if he is a member of a suspect or unpopular minority, and saving those who by social position may be in a more protected position."[42]

Yet Chief Justice Warren Burger saw something quite different in the discretion left to juries, namely an opportunity for them to accord mercy based on their own cultivated moral sentiments. Criticizing Justice Stewart's concurring opinion in *Furman* he said,

> If the reservations expressed by my Brother Stewart . . . were to command support, namely, that capital punishment may not be unconstitutional so long as it be mandatorily imposed, the result, I fear, will be that statutes struck down today will be reenacted by state legislatures to prescribe the death penalty for specified crimes without any alternative for the imposition of a lesser punishment in the discretion of the judge or jury, as the case may be. This approach, it seems to me, encourages legislation that is regressive and of an antique mold, for it eliminates the element of mercy in the imposition of punishment. I thought we had passed beyond that point in our criminology long ago.[43]

Turning from his critique of Stewart to Douglas, Burger concluded, "that the flexible sentencing system created by the legislatures, and carried out by juries and judges, has yielded more mercy than the Eighth Amendment can stand."[44]

One person's risk of discrimination is another's opportunity for leniency. One person's fear of prejudice is another's hope for sober moral deliberation. And neither law nor any set of fixed moral norms can forbid the former or ensure the later. This is the risk that embracing mercy requires we take. And where life is at stake, it is a risk worth taking.

Like the jury's power in a capital case, clemency is a place where law runs out, where law authorizes what it cannot subject to rule.[45] Moreover, in both of these situations we see a tension endemic to modern liberal democracies, committed as they are to popular sovereignty and the rule of law, when those societies confront the exercise of unfettered discretion. In these cases law acknowledges its own limits and invites the embrace of mercy's risks.

In this invitation I am reminded of Supreme Court Justice Robert Jackson's remarkable dissenting opinion in *Korematsu v. United States*, a case in which the court upheld the mass internment of Japanese Americans during World War II on the grounds of an alleged military necessity. "The very essence of the military job," he wrote,

> is to marshal physical force, to remove every obstacle to its effectiveness, to give it every strategic advantage. Defense measures will not, and often should not, be held within the limits that bind civil authority in peace. No court can require such a commander in such circumstances to act as a reasonable man; he may be unreasonably cautious and exacting. Perhaps he should be. . . . Of course the existence of a military power resting on force, so vagrant, so centralized, so necessarily heedless of the individual, is an inherent threat to liberty. But I would not lead people to rely on this Court for a review that seems to me wholly delusive. . . . If the people ever let command of the war power fall into irresponsible and unscrupulous hands, the courts wield no power equal to its restraint. The chief restraint upon those who command the

> physical forces of the country, in the future as in the past, must be their responsibility to the political judgments of their contemporaries and to the moral judgments of history.[46]

Jackson's dissent highlights convergence between the jurisprudence of emergency and clemency. What he says about military power in times of emergency can also be applied to gubernatorial clemency in capital cases. The power that governors exercise is, like the military's, "forceful," "vagrant," and threatening. And as we saw in chapter 3, like military power, law can barely contain it. Moreover, it is precisely to the political judgments of their contemporaries and the moral judgments of history that governors like Ryan, Brown, and DiSalle address themselves in their exercise of capital clemency.

Perhaps the major risks associated with clemency and mercy are that we will come to believe that courts can bring them to heel, that law can restrain them, or that we will shy away from them precisely because we come to understand their uncontainable quality. But here too Jackson is an apt tutor. He reminds us of the limits, as well as the value, of law and morality and of the need to take responsibility for the cultivation, in ourselves, our political culture, and our leaders, of the kind of "scrupulousness and caution" about which Hamilton wrote.[47] While embracing mercy in capital cases does not require that we reject either law or justice, it does require that we be worldly enough to see what both law and justice can and *cannot* do for us and to accept that neither can protect us from the dangers that accompany the exercise of mercy.

Jackson calls the citizens of a constitutional democracy to an ethic of responsibility, an ethic which demands that we look to ourselves and what we tolerate from public officials as the only real security in the face of risk. His admonitions suggest that, in the trial of mercy, citizens must make sure that the power over life and death does not fall into "irresponsible and unscrupulous hands."[48] He offers hope of political life without illusion, of political life genuinely worthy of constitutional democracy.

Jackson suggests that what is beyond law exists in time, connected to past uses of power as well as to a future in which new judgments will be made. In so doing, he invites us to join an ongoing conversation about memory and aspiration, a conversation about sovereign prerogative and its associated risks. He invites us to that conversation with a full awareness of what is ultimately at stake, namely life and death. In the end, living with the indeterminacy of capital clemency and mercy requires all of us to embrace Jackson's ethic of responsibility and tend to its cultivation in ourselves and our community. In the end, putting mercy on trial means putting ourselves and our political system on trial as well.

Appendix A

GEORGE RYAN

"I MUST ACT"

The following is the prepared text of Gov. George Ryan's speech delivered at Northwestern University College of Law on January 11, 2003.*

FOUR YEARS AGO I was sworn in as the 39th Governor of Illinois. That was just four short years ago; that's when I was a firm believer in the American System of Justice and the death penalty. I believed that the ultimate penalty for the taking of a life was administrated in a just and fair manner.

Today, 3 days before I end my term as Governor, I stand before you to explain my frustrations and deep concerns about both the administration and the penalty of death. It is fitting that we are gathered here today at Northwestern University with the students, teachers, lawyers and investigators who first shed light on the sorrowful condition of Illinois' death penalty system. Professors Larry Marshall, Dave Protess have and their students along with investigators Paul Ciolino have gone above the call. They freed the falsely accused Ford Heights Four, they saved Anthony Porter's life, they fought for Rolando Cruz and Alex Hernandez. They devoted time and effort on behalf of Aaron Patterson, a young man who lost 15 years of his youth sitting among the condemned, and LeRoy Orange, who lost 17 of the best years of his life on death row.

It is also proper that we are together with dedicated people like Andrea Lyon who has labored on the front lines trying capital cases for many years and who is now devoting her passion

* Found at http://www.deathpenaltyinfo.org/article.php?scid=13&did=551.

to creating an innocence center at De Paul University. You saved Madison Hobley's life.

Together you spared the lives and secured the freedom of 17 men—men who were wrongfully convicted and rotting in the condemned units of our state prisons. What you have achieved is of the highest calling—Thank You!

Yes, it is right that I am here with you, where, in a manner of speaking, my journey from staunch supporters [*sic*] of capital punishment to reformer all began. But I must tell you—since the beginning of our journey—my thoughts and feelings about the death penalty have changed many, many times. I realize that over the course of my reviews I had said that I would not do blanket commutation. I have also said it was an option that was there and I would consider all options.

During my time in public office I have always reserved my right to change my mind if I believed it to be in the best public interest, whether it be about taxes, abortions or the death penalty. But I must confess that the debate with myself has been the toughest concerning the death penalty. I suppose the reason the death penalty has been the toughest is because it is so final—the only public policy that determines who lives and who dies. In addition it is the only issue that attracts most of the legal minds across the country. I have received more advice on this issue than any other policy issue I have dealt with in my 35 years of public service. I have kept an open mind on both sides of the issues of commutation for life or death.

I have read, listened to and discussed the issue with the families of the victims as well as the families of the condemned. I know that any decision I make will not be accepted by one side or the other. I know that my decision will be just that—my decision—based on all the facts I could gather over the past 3 years. I may never be comfortable with my final decision, but I will know in my heart, that I did my very best to do the right thing.

Having said that I want to share a story with you:

I grew up in Kankakee which even today is still a small midwestern town, a place where people tend to know each other.

Steve Small was a neighbor. I watched him grow up. He would babysit my young children—which was not for the faint of heart since Lura Lynn and I had six children, 5 of them under the age of 3. He was a bright young man who helped run the family business. He got married and he and his wife had three children of their own. Lura Lynn was especially close to him and his family. We took comfort in knowing he was there for us and we for him.

One September midnight he received a call at his home. There had been a break-in at the nearby house he was renovating. But as he left his house, he was seized at gunpoint by kidnappers. His captors buried him alive in a shallow hole. He suffocated to death before police could find him.

His killer led investigators to where Steve's body was buried. The killer, Danny Edward was also from my hometown. He now sits on death row. I also know his family. I share this story with you so that you know I do not come to this as a neophyte without having experienced a small bit of the bitter pill the survivors of murder must swallow.

My responsibilities and obligations are more than my neighbors and my family. I represent all the people of Illinois, like it or not. The decision I make about our criminal justice system is felt not only here, but the world over.

The other day, I received a call from former South African President Nelson Mandela who reminded me that the United States sets the example for justice and fairness for the rest of the world. Today the United States is not in league with most of our major allies: Europe, Canada, Mexico, most of South and Central America. These countries rejected the death penalty. We are partners in death with several third world countries. Even Russia has called a moratorium.

The death penalty has been abolished in 12 states. In none of these states has the homicide rate increased. In Illinois last year we had about 1000 murders, only 2 percent of that 1000 were sentenced to death. Where is the fairness and equality in that? The death penalty in Illinois is not imposed fairly or uniformly because of the absence of standards for the 102 Illinois State Attorneys, who must decide whether to request the death sentence. Should geography be a factor in determining who gets the death sentence? I don't think so but in Illinois it makes a difference. You are 5 times more likely to get a death sentence for first degree murder in the rural area of Illinois than you are in Cook County. Where is the justice and fairness in that—where is the proportionality?

The Most Reverend Desmond Tutu wrote to me this week stating that "to take a life when a life has been lost is revenge, it is not justice. He says justice allows for mercy, clemency and compassion. These virtues are not weakness."

"In fact the most glaring weakness is that no matter how efficient and fair the death penalty may seem in theory, in actual practice it is primarily inflicted upon the weak, the poor, the ignorant and against racial minorities." That was a quote from Former California Governor Pat Brown. He wrote that in his book—*Public Justice, Private Mercy* he wrote that nearly 50 years ago—nothing has changed in nearly 50 years.

I never intended to be an activist on this issue. I watched in surprise as freed death row inmate Anthony Porter was released from jail. A free man, he ran into the arms of Northwestern University Professor Dave Protess who poured his heart and soul into proving Porter's innocence with his journalism students.

He was 48 hours away from being wheeled into the execution chamber where the state would kill him.

It would all be so antiseptic and most of us would not have even paused, except that Anthony Porter was innocent of the double murder for which he had been condemned to die.

After Mr. Porter's case there was the report by Chicago Tribune reporters Steve Mills and Ken Armstrong documenting the systemic failures of our capital punishment system. Half of the nearly 300 capital cases in Illinois had been reversed for a new trial or resentencing.

Nearly Half!

33 of the death row inmates were represented at trial by an attorney who had later been disbarred or at some point suspended from practicing law.

Of the more than 160 death row inmates, 35 were African American defendants who had been convicted or condemned to die by all-white juries.

More than two-thirds of the inmates on death row were African American.

46 inmates were convicted on the basis of testimony from jailhouse informants.

I can recall looking at these cases and the information from the Mills/Armstrong series and asking my staff: How does that happen? How in God's name does that happen? I'm not a lawyer, so somebody explain it to me.

But no one could. Not to this day.

Then over the next few months. There were three more exonerated men, freed because their sentence hinged on a jailhouse informant or new DNA technology proved beyond a shadow of doubt their innocence.

We then had the dubious distinction of exonerating more men than we had executed. 13 men found innocent, 12 executed.

As I reported yesterday, there is not a doubt in my mind that the number of innocent men freed from our Death Row stands at 17, with the pardons of Aaron Patterson, Madison Hobley, Stanley Howard and Leroy Orange.

That is an absolute embarrassment. 17 exonerated death row inmates is nothing short of a catastrophic failure. But the 13, now 17 men, is just the beginning of our sad arithmetic in prosecuting murder cases. During the time we have had capital punishment in Illinois, there were at least 33 other people wrongly convicted on murder charges and exonerated. Since we reinstated the death penalty there are also 93 people—93—where our criminal justice system imposed the most severe sanction and later rescinded the sentence or even released them from custody because they were innocent.

How many more cases of wrongful conviction have to occur before we can all agree that the system is broken?

Throughout this process, I have heard many different points of view expressed. I have had the opportunity to review all of the cases involving the inmates on death row. I have conducted private group meetings, one in Springfield and one in Chicago, with the surviving family members of homicide victims. Everyone in the room who wanted to speak had the opportunity to do so. Some wanted to express their grief, others wanted to express their anger. I took it all in.

My commission and my staff had been reviewing each and every case for three years. But, I redoubled my effort to review each case personally in order to respond to the concerns of prosecutors and victims' families. This individual review also naturally resulted in a collective examination of our entire death penalty system.

I also had a meeting with a group of people who are less often heard from, and who are not as popular with the media. The family members of death row inmates have a special challenge to face. I spent an afternoon with those family members at a Catholic church here in Chicago. At that meeting, I heard a different kind of pain expressed. Many of these families live with the twin pain of knowing not only that, in some cases, their family member may have been responsible for inflicting a terrible trauma on another family, but also the pain of knowing that society has called for another killing. These parents, siblings and children are not to blame for the crime committed, yet these innocent stand to have their loved ones killed by the state. As Mr. Mandela told me, they are also branded and scarred for life because of the awful crime committed by their family member.

Others were even more tormented by the fact that their loved one was another victim, that they were truly innocent of the crime for which they were sentenced to die.

It was at this meeting that I looked into the face of Claude Lee, the father of Eric Lee, who was convicted of killing Kankakee police officer Anthony Samfay a few years ago. It was a traumatic moment, once again, for my hometown. A brave officer, part of that thin blue line that protects each of us, was struck down by wanton violence. If you will kill a police officer, you have absolutely no respect for the laws of man or God.

I've know the Lee family for a number of years. There does not appear to be much question that Eric was guilty of killing the officer. However, I can say now after our review, there is also not much question that Eric is seriously ill, with a history of treatment for mental illness going back a number of years.

The crime he committed was a terrible one—killing a police officer. Society demands that the highest penalty be paid.

But I had to ask myself—could I send another man's son to death under the deeply flawed system of capital punishment we have in Illinois? A troubled young man, with a history of mental illness? Could I rely on the system of justice we have in Illinois not to make another horrible mistake? Could I rely on a fair sentencing?

In the United States the overwhelming majority of those executed are psychotic, alcoholic, drug addicted or mentally unstable. They frequently are raised in an impoverished and abusive environment.

Seldom are people with money or prestige convicted of capital offenses, even more seldom are they executed.

To quote Governor Brown again, he said "society has both the right and the moral duty to protect itself against its enemies. This natural and prehistoric axiom has never successfully been refuted. If by ordered death, society is really protected and our homes and institutions guarded, then even the most extreme of all penalties can be justified."

"Beyond its honor and incredibility, it has neither protected the innocent nor deterred the killers. Publicly sanctioned killing has cheapened human life and dignity without the redeeming grace which comes from justice metered out swiftly, evenly, humanely."

At stake throughout the clemency process, was whether some, all or none of these inmates on death row would have their sentences commuted from death to life without the possibility [*sic*] parole.

One of the things discussed with family members was life without parole was seen as a life filled with perks and benefits.

Some inmates on death row don't want a sentence of life without parole. Danny Edwards wrote me and told me not to do him any favors because he didn't want to face a prospect of a life in prison without parole. They will be confined in a cell that is about 5-feet-by-12 feet, usually double-bunked. Our prisons have no air conditioning, except at our supermax facility where inmates are kept in their cell 23 hours a day. In summer months, temperatures in these prisons exceed one hundred degrees. It is a stark and dreary existence. They can think about their crimes. Life without parole has even, at times, been described by prosecutors as a fate worse than death.

Yesterday, I mentioned a lawsuit in Livingston County where a judge ruled the state corrections department cannot force feed two corrections inmates who are on a hunger strike. The judge ruled that suicide by hunger strike was not an irrational action by the inmates, given what their future holds.

Earlier this year, the U.S. Supreme Court held that it is unconstitutional and cruel and unusual punishment to execute the mentally retarded. It is now the law of the land. How many people have we already executed who were mentally retarded and are now dead and buried? Although we now know that they have been killed by the state unconstitutionally and illegally. Is that fair? Is that right?

This court decision was last spring. The General Assembly failed to pass any measure defining what constitutes mental retardation. We are a rudderless ship because they failed to act.

This is even after the Illinois Supreme Court also told lawmakers that it is their job and it must be done.

I started with this issue concerned about innocence. But once I studied, once I pondered what had become of our justice system, I came to care above all about fairness. Fairness is fundamental to the American system of justice and our way of life.

The facts I have seen in reviewing each and every one of these cases raised questions not only about the innocence of people on death row, but about the fairness of the death penalty system as a whole.

If the system was making so many errors in determining whether someone was guilty in the first place, how fairly and accurately was it determining which guilty defendants deserved to live and which deserved to die? What effect was race having? What effect was poverty having?

And in almost every one of the exonerated 17, we not only have breakdowns in the system with police, prosecutors and judges, we have terrible cases of shabby defense lawyers. There is just no way to sugar coat it. There are defense attorneys that did not consult with their clients, did not investigate the case and were completely unqualified to handle complex death penalty cases. They often didn't put much effort into fighting a death sentence. If your life is on the line, your lawyer ought to be fighting for you. As I have said before, there is more than enough blame to go around.

I had more questions.

In Illinois, I have learned, we have 102 decision makers. Each of them are politically elected, each beholden to the demands of their community and, in some cases, to the media or especially vocal victims' families. In cases that have the attention of the media and the public, are decisions to seek the death penalty more likely to occur? What standards are these prosecutors using?

Some people have assailed my power to commute sentences, a power that literally hundreds of legal scholars from across the country have defended. But prosecutors in Illinois have the ultimate commutation power, a power that is exercised every day. They decide who will be subject to the death penalty, who will get a plea deal or even who may get a complete pass on prosecution. By what objective standards do they make these decisions? We do not know, they are not public. There were more than 1000 murders last year in Illinois. There is no doubt that all murders are horrific and cruel. Yet, less than 2 percent of those murder defendants will receive the death penalty. That means more than 98% of victims families do not get, and will not receive whatever satisfaction can be derived from the execution of the murderer. Moreover, if you look at the cases, as I have done—both individually and collectively—a killing with the same circumstances might get 40 years in one county and death in another county. I have also seen where co-defendants who are equally or even more culpable get sentenced to a term of years, while another less culpable defendant ends up on death row.

In my case-by-case review, I found three people that fell into this category, Mario Flores, Montel Johnson and William Franklin. Today I have commuted their sentences to a term of 40 years to bring their sentences into line with their co-defendants and to reflect the other extraordinary circumstances of these cases.

Supreme Court Justice Potter Stewart has said that the imposition of the death penalty on defendants in this country is as freakish and arbitrary as who gets hit by a bolt of lightning.

For years the criminal justice system defended and upheld the imposition of the death penalty for the 17 exonerated inmates from Illinois Death row. Yet when the real killers are charged, prosecutors have often sought sentences of less than death. In the Ford Heights Four Case, Verneal Jimerson and Dennis Williams fought the death sentences imposed upon them for 18 years before they were exonerated. Later, Cook County prosecutors sought life in prison for two of the real killers and a sentence of 80 years for a third.

What made the murder for which the Ford Heights Four were sentenced to die less heinous and worthy of the death penalty twenty years later with a new set of defendants?

We have come very close to having our state Supreme Court rule our death penalty statute—the one that I helped enact in 1977—unconstitutional. Former State Supreme Court Justice Seymour Simon wrote to me that it was only happenstance that our statute was not struck down by the state's high court. When he joined the bench in 1980, three other justices had already said Illinois' death penalty was unconstitutional. But they got cold feet when a case came along to revisit the question. One judge wrote that he wanted to wait and see if the Supreme Court of the United States would rule on the constitutionality of the new Illinois law. Another said precedent required him to follow the old state Supreme Court ruling with which he disagreed.

Even a pharmacist knows that doesn't make sense. We wouldn't have a death penalty today, and we all wouldn't be struggling with this issue, if those votes had been different. How arbitrary.

Several years after we enacted our death penalty statute, Girvies Davis was executed. Justice Simon writes that he was executed because of this unconstitutional aspect of the Illinois law—the wide latitude that each Illinois State's Attorney has to determine what cases qualify for the death penalty. One State's Attorney waived his request for the death sentence when Davis' first sentencing was sent back to the trial court for a new sentencing hearing. The prosecutor was going to seek a life sentence. But in the interim, a new State's Attorney took office and changed directions. He once again sought and secured a death sentence. Davies was executed.

How fair is that?

After the flaws in our system were exposed, the Supreme Court of Illinois took it upon itself to begin to reform its' [*sic*] rules and improve the trial of capital cases. It changed the rule to require that State's Attorney's [*sic*] give advance notice to defendants that they plan to seek the death penalty to require notice before trial instead of after conviction. The Supreme Court also enacted new discovery rules designed to prevent trials by ambush and to allow for better investigation of cases from the beginning.

But shouldn't that mean if you were tried or sentenced before the rules changed, you ought to get a new trial or sentencing with the new safeguards of the rules? This issue has divided our Supreme Court, some saying yes, a majority saying no. These justices have a lifetime of experience with the criminal justice system and it concerns me that these great minds so strenuously differ on an issue of such importance, especially where life or death hangs in the balance.

What are we to make of the studies that showed that more than 50% of Illinois jurors could not understand the confusing and obscure sentencing instructions that were being used? What effect did that problem have on the trustworthiness of death sentences? A review of the cases shows that often even the lawyers and judges are confused about the instructions—let alone the jurors sitting in judgment. Cases still come before the Supreme Court with arguments about whether the jury instructions were proper.

I spent a good deal of time reviewing these death row cases. My staff, many of whom are lawyers, spent busy days and many sleepless nights answering my questions, providing me with information, giving me advice. It became clear to me that whatever decision I made, I would be criticized. It also became clear to me that it was impossible to make reliable choices about whether our capital punishment system had really done its job.

As I came closer to my decision, I knew that I was going to have to face the question of whether I believed so completely in the choice I wanted to make that I could face the prospect of even commuting the death sentence of Daniel Edwards—the man who had killed a close family friend of mine. I discussed it with my wife, Lura Lynn, who has stood by me all these years. She was angry and disappointed at my decision like many of the families of other victims will be.

I was struck by the anger of the families of murder victims. To a family they talked about closure. They pleaded with me to allow the state to kill an inmate in its name to provide the families with closure. But is that the purpose of capital punishment? Is it to soothe the families? And is that truly what the families experience.

I cannot imagine losing a family member to murder. Nor can I imagine spending every waking day for 20 years with a single minded focus to execute the killer. The system of death in Illinois is so unsure that it is not unusual for cases to take 20 years before they are resolved. And thank God. If it had moved any faster, then Anthony Porter, the Ford Heights Four, Ronald Jones, Madison Hobley and the other innocent men we've exonerated might be dead and buried.

But it is cruel and unusual punishment for family members to go through this pain, this legal limbo for 20 years. Perhaps it would be less cruel if we sentenced the killers to TAMS to life, and used our resources to better serve victims.

My heart ached when I heard one grandmother who lost children in an arson fire. She said she could not afford proper grave markers for her grandchildren who died. Why can't the state help families provide a proper burial?

Another crime victim came to our family meetings. He believes an inmate sent to death row for another crime also shot and paralyzed him. The inmate he says gets free health care while the victim is struggling to pay his substantial medical bills and, as a result, he has forgone getting proper medical care to alleviate the physical pain he endures.

What kind of victims services are we providing? Are all of our resources geared toward providing this notion of closure by execution instead of tending to the physical and social service needs of victim families? And what kind of values are we instilling in these wounded families and in the young people? As Gandhi said, an eye for an eye only leaves the whole world blind.

President Lincoln often talked of binding up wounds as he sought to preserve the Union. "We are not enemies, but friends. We must not be enemies. Though passion may have strained, it must not break our bonds of affection."

I have had to consider not only the horrible nature of the crimes that put men on death row in the first place, the terrible suffering of the surviving family members of the victims, the despair of the family members of the inmates, but I have also had to watch in frustration as members of the Illinois General Assembly failed to pass even one substantive death penalty reform. Not one. They couldn't even agree on ONE. How much more evidence is needed before the General Assembly will take its responsibility in this area seriously?

The fact is that the failure of the General Assembly to act is merely a symptom of the larger problem. Many people express the desire to have capital punishment. Few, however, seem prepared to address the tough questions that arise when the system fails. It is easier and more comfortable for politicians to be tough on crime and support the death penalty. It wins votes. But when it comes to admitting that we have a problem, most run for cover. Prosecutors across our state continue to deny that our death penalty system is broken—or they say if there is a problem, it is really a small one and we can fix it somehow. It is difficult to see how the system can be fixed when not a single one of the reforms proposed by my Capital Punishment Commission has been adopted. Even the reforms the prosecutors agree with haven't been adopted.

So when will the system be fixed? How much more risk can we afford? Will we actually have to execute an innocent person before the tragedy that is our capital punishment system in Illinois is really understood? This summer, a United States District court judge held the federal death penalty was unconstitutional and noted that with the number of recent exonerations based on DNA and new scientific technology we undoubtedly executed innocent people before this technology emerged.

As I prepare to leave office, I had to ask myself whether I could really live with the prospect of knowing that I had the opportunity to act, but that I failed to do so because I might be criticized. Could I take the chance that our capital punishment system might be reformed, that wrongful convictions might not occur, that enterprising journalism students might free more men from death row? A system that's so fragile that it depends on young journalism students is seriously flawed.

"There is no honorable way to kill, no gentle way to destroy. There is nothing good in war. Except its ending."

That's what Abraham Lincoln said about the bloody war between the states. It was a war fought to end the sorriest chapter in American history—the institution of slavery. While we are not in a civil war now, we are facing what is shaping up to be one of the great civil rights struggles of our time. Stephen Bright of the Southern Center for Human Rights has taken the position that the death penalty is being sought with increasing frequency in some states against the poor and minorities.

Our own study showed that juries were more likely to sentence to death if the victim were white than if the victim were black—three-and-a-half times more likely to be exact. We are not alone. Just this month Maryland released a study of their death penalty system and racial disparities exist there too.

This week, Mamie Till died. Her son Emmett was lynched in Mississippi in the 1950s. She was a strong advocate for civil rights and reconciliation. In fact just three weeks ago, she was the keynote speaker at the Murder Victims' Families for Reconciliation Event in Chicago. This group, many of whom I've met, opposes the death penalty even though their family members have been lost to senseless killing. Mamie's strength and grace not only ignited the civil rights movement—including inspiring Rosa Parks to refuse to go to the back of the bus—but inspired murder victims' families until her dying day.

Is our system fair to all? Is justice blind? These are important human rights issues.

Another issue that came up in my individual, case-by-case review was the issue of international law. The Vienna Convention protects U.S. citizens abroad and foreign nationals in the United States. It provides that if you [*sic*] arrested, you should be afforded the opportunity to contact your consulate. There are five men on death row who were denied that internationally recognized human right. Mexico's President Vicente Fox contacted me to express his deep concern for the Vienna Convention violations. If we do not uphold international law here, we cannot expect our citizens to be protected outside the United States.

My Commission recommended the Supreme Court conduct a proportionality review of our system in Illinois. While our appellate courts perform a case by case review of the appellate record, they have not done such a big picture study. Instead, we tinker with a case-by-case review as each appeal lands on their docket.

In 1994, near the end of his distinguished career on the Supreme Court of the United States, Justice Harry Blackmun wrote an influential dissent in the body of law on capital punishment. 20 years earlier he was part of the court that issued the landmark Furman decision. The Court decided that the death penalty statutes in use throughout the country were fraught with severe flaws that rendered them unconstitutional. Quite frankly, they were the same problems we see here in Illinois. To many, it looked liked the Furman decision meant the end of the death penalty in the United States.

This was not the case. Many states responded to Furman by developing and enacting new and improved death penalty statutes. In 1976, four years after it had decided Furman, Justice Blackmun joined the majority of the United States Supreme Court in deciding to give the States a chance with these new and improved death penalty statutes. There was great optimism in the air.

This was the climate in 1977, when the Illinois legislature was faced with the momentous decision of whether to reinstate the death penalty in Illinois. I was a member of the General Assembly at that time and when I pushed the green button in favor of reinstating the death penalty in this great State, I did so with the belief that whatever problems had plagued the capital punishment system in the past were now being cured. I am sure that most of my colleagues who voted with me that day shared that view.

But 20 years later, after affirming hundreds of death penalty decisions, Justice Blackmun came to the realization, in the twilight of his distinguished career that the death penalty remains [“]fraught with arbitrariness, discrimination, caprice and mistake.” He expressed frustration with a 20-year struggle to develop procedural and substantive safeguards. In a now famous dissent he wrote in 1994, “From this day forward, I no longer shall tinker with the machinery of death.”

One of the few disappointments of my legislative and executive career is that the General Assembly failed to work with me to reform our deeply flawed system.

I don't know why legislators could not heed the rising voices of reform. I don't know how many more systemic flaws we needed to uncover before they would be spurred to action.

Three times I proposed reforming the system with a package that would restrict the use of jailhouse snitches, create a statewide panel to determine death eligible cases, and reduce the number of crimes eligible for death. These reforms would not have created a perfect system, but they would have dramatically reduced the chance for error in the administration of the ultimate penalty.

The Governor has the constitutional role in our state of acting in the interest of justice and fairness. Our state constitution provides broad power to the Governor to issue reprieves, pardons and commutations. Our Supreme Court has reminded inmates petitioning them that the last resort for relief is the governor.

At times the executive clemency power has perhaps been a crutch for courts to avoid making the kind of major change that I believe our system needs.

Our systemic case-by-case review has found more cases of innocent men wrongfully sentenced to death row. Because our three year study has found only more questions about the fairness of the sentencing; because of the spectacular failure to reform the system; because we have seen justice delayed for countless death row inmates with potentially meritorious claims; because the Illinois death penalty system is arbitrary and capricious—and therefore immoral—I no longer shall tinker with the machinery of death.

I cannot say it more eloquently than Justice Blackmun.

The legislature couldn't reform it.

Lawmakers won't repeal it.

But I will not stand for it.

I must act.

Our capital system is haunted by the demon of error, error in determining guilt, and error in determining who among the guilty deserves to die. Because of all of these reasons today I am commuting the sentences of all death row inmates.

This is a blanket commutation. I realize it will draw ridicule, scorn and anger from many who oppose this decision. They will say I am usurping the decisions of judges and juries and state legislators. But as I have said, the people of our state have vested in me to act in the interest of justice. Even if the exercise of my power becomes my burden I will bear it. Our constitution compels it. I sought this office, and even in my final days of holding it I cannot shrink from the obligations to justice and fairness that it demands.

There have been many nights where my staff and I have been deprived of sleep in order to conduct our exhaustive review of the system. But I can tell you this: I will sleep well knowing I made the right decision.

As I said when I declared the moratorium, it is time for a rational discussion on the death penalty. While our experience in Illinois has indeed sparked a debate, we have fallen short of a rational discussion. Yet if I did not take this action, I feared that there would be no comprehensive and thorough inquiry into the guilt of the individuals on death row or of the fairness of the sentences applied.

To say it plainly one more time—the Illinois capital punishment system is broken. It has taken innocent men to a hair's breadth escape from their unjust execution. Legislatures past have refused to fix it. Our new legislature and our new Governor must act to rid our state of the shame of threatening the innocent with execution and the guilty with unfairness.

In the days ahead, I will pray that we can open our hearts and provide something for victims' families other than the hope of revenge. Lincoln once said: "I have always found that mercy bears richer fruits than strict justice." I can only hope that will be so. God bless you. And God bless the people of Illinois.

Appendix B

CAPITAL CLEMENCY, 1900–2004

Commutations by State

	1900	1901	1902	1903	1904	1905	1906	1907	1908	1909	1910	1911	1912	1913	1914	1915
Alabama																
Alaska	0	0	0	0	0	0	0	0	0	0	0	0	0	0	0	0
Arizona	0	0	0	0	0	0	0	0	0	0	nd	nd	13			nd
Arkansas	1															
California	nd	nd	nd	0	0	nd	1	nd	nd	2	1	2	3	3	0	1
Colorado	0	0														
Connecticut																
Delaware																
Florida	nd	nd	1													
Georgia														1		
Hawaii	0	0	0	0	0	0	0	0	0	0	0	0	0	0	0	0
Idaho									1							
Illinois								0	0	1	0					
Indiana																
Iowa																
Kansas								0	0	0	0	0	0	0	0	0
Kentucky																
Louisiana																
Maine	0	0	0	0	0	0	0	0	0	0	0	0	0	0	0	0
Maryland																
Massachusetts																
Michigan	0	0	0	0	0	0	0	0	0	0	0	0	0	0	0	0
Minnesota												0	0	0	0	0
Mississippi																
Missouri																
Montana																
Nebraska																
Nevada																
New Hampshire																
New Jersey	nd	nd	nd	nd	nd	nd	nd	0	0	2	0	2	2	2	1	2
New Mexico	0	0	0	0	0	0	0	0	0	0	0	0	nd	nd	nd	nd
New York	nd	nd	nd	1	nd	nd	1	nd	nd	0	0	1	nd	nd	nd	nd
North Carolina	nd	nd	nd							1909–1912: 7				1913–1916: 29		
North Dakota																0
Ohio																
Oklahoma	0	0	0	0	0	0	0	nd	nd	nd	nd	8		14		
Oregon	nd	nd	nd	1	0	1	0	0	0	1	0	3	1	3	2	0
Pennsylvania																
Rhode Island	0	0	0	0	0	0	0	0	0	0	0	0	0	0	0	0
South Carolina												1				
South Dakota																0
Tennessee									1							
Texas																
Utah																
Vermont																
Virginia																
Washington														0	0	0
West Virginia																
Wisconsin	0	0	0	0	0	0	0	0	0	0	0	0	0	0	0	0
Wyoming																
Total	**1**	**0**	**1**	**2**	**0**	**1**	**2**	**0**	**2**	**6**	**1**	**24**	**6**	**36**	**3**	**32**

Years of Legislative Abolition
Furman v. Georgia Decision
Pre-Statehood Years
No Data Found

Note*: Where annual clemency totals (along the bottom) are highlighted in darkest gray, that number is distorted by composite data calculated into a single year total.

Row	1916	1917	1918	1919	1920	1921	1922	1923	1924	1925	1926	1927	1928	1929	1930	1931	1932	1933	1934
	0	0	0	0	0	0	0	0	0	0	0	0	0	0	0	0	0	0	0
	0	0	0												0	0	0	0	0
									6										
	0	nd	1	nd	nd	nd	nd	0	1	0	0	2	1	2	0	4	2	1	8
					1920–1962: 8														
									1	2	0	3	2	6	0	1	1	1	0
	0	0	0	0	0	0	0	0	0	0	0	0	0	0	0	0	0	0	0
															1930–1963: 10				
															1930–1963: 5				
	0	0	0	0	0	0	0	0	0	0	0	0	0	0	0	0	0	0	0
			2	2	3	0	1	1	1	0	0	0	0	0	5	6	1	4	1
	0	0	0	0	0	0	0	0	0	0	0	0	0	0	0	0	0	0	0
	1900–1958: 30																		
	0	0	0	0	0	0	0	0	0	0	0	0	0	0	0	0	0	0	0
	0	0	0	0	0	0	0	0	0	0	0	0	0	0	0	0	0	0	0
	2	0	0	0	0	1	2	2	1	2	0	0	0	0	4	0	0	0	0
	nd	nd	nd	1															
	1	nd	1	3	8	2	2	7	4	2	3	7	3	1	4	4	13	9	5
		19				23				17				25					
	0	0	0	0	0	0	0	0	0	0	0	0	0	0	0	0	0	0	0
	0	0	0	0	0	0	0	0	2	0	0	0	0	0	0	0	0	0	2
	1914–1952: 72																		
	0	0	0	0	0	0	0	0	0	0	0	0	0	0	0	0	0	0	0
																		1	0
	0	0	0	0	0	0	0	0	0	0	0	0	0	0	0	0	0	0	0
												13							
								0	0	5	2	1	3	2	3	2	0	8	4
															1				
	0	0	0	0															
														1					
	0	0	0	0	0	0	0	0	0	0	0	0	0	0	0	0	0	0	0
	3	**0**	**4**	**25**	**11**	**3**	**5**	**33**	**16**	**11**	**5**	**30**	**9**	**12**	**60**	**42**	**17**	**96**	**20**

States with Fewer than 20 Years of Data Pre-*Furman*

Alabama
Colorado
Delaware
Idaho
Indiana
Louisiana
Mississippi
Missouri
Montana
Nebraska
Nevada
New Hampshire
New Mexico
Ohio
Oklahoma
South Carolina
Tennessee
Utah
Vermont
Virginia
Washington
West Virginia
Wyoming

	1935	1936	1937	1938	1939	1940	1941	1942	1943	1944	1945	1946	1947	1948	1949	1950
Alabama															0	1
Alaska	0	0	0	0	0	0	0	0	0	0	0	0	0	0	0	0
Arizona	0	0	0	0	0	0	0	0	0	0	0	0	0	0	0	0
Arkansas		1														
California	nd	nd	nd	nd	nd	nd	2	1	0	1	1	1	2	1	1	0
Colorado																
Connecticut	1920–1962: 8															
Delaware																
Florida	0	1	1	1	4	4	2	1	0	1	2	1	1	0	1	0
Georgia									10		13		7		6	
Hawaii	0	0	0	0	0	0	0	0	0	0	0	0	0	0	0	0
Idaho																
Illinois	1930–1963: 10															
Indiana																
Iowa	1930–1963: 5															
Kansas	0															
Kentucky	1	0	0	0	0	0	0	0	0	0	2	0	1	0	0	0
Louisiana																
Maine	0	0	0	0	0	0	0	0	0	0	0	0	0	0	0	0
Maryland			1937–1961: 34													
Massachusetts	1900–1958: 30															
Michigan	0	0	0	0	0	0	0	0	0	0	0	0	0	0	0	0
Minnesota	0	0	0	0	0	0	0	0	0	0	0	0	0	0	0	0
Mississippi																
Missouri																
Montana																
Nebraska																
Nevada																
New Hampshire																
New Jersey	3	2	0	0	1	0	0	0	0	2	0	0	0	0	0	0
New Mexico																
New York	9	0	6	1	2	4	4	2	1943–1954: 31							
North Carolina	28		1937–1954: 54													
North Dakota	0	0	0	0	0	0	0	0	0	0	0	0	0	0	0	0
Ohio																
Oklahoma																
Oregon	0	0	0	0	0	0	0	0	0	0	0	0	0	0	0	0
Pennsylvania	1914–1952: 72															
Rhode Island	0	0	0	0	0	0	0	0	0	0	0	0	0	0	0	0
South Carolina																
South Dakota	0	0	0	0	0											
Tennessee																
Texas	3	3	3	3	2	0	0	0	1	3	4	3	2	3	1	1
Utah																
Vermont																
Virginia																
Washington																
West Virginia																
Wisconsin	0	0	0	0	0	0	0	0	0	0	0	0	0	0	0	0
Wyoming																
Total	44	7	10	5	9	8	31	4	11	7	22	59	13	38	40	2

Years of Legislative Abolition
Furman v. Georgia Decision
Pre-Statehood Years
No Data Found

Note*: Where annual clemency totals (along the bottom) are highlighted in darkest gray, that number is distorted by composite data calculated into a single year total.

1951	1952	1953	1954	1955	1956	1957	1958	1959	1960	1961	1962	1963	1964	1965	1966	1967	1968	1969
										2								
0	0	0	0	0	0	0	0	0	0	0	0	0	0	0	0	0	0	0
0	2	0	0	0	0	0	0	0	0	0	0	0	0	0	0	0	0	nd
									0	0	0	nd	nd	nd	nd	0	0	0
0	0	1	3	0	0	0	3	4	4	2	4	4	0	0	4	1	0	0
									0	0	0							
							0	0	0	0	0	0						
0	1	1	2	2	2	0	2	1	2	0	0	3	2	0	3	nd	nd	nd
7		4		7		5		2		3	4	0	1	2	0	2	5	1
0	0	0	0	0	0	0	0	0	0	0	0	0	0	0	0	0	0	0
										1								
									0	0	0							
													nd	0	0	0	0	0
									0	0	0	0						
0	0	0	0	0	0	0	0	0	0	0	0	0	0	0	0	3	nd	nd
										1								
0	0	0	0	0	0	0	0	0	0	0	0	0	0	0	0	0	0	0
											nd	3						
										1	0	nd	nd	nd	0	0	0	0
0	0	0	0	0	0	0	0	0	0	0	0	0	0	0	0	0	0	0
0	0	0	0	0	0	0	0	0	0	0	0	0	0	0	0	0	0	0
										1								
										1								
									0	0	0							
										1								
									0	0	0							
									0	0	0							
0	0	0	0	0	0	0	1	0	1	0	0							
									0	0	0	nd	nd	nd	nd	nd	nd	0
				2	0	0	2			9				0	0	0	0	0
								32										
0	0	0	0	0	0	0	0	0	0	0	0	0	0	0	0	0	0	0
				23						5								
										1								
0	0	0	0	1	0	2	0	1	1	0	0	0	3	nd	nd	nd	nd	nd
				14					2									
0	0	0	0	0	0	0	0	0	0	0	0	0	0	0	0	0	0	0
									2	0	0	0	0	0	0	0	0	0
									0	0	0							
										7		0	0	5	nd	nd	nd	nd
1	7	1	0	2	0	1	2	1	2	2	1	1	0	2	2	0	1	5
										1								
									0	0	0	nd	nd	0	0	0	0	0
	1								2									
														0	0	0	0	0
								1					nd	0	0	0	0	0
0	0	0	0	0	0	0	0	0	0	0	0	0	0	0	0	0	0	0
									0	0	0							
8	**11**	**7**	**28**	**28**	**2**	**8**	**10**	**42**	**16**	**38**	**9**	**11**	**6**	**9**	**9**	**6**	**6**	**6**

	1970	1971	1972	1973	1974	1975	1976	1977	1978	1979	1980	1981	1982	1983	1984	1985
Alabama			0	0	0	0	0	0	0	0	0	0	0	0	0	0
Alaska	0	0	0	0	0	0	0	0	0	0	0	0	0	0	0	0
Arizona	nd	nd	0	0	0	0	0	0	0	0	0	0	0	0	0	0
Arkansas	15	1	0	0	0	0	0	0	0	0	0	0	0	0	0	0
California	0	0	0	0	0	0	0	0	0	0	0	0	0	0	0	0
Colorado			0	0	0	0	0	0	0	0	0	0	0	0	0	0
Connecticut			0	0	0	0	0	0	0	0	0	0	0	0	0	0
Delaware			0	0	0	0	0	0	0	0	0	0	0	0	0	0
Florida	nd	nd	0	0	0	2	0	0	0	2	2	1	0	1	0	0
Georgia	0	0	0	0	0	0	0	1	0	0	0	0	0	0	0	0
Hawaii	0	0	0	0	0	0	0	0	0	0	0	0	0	0	0	0
Idaho			0	0	0	0	0	0	0	0	0	0	0	0	0	0
Illinois			0	0	0	0	0	0	0	0	0	0	0	0	0	0
Indiana			0	0	0	0	0	0	0	0	0	0	0	0	0	0
Iowa	0	0	0	0	0	0	0	0	0	0	0	0	0	0	0	0
Kansas			0	0	0	0	0	0	0	0	0	0	0	0	0	0
Kentucky	nd	nd	0	0	0	0	0	0	0	0	0	0	0	0	0	0
Louisiana			0	0	0	0	0	0	0	0	0	0	0	0	0	0
Maine	0	0	0	0	0	0	0	0	0	0	0	0	0	0	0	0
Maryland			0	0	0	0	0	0	0	0	0	0	0	0	0	0
Massachusetts	nd	nd	0	0	0	0	0	0	0	0	0	0	0	0	0	0
Michigan	0	0	0	0	0	0	0	0	0	0	0	0	0	0	0	0
Minnesota	0	0	0	0	0	0	0	0	0	0	0	0	0	0	0	0
Mississippi			0	0	0	0	0	0	0	0	0	0	0	0	0	0
Missouri			0	0	0	0	0	0	0	0	0	0	0	0	0	0
Montana			0	0	0	0	0	0	0	0	0	0	0	0	0	0
Nebraska			0	0	0	0	0	0	0	0	0	0	0	0	0	0
Nevada			0	0	0	0	0	0	0	0	0	0	0	0	0	0
New Hampshire			0	0	0	0	0	0	0	0	0	0	0	0	0	0
New Jersey			0	0	0	0	0	0	0	0	0	0	0	0	0	0
New Mexico	0	0	0	0	0	0	0	0	0	0	0	0	0	0	0	0
New York	0	0	0	0	0	0	0	0	0	0	0	0	0	0	0	0
North Carolina			0	0	0	0	0	0	0	0	0	0	0	0	0	0
North Dakota	0	0	0	0	0	0	0	0	0	0	0	0	0	0	0	0
Ohio			0	0	0	0	0	0	0	0	0	0	0	0	0	0
Oklahoma			0	0	0	0	0	0	0	0	0	0	0	0	0	0
Oregon	nd	nd	0	0	0	0	0	0	0	0	0	0	0	0	0	0
Pennsylvania			0	0	0	0	0	0	0	0	0	0	0	0	0	0
Rhode Island	0	0	0	0	0	0	0	0	0	0	0	0	0	0	0	0
South Carolina	0	3	0	0	0	0	0	0	0	0	0	0	0	0	0	0
South Dakota			0	0	0	0	0	0	0	0	0	0	0	0	0	0
Tennessee	nd	3	0	0	0	0	0	0	0	0	0	0	0	0	0	0
Texas	0	5	0	0	0	0	0	0	0	0	0	0	0	0	0	0
Utah			0	0	0	0	0	0	0	0	0	0	0	0	0	0
Vermont	0	0	0	0	0	0	0	0	0	0	0	0	0	0	0	0
Virginia			0	0	0	0	0	0	0	0	0	0	0	0	0	0
Washington	0	0	0	0	0	0	0	0	0	0	0	0	0	0	0	0
West Virginia	0	0	0	0	0	0	0	0	0	0	0	0	0	0	0	0
Wisconsin	0	0	0	0	0	0	0	0	0	0	0	0	0	0	0	0
Wyoming			0	0	0	0	0	0	0	0	0	0	0	0	0	0
Total	**15**	**12**	**0**	**0**	**0**	**2**	**0**	**1**	**0**	**2**	**2**	**1**	**0**	**1**	**0**	**0**

- Years of Legislative Abolition
- *Furman v. Georgia* Decision
- Pre-Statehood Years
- No Data Found

Note: Over 600 death row prisoners under state civil authority nationwide had their sentences commuted between 1972 and 1974, in direct response to the Supreme Court's decision in *Furman v. Georgia*. While many of these commutations were technically granted by governors, none is included on this chart. Governors took such action simply to expedite a process made necessary after Furman effectively vacated all death sentences nationwide.

1986	1987	1988	1989	1990	1991	1992	1993	1994	1995	1996	1997	1998	1999	2000	2001	2002	2003	2004	Total
0	0	0	0	0	0	0	0	0	0	0	0	0	1	0	0	0	0	0	**4**
0	0	0	0	0	0	0	0	0	0	0	0	0	0	0	0	0	0	0	**0**
0	0	0	0	0	0	0	0	0	0	0	0	0	0	0	0	0	0	0	**15**
0	0	0	0	0	0	0	0	0	0	0	0	0	1	0	0	0	0	0	**25**
0	0	0	0	0	0	0	0	0	0	0	0	0	0	0	0	0	0	0	**75**
0	0	0	0	0	0	0	0	0	0	0	0	0	0	0	0	0	0	0	**0**
0	0	0	0	0	0	0	0	0	0	0	0	0	0	0	0	0	0	0	**8**
0	0	0	0	0	0	0	0	0	0	0	0	0	0	0	0	0	0	0	**0**
0	0	0	0	0	0	0	0	0	0	0	0	0	0	0	0	0	0	0	**67**
0	0	1	0	1	0	0	0	0	0	0	0	0	0	0	0	1	0	1	**85**
0	0	0	0	0	0	0	0	0	0	0	0	0	0	0	0	0	0	0	**0**
0	0	0	0	0	0	0	0	0	0	1	0	0	0	0	0	0	0	0	**3**
0	0	0	0	0	0	0	0	0	0	1	0	0	0	0	0	0	171	0	**183**
0	0	0	0	0	0	0	0	0	0	0	0	0	0	0	0	0	0	1	**1**
0	0	0	0	0	0	0	0	0	0	0	0	0	0	0	0	0	0	0	**5**
0	0	0	0	0	0	0	0	0	0	0	0	0	0	0	0	0	0	0	**0**
0	0	0	0	0	0	0	0	0	0	0	0	0	0	0	0	0	1	0	**35**
0	0	0	1	0	0	0	0	0	0	0	0	0	0	0	0	0	1	0	**3**
0	0	0	0	0	0	0	0	0	0	0	0	0	0	0	0	0	0	0	**0**
0	1	0	0	0	0	0	0	0	0	0	0	0	0	1	0	0	0	0	**39**
0	0	0	0	0	0	0	0	0	0	0	0	0	0	0	0	0	0	0	**31**
0	0	0	0	0	0	0	0	0	0	0	0	0	0	0	0	0	0	0	**0**
0	0	0	0	0	0	0	0	0	0	0	0	0	0	0	0	0	0	0	**0**
0	0	0	0	0	0	0	0	0	0	0	0	0	0	0	0	0	0	0	**1**
0	0	0	0	0	0	0	1	0	0	0	0	0	1	0	0	0	0	0	**3**
0	0	1	0	0	0	0	0	0	0	0	0	0	0	0	0	0	0	0	**1**
0	0	0	0	0	0	0	0	0	0	0	0	0	0	0	0	0	0	0	**1**
0	0	0	0	0	0	0	0	0	0	0	0	0	0	0	0	1	0	0	**1**
0	0	0	0	0	0	0	0	0	0	0	0	0	0	0	0	0	0	0	**0**
0	0	0	0	0	0	0	0	0	0	0	0	0	0	0	0	0	0	0	**35**
0	5	0	0	0	0	0	0	0	0	0	0	0	0	0	0	0	0	0	**6**
0	0	0	0	0	0	0	0	0	0	0	0	0	0	0	0	0	0	0	**154**
0	0	0	0	0	0	1	0	0	0	0	0	0	1	1	1	1	0	0	**239**
0	0	0	0	0	0	0	0	0	0	0	0	0	0	0	0	0	0	0	**0**
0	0	0	0	0	0	0	0	0	0	0	0	0	0	0	0	0	1	0	**37**
0	0	0	0	0	0	0	0	0	0	0	0	0	0	0	1	0	0	1	**25**
0	0	0	0	0	0	0	0	0	0	0	0	0	0	0	0	0	0	0	**24**
0	0	0	0	0	0	0	0	0	0	0	0	0	0	0	0	0	0	0	**88**
0	0	0	0	0	0	0	0	0	0	0	0	0	0	0	0	0	0	0	**0**
0	0	0	0	0	0	0	0	0	0	0	0	0	0	0	0	0	0	0	**7**
0	0	0	0	0	0	0	0	0	0	0	0	0	0	0	0	0	0	0	**0**
0	0	0	0	0	0	0	0	0	0	0	0	0	0	0	0	0	0	0	**29**
0	0	0	0	0	0	0	0	0	0	0	0	1	0	0	0	0	0	1	**100**
0	0	0	0	0	0	0	0	0	0	0	0	0	0	0	0	0	0	0	**1**
0	0	0	0	0	0	0	0	0	0	0	0	0	0	0	0	0	0	0	**0**
0	0	0	0	1	0	1	0	1	0	1	1	0	1	0	0	0	0	0	**10**
0	0	0	0	0	0	0	0	0	0	0	0	0	0	0	0	0	0	0	**0**
0	0	0	0	0	0	0	0	0	0	0	0	0	0	0	0	0	0	0	**2**
0	0	0	0	0	0	0	0	0	0	0	0	0	0	0	0	0	0	0	**0**
0	0	0	0	0	0	0	0	0	0	0	0	0	0	0	0	0	0	0	**0**
0	**6**	**2**	**1**	**2**	**8**	**2**	**1**	**1**	**0**	**3**	**1**	**1**	**5**	**2**	**2**	**3**	**174**	**4**	
															Total Commutations				**1343**

Appendix C

CHRONOLOGY OF CAPITAL CLEMENCY, 1900–2004

Commutations by Governor

Year(s)/State	*Governor*	*Number*	*Inmate names, circumstances of the clemency, etc.*	*Source*
1900/Arkansas	Daniel W. Jones	1	**Charles Colbert.** Pardoned by the Governor (11/15/1900) on grounds of actual innocence.	"Arkansas Man, Condemned to be Hanged, Found to be Guiltless." *New York Times.* 11/24/1900.
1900–1958/Massachusetts	W.M. Crane (1900–03); John L. Bates (1903–05); William Douglas (1905–06); Curtis Guild, Jr. (1906–09); Eben S. Draper (1909–11); Eugene N. Foss (1911–14); David I. Walsh (1914–16); Samuel McCall (1916–19); Calvin Coolidge (1919–21); Channing H. Cox (1921–25); Alvan T. Fuller (1925–29); Frank G Allen (1929–31); Joseph B. Ely (1931–35); James M. Curley (1935–37); Charles Hurley (1937–39); Leveret Salonstall (1939–45); Maurice Tobin (1945–47); Robert Bradford (1947–49); Paul A. Dever (1949–1953); Christian Harter (1953–57)	29	30 capital commutations total by governors between 1900 and 1958 according to statistical executive clemency data complied by House report on the death penalty. No specific individual information furnished, but one of these was Lena Cusumano in 1912 (counted separately in an individual entry on this chart).	Massachusetts House of Representatives. Commonwealth of Massachusetts Report and Recommendations of the Special Committee Established for the Purpose of Investigating and Studying the Abolition of the Death Penalty in Capital Cases. H. Rep. No. 2575 at 29 (1958).
1902/Florida	William Sherman Jennings	1	**J.B. Brown** was sentenced to hang in 1901 but had his sentence commuted to life in prison in 1902. In 1913 another man would confess to the crime on his deathbed, and Gov. Park Trammell would grant a full pardon to Brown.	Radelet, Bedau, and Putnam. *In Spite of Innocence* (1992).

1903/New York	Benjamin Odell	1	**Luigi Fillipelli.** Death sentence commuted to life 3/24/1903. Would later have sentence further reduced by Governor Alfred Smith in 1919 on recommendation of the presiding judge in the case.	State of New York. "Pardons, Commutations and Reprieves." *Public Papers of Governor Alfred E. Smith.* Albany (1920).
1903–1908 and 1955–1963/North Carolina	Charles Aycock (1901–05); Robert B. Glenn (1905–09); Luther Hodges (1954–61); Terry Sanford (1961–65)	32	According to Abramowitz and Paget's statistical summary of capital clemencies in North Carolina, 234 total were granted between 1903 and 1963. Annual distribution information was not furnished. 202 of these capital clemencies are documented later on this chart, between 1909 and 1954, using other sources. The remaining 32 commutations must have been granted sometime between 1903–1909 and 1955–1983, but with the data provided, it is not possible to discern the specific distribution.	Elkan Abramowitz and David Paget. *Executive Clemency in Capital Cases.* 39 *NYU L Rev.* 191 (1964).
1903/Oregon	George E. Chamberlain	1	From statistical summary of capital commutations in Oregon, 1903–1964. No individualized information provided.	Bedau, Hugo. 45 *Or. L Rev.* 8 (1965–66) "Capital Punishment in Oregon, 1903–1964."
1905/Oregon	George E. Chamberlain	1	From statistical summary of capital commutations in Oregon, 1903–1964. No individualized information provided.	Bedau, Hugo. 45 *Or. L Rev.* 8 (1965–66) "Capital Punishment in Oregon, 1903–1964."
1906/California	George C. Pardee	1	**Will Johnson.** After 5 years awaiting hanging, Johnson was granted commutation when his co-defendant claimed sole responsibility for the murder.	Radelet, Bedau, and Putnam. *In Spite of Innocence* (1992).

Year(s)/State	*Governor*	*Number*	*Inmate names, circumstances of the clemency, etc.*	*Source*
1906/New York	Frank Higgins	1	**Albert T. Patrick**. Sentence commuted to life by governor (12/20/1906).	"Wife Chief Factor in Patrick's Plea." *New York Times*. 1/7/1913.
1908/Idaho	Frank R. Gooding	1	**Harry Orchard** (7/1/1908). Death sentence commuted to life by Board of Pardons and Paroles.	Jensen, Christen. *The Pardoning Power in Some Western States*. Dissertation, U. Chicago, Dept. of Political Science. (1922).
1908/Tennessee	Malcom Patterson	1	**David Sherman**. Gov. Patterson first commuted Sherman's sentence because of doubts about his guilt, and later (in 1911) pardoned Sherman completely when it became clear that he had "absolutely nothing to do with the murder."	Radelet, Bedau, and Putnam. *In Spite of Innocence* (1992).
1909/California	James N. Gillett	2	**Ed Silver** (2/11/09) and **William Buckley** (9/21/09) commuted to life by Gov. Gillett.	State of California. Second Biennial Message of Governor James N. Gillett, 1911.
1909/Illinois	Charles Deneen	1	**Herman Zajicek** had his death sentence commuted to life in prison by Gov. Deneen. Eight years later, when the prosecution admitted its star witness had given perjured testimony, Gov. Dunne granted Zajicek a full pardon.	Radelet, Bedau, and Putnam. *In Spite of Innocence* (1992).

1909/New Jersey	John Franklin Fort	2	From statistical summary of capital commutations in New Jersey, 1907–1960. No individualized information provided.	Bedau, Hugo. "Death Sentences in New Jersey 1907–1960." 19 *Rutgers Law Review* 1 (1964).
1909–1913/North Carolina	William Kitchin	7	7 commutations of death sentence to life, by Governor William Kitchin during his term.	*Executive Clemency in Relation to Capital Punishment: A Report.* State of North Carolina (1937).
1909/Oregon	Frank Benson	1	From statistical summary of capital commutations in Oregon, 1903–1964. No individualized information provided.	Bedau, Hugo. 45 *Or. L. Rev.* 8 (1965–66) "Capital Punishment in Oregon, 1903–1964."
1910/California	James N. Gillett	1	**Fabronio Machuca** (8/23/10). Sentence commuted to life by Gov. Gillett.	State of California. Second Biennial Message of Governor James N. Gillett, 1911.
1911/California	Hiram Johnson	2	**Louie Augustine** (6/6/11) and **Horace Bennett** (12/13/11). Sentences commuted by Gov. Johnson.	State of California. Biennial Message of Governor Hiram Johnson to the Legislature of the State of California, 1913.
1911/New Jersey	John Franklin Fort	2	From statistical summary of capital commutations in New Jersey, 1907–1960. No individualized information provided.	Bedau, Hugo. "Death Sentences in New Jersey 1907–1960." 19 *Rutgers Law Review* 1 (1964).
1911/New York	John Alden Dix	1	**Peter C. Hains.** Sentence commuted to life by governor (9/28/1911).	"Pardon for Capt. Hains." *New York Times.* 9/29/1911.

Year(s)/State	*Governor*	*Number*	*Inmate names, circumstances of the clemency, etc.*	*Source*
1911–1915/Oklahoma	Lee Cruce	22	**John Henry Prather** (July 28, 1911), **John Cotton** (Dec. 1912), and six unspecified inmates between July and December. **Newton Henry** (4/14/14) and thirteen unspecified commutations between 1913 and 1914. Due to personal opposition to death penalty, Gov. Cruce refused to sign any execution warrants while in office.	*39 N.Y.U. Law Rev.* 136 (1964) Solie M. Ringold. "The Dynamics of Executive Clemency." *52 ABA Journal 240 (1966).* O'Brien, Joe. "He Killed Oklahoma's Death Penalty." *Daily Oklahoman.* July 31, 1927, D1.
1911/Oregon	Jay Bowerman	3	From statistical summary of capital commutations in Oregon, 1903–1964. No individualized information provided.	Bedau, Hugo. 45 *Or. L. Rev.* 8 (1965–66) "Capital Punishment in Oregon, 1903–1964."
1911/South Carolina	Coleman Blease	1	**Joe Bates.** Sentence commuted by governor (7/8/1911).	"Blease in Message Lauds his Pardons." *New York Times.* 2/22/1914.
1912–1915/Arizona	George W.P. Hunt	13	Upon entering office in 1912, Governor Hunt declared that no executions would take place in Arizona during his tenure. He granted 13 capital commutations in his first term before backing off his crusade against the death penalty.	Tingley, Katherine, "Theosophy and Some Vital Problems of the Day." Address delivered 1/17/1915 at the Isis Theater in San Diego, CA.
1912/California	Hiram Johnson and acting governor A.J. Wallace	3	**John Byrne** (1/10/12). Sentence commuted to life by Gov. Hiram Johnson. **William Burke** (9/10/12) and **George E. Figueroa** (9/17/12). Death sentences commuted to life by acting governor A.J. Wallace.	State of California. *Biennial Message of Governor Hiram Johnson to the Legislature of the State of California.* (1913).

1912/Massachusetts	Eugene N. Foss	1	**Lena Cusumano**: Hanging sentence commuted to life by Gov. Foss, a Massachusetts governor who earned the nickname "the pardoning governor" by pardoning 132 non-capital offenders his first year and a half in office. Ms. Cusumano, the only woman on death row in Massachusetts, was the only capital commutation he granted during that time.	July 8, 1912. "Foss has Pardoned 132." *New York Times*, p. 9.
1912/New Jersey	Woodrow Wilson	2	From statistical summary of capital commutations in New Jersey, 1907–1960. No individualized information provided.	Bedau, Hugo. "Death Sentences in New Jersey 1907–1960." 19 *Rutgers Law Review* 1 (1964).
1912/Oregon	Oswald West	1	From statistical summary of capital commutations in Oregon, 1903–1964. No individualized information provided.	Bedau, Hugo. 45 *Or. L. Rev.* 8 (1965–66) "Capital Punishment in Oregon, 1903–1964."
1913/California	Hiram Johnson	3	**Manuel Bombela** (2/1/13), **August Gerber** (9/22/13) and **James W. Finley** (10/11/13). Sentences commuted from death to life by Gov. Johnson.	State of California. *Second Biennial Message of Governor Hiram Johnson to the Legislature of the State of California* (1915).
1913/Georgia	John Slanton	1	**Leo M. Frank**. After two years on death row, Gov. Slanton commuted Frank's sentence to life in prison because of doubts about his guilt.	Radelet, Bedau, and Putnam. *In Spite of Innocence* (1992).
1913/New Jersey	Woodrow Wilson	2	From statistical summary of capital commutations in New Jersey, 1907–1960. No individualized information provided.	Bedau, Hugo. "Death Sentences in New Jersey 1907–1960." 19 *Rutgers Law Review* 1 (1964).

Year(s)/State	*Governor*	*Number*	*Inmate names, circumstances of the clemency, etc.*	*Source*
1913–1917/North Carolina	Locke Craig	29	29 commutations of death sentence to life in prison, by Governor Locke Craig during his term.	*Executive Clemency in Relation to Capital Punishment. A Report.* State of North Carolina *(1937).*
1913/Oregon	Oswald West	3	From statistical summary of capital commutations in Oregon, 1903–1964. No individualized information provided.	Bedau, Hugo. 45 *Or. L. Rev.* 8 (1965–66) "Capital Punishment in Oregon, 1903–1964."
1914/New Jersey	Edward Stokes	1	**John Edward Schuyler.** Having spent 7 years on death row, Schuyler was pardoned by Gov. Stokes after the actual culprit confessed.	Radelet, Bedau, and Putnam. *In Spite of Innocence* (1992).
1914–1952/Pennsylvania	Martin Grove Brumbaugh (1915–1919); William Sproul (1919–1923); Gifford Pinchot (1923–27); John S. Fisher (1927–31); Gifford Pinchot (1931–35); George H. Earle (1935–39); Arthur H. James (1939–43); Edward Martin (1943–47); John Cromwel Bell Jr. (1947); James Duff (1947–51)	72	72 capital offenders had their sentences commuted between 1914 and 1952 according to data furnished to the authors by the Commonwealth of Pennsylvania. Annual breakdown not published in Giardiani and Farrow article. Two of these 72 were **Grace Giovanetti** and **Josephine Romulado.** Giovanetti and Romulado were the only two of 24 "arsenic widows" (a ring of women accused of poisoning their husbands) in Pennsylvania to receive the death sentence. By coincidence, the two were sentenced on the same day—Oct. 24, 1940. According to Kathleen O'Shea, both women had their death sentences commuted, though she does not specify the year.	G.I. Giardiani and R.G. Farrow. "The Paroling of Capital Offenders." *Annals of the American Academy of Political and Social Science.* Vol. 284 (1957), pp. 90–93. O'Shea, Kathleen. *Women and the Death Penalty in the United States 1900–1998* (1999), and "Two Women Sentenced to Die." *New York Times,* 10/26/1940, p.17.

1914/Oregon	Oswald West	2	**John Pender** and one other man. Pender had his sentence commuted to life in prison by Gov. West. Another man confessed to the crime in 1920, at which time Gov. Ben Olcott granted John Pender a full pardon. Pender was one of two men to receive commutation of a capital sentence according to a statistical summary of capital commutations in Oregon, 1903–1964. No individualized information provided for the other inmate.	Radelet, Bedau, and Putnam. *In Spite of Innocence* (1992) and Bedau, Hugo. 45 *Or. L. Rev.* 8 (1965–66) "Capital Punishment in Oregon, 1903–1964."
1915/California	Hiram Johnson	1	**Louis Choukalas** (1/30/15). Sentence commuted from death to life by Gov. Johnson.	State of California. Third Second Biennial Message of Governor Hiram Johnson to the Legislature of the State of California, 1917.
1915/New Jersey	James F. Fielder	2	Number taken from statistical summary of capital commutations in New Jersey, 1907–1960. No individualized information provided. One may have been **Madeline Ciccone** who was sentenced to die in New Jersey but, according to Kathleen O'Shea, had her sentence "later commuted."	Bedau, Hugo. "Death Sentences in New Jersey 1907–1960." 19 *Rutgers Law Review* 1 (1964), and O'Shea, Kathleen. *Women and the Death Penalty in the United States 1900–1998.* (1999).
1916/New Jersey	James F. Fielder	2	From statistical summary of capital commutations in New Jersey, 1907–1960. No individualized information provided.	Bedau, Hugo. "Death Sentences in New Jersey 1907–1960." 19 *Rutgers Law Review* 1 (1964).

Year(s)/State	*Governor*	*Number*	*Inmate names, circumstances of the clemency, etc.*	*Source*
1916/New York	Charles S. Whitman	1	**Charles Stielow.** Sentence commuted to life by Gov. Charles Whitman. Would receive a full pardon in 1918 (along with co-defendant who had been serving life term)	Harriman, Averell. "Mercy is a Lonely Business" *Saturday Evening Post* March 22, 1958, pp.24–25, 83–84.
1917–1921/North Carolina	Thomas Bickett	19	19 commutations of death sentence to life, by Governor Thomas Bickett during his term.	*Executive Clemency in Relation to Capital Punishment: A Report.* State of North Carolina (1937).
1918/California	William D. Stephens	1	**Thomas J. Mooney**, known labor agitator and anarcho-socialist, was convicted of a deadly bombing at patriotic, prowar parade in San Francisco, July 22, 1916. Despite strong evidence in support of his innocence, Mooney was sentenced to die in the gallows. Two years later, Mooney's life was spared by Gov. William D. Stephens, but the governor, facing a tough reelection battle, declined to grant a full pardon, instead commuting the sentence to life in prison. Mooney would not receive a full pardon until January 1939, from Gov. Culbert L. Olson.	Radelet, Bedau, and Putnam. *In Spite of Innocence* (1992).

1918/Kentucky	James D. Black	2	**Julius Babey** and **John Ratliffe** by Gov. Augustus O. Stanley.	*The Power, Practice and Process of Commutation of Persons Sentenced to Death* (Kentucky Department of Public Advocacy), http://dpa.ky.gov/text/cppp.pdf.
1918/New York	Charles S. Whitman	1	**Paul Chapman,** 16 years old, was spared execution by Gov. Whitman in December of 1918.	"Sing Sing's Varsity Adds Third Victory," *New York Times* (12/7/1931).
1919/Kentucky	James D. Black	2	**Delbert Thomas** (12/03/19) and **Bradley McDaniel** (11/28/19) by Gov. James D. Black	*The Power, Practice and Process of Commutation of Persons Sentenced to Death* (Kentucky Department of Public Advocacy), http://dpa.ky. gov/text/cppp.pdf.
1919/New Mexico	O.A. Larrazolo	1	**Ysidoro Miranda.** Executive pardon of 1905 death sentence granted by Gov. O.A. Larrazolo.	Museum of New Mexico Library. *Ray Dewey Collection of New Mexico Historical Documents (1902–1919).*
1919/New York	Alfred E. Smith	3	**Antonio Verrino** (3/18/1919), **Thomas Abbruzzo** (8/22/1919), and **George DeSoma** (12/3/1919) all commuted according to Governor Smith's policy to only grant capital commutations in the case of one or more dissenting appellate judge, the request of the D.A. and/or the request of the presiding judge in the original trial.	State of New York. "Pardons, Commutations and Reprieves." Public Papers of Governor Alfred E. Smith. Albany (1920).

Year(s)/State	*Governor*	*Number*	*Inmate names, circumstances of the clemency, etc.*	*Source*
1920–1962/Connecticut	Everett John Lake (1921–23); Charles Augustus Templeton (1923–25); Hiram Bingham (1925); John H. Trumbull (1925–31); Wilbur L. Cross (1931–39); Ray Baldwin (1939–41); Robert A. Hurley (1941–43); Ray Baldwin (1943–46); C. Wilbert Snow (1946–47); James L. McConaughy (1947–48); James Shannon (1948–49); Chester Bowles (1949–51); John Davis Lodge (1951–55); Abraham Ribicoff (1955–61)	8	8 capital commutations by governors between 1920 and 1962 according to statistical executive clemency data compiled by Abramowitz and Paget. No specific individual information furnished.	Elkan Abramowitz and David Paget. *Executive Clemency in Capital Cases.* 39 *NYU L. Rev.* 191 (1964).
1920/Kentucky	Edwin Morrow	3	**Joe Hughes** (05/10/20), **Charles Douthitt** (03/23/20) and **A.A. Garman** by Gov. Edwin Morrow.	*The Power, Practice and Process of Commutation of Persons Sentenced to Death* (Kentucky Department of Public Advocacy), http://dpa.ky.gov/text/cppp.pdf.
1920/New York	Alfred E. Smith	8	From statistical chart released to press by governor's office in 1937. No case-specifics given.	"Lehman Leniency Criticized in Court." *New York Times* 1/19/1937, p. 3.

1921/New Jersey	Edward Edwards	1	From statistical summary of capital commutations in New Jersey, 1907–1960. No individualized information provided.	Bedau, Hugo. "Death Sentences in New Jersey 1907–1960." 19 *Rutgers Law Review* 1 (1964).
1921/New York	Nathan Miller	2	From statistical chart released to press by governor's office in 1937. No case-specifics given.	Lehman Leniency Criticised in Court. *New York Times* 1/19/1937, p. 3.
1921–1925/North Carolina	Cameron Morrison	23	23 commutations of sentence, death to life in prison, by Governor Morrison during his term. Among these were **Joe Bowies** (1921) and **Frank Dove, Fred Dove,** and **George Williams** (1923) (as documented by Radelet, Bedau and Putnam, *in Spite of Innocence*) who had their death sentences commuted to life in prison when a fourth defendant declared on the morning of his execution, that he had been coerced into perjuring himself and wrongfully implicating the three others. Upon the urging of the trial judge, Gov. Morrison granted the commutation.	*Executive Clemency in Relation to Capital Punishment: A Report.* State of North Carolina (1937).
1922/Kentucky	Edwin Morrow	1	**Ferdinande Sayre** (6/19/22) by Gov. Edwin Morrow.	*The Power, Practice and Process of Commutation of Persons Sentenced to Death* (Kentucky Department of Public Advocacy). http://dpa.ky.gov/text/cppp.pdf.

Year(s)/State	*Governor*	*Number*	*Inmate names, circumstances of the clemency, etc.*	*Source*
1922/New Jersey	Edward Edwards	2	From statistical summary of capital commutations in New Jersey, 1907–1960. No individualized information provided.	Bedau, Hugo. "Death Sentences in New Jersey 1907–1960." 19 *Rutgers Law Review* 1 (1964).
1922/New York	Nathan Miller	2	Total number from statistical chart released to press by governor's office in 1937. One of these was **Russell Jones.** Originally commuted from death to life sentence in 1922 by Gov. Nathan Miller, Jones would receive further commutation of sentence by Gov. Harriman in 1958.	"Lehman Leniency Criticised in Court." *New York Times* 1/19/1937, p. 3. And State of New York, Public Papers of Governor Averell Harriman, 1958. "Pardons, Commutations and Reprieves." New York, 1959, pp. 839–845.
1923/Kentucky	Edwin Morrow	1	**Campbell Graham** (12/4/23) by Gov. Edwin Morrow.	*The Power, Practice and Process of Commutation of Persons Sentenced to Death* (Kentucky Department of Public Advocacy), http://dpa.ky.gov/text/cppp.pdf.
1923/New Jersey	Edward Edwards	2	From statistical summary of capital commutations in New Jersey, 1907–1960. No individualized information provided.	Bedau, Hugo. "Death Sentences in New Jersey 1907–1960." 19 *Rutgers Law Review* 1 (1964).

1923/New York	Alfred E. Smith	7	From statistical chart released to press by governor's office in 1937. No case-specifics given.	Lehman Leniency Criticised in Court. *New York Times* 1/19/1937, p. 3.
1924/Arkansas	Thomas McRae	6	**Frank Moore, J.E. Knox, Ed Hicks, Frank Hicks, Paul Hall**, and **Ed Coleman.** In 1919, following an alleged race riot, a dozen black men were convicted of first degree murder and sentenced to die (a total of 67 black men had been incarcerated on charges related to the incident). In reality, the men had been conducting a peaceful farm laborers' meeting in their community church when they were surrounded and fired upon by a crowd of heavily armed white supremacists. In the years following the convictions, the NAACP managed to thoroughly and publicly discredit the story of the riot, to the point where Arkansas courts and government officials sought to save face by freeing the wrongly convicted men. Half of the men awaiting death had their convictions overturned by the state Supreme Court, but the other 6—Frank Moore, J.E. Knox, Ed Hicks, Frank Hicks, Paul Hall, and Ed Coleman—remained on death row until Gov. McRae commuted their sentences, first (in Nov. 1924) to 12 years imprisonment, and finally (in Jan. 1925, as he was about to leave office) to time served.	Radelet, Bedau, and Putnam. *In Spite of Innocence* (1992).

Year(s)/State	*Governor*	*Number*	*Inmate names, circumstances of the clemency, etc.*	*Source*
1924/California	Wm Richardson	1	**William Alexander Hard** (4/14/1924). Death sentence commuted by the governor due to the defendants age (younger than 18 at the commission of the crime).	State of California. *Message from Gov. Wm Richardson Regarding Acts of Executive Clemency* (1925).
1924/Florida	Carey Hardee	1	**Burnard Whitten**. Sentence commuted by Governor Carey Hardee, 7/23/1924.	Vandiver, Margaret. PhD diss. chart "Florida Capital Cases, 1923–1966."
1924/Kentucky	William Fields	1	**Sam Archie** by Gov. William Fields.	*The Power, Practice and Process of Commutation of Persons Sentenced to Death* (Kentucky Department of Public Advocacy). http://dpa.ky.gov/text/cppp.pdf.
1924/New Jersey	George Silzer	1	From statistical summary of capital commutations in New Jersey, 1907–1960. No individualized information provided.	Bedau, Hugo. "Death Sentences in New Jersey 1907–1960." 19 *Rutgers Law Review* 1 (1964).
1924/New York	Alfred E. Smith	4	Total Number from statistical chart released to press by governor's office in 1937. One of these was **Guiseppe DeMatteo**. Commuted to life sentence by Gov. Alfred E. Smith. Would received further reduction in sentence almost 35 years later by Gov. Averill Harriman.	"Lehman Leniency Criticised in Court." *New York Times* 1/19/1937, p. 3, and State of New York. Public Papers of Governor Averill Harriman, 1958. "Pardons, Commutations and Reprieves." New York, 1959, pp. 839–845.

1924/Oregon	Walter Pierce	2	From statistical summary of capital commutations in Oregon, 1903–1964. No individualized information provided.	Bedau, Hugo. 45 Or. L. Rev. 8 (1965–66) "Capital Punishment in Oregon, 1903–1964."
1925/Florida	John Martin	2	**Fred Meyer** (9/15/25) and **Nathan Lowe** (11/3/25). Sentences commuted by Governor John Martin.	Vandiver, Margaret. PhD diss. chart "Florida Capital Cases, 1923–1966."
1925/New Jersey	George Silzer	2	From statistical summary of capital commutations in New Jersey, 1907–1960. No individualized information provided.	Bedau, Hugo. "Death Sentences in New Jersey 1907–1960." 19 *Rutgers Law Review* 1 (1964).
1925/New York	Alfred E. Smith	2	From statistical chart released to press by governor's office in 1937. No case-specifics given.	"Lehman Leniency Criticised in Court." *New York Times* 1/19/1937, p. 3.
1925–1928/North Carolina	Angus McLean	17	17 commutations of sentence, death to life in prison, by Governor Angus McLean during his term. One of these was a commutation granted to **Alvin Mansell** (1926) as documented by Radelet, Bedau, and Putnam, in *Spite of Innocence.*	*Executive Clemency in Relation to Capital Punishment: A Report.* State of North Carolina (1937). And Radelet, Bedau, and Putnam. *In Spite of Innocence* (1992).
1925/Texas	Miriam Amanda Wallace Ferguson	5	**Roy Mitchell** (4/29/25), **Newt DeSilva** (3/20/25), **Jacques Salvador** (7/22/25), **Joe Brown** (7/19/25), and **Arnuflo Valles** (7/30/25).	Texas Department of Criminal Justice. *Death Row Commutations, 1923–1973.*

Year(s)/State	*Governor*	*Number*	*Inmate names, circumstances of the clemency, etc.*	*Source*
1926/New York	Alfred E. Smith	3	Total number from statistical chart released to press by governor's office in 1937. These three were **John Slattery** (1/21/1926), **Anthony J. Pantano** (3/5/1926) and **Ambrose Ross** (12/8/1926). Slattery's sentence was commuted to life by the governor due to dissent on the Court of Appeals. Patano's death sentence was commuted to life in March of the same year. He would receive further commutation from Gov. Harriman in 1958. Ross had his sentence commuted to life in December after helping the state convict 3 of his robbery/murder co-conspirators.	"Lehman Leniency Criticised in Court." *New York Times* 1/19/1937, p. 3, and "Governor Smith Saves One Bellmore Slayer." *New York Times* (1/21/1926) and "Patano is Saved from Electric Chair." *New York Times* (3/5/1926) and "Smith Commutes Sentence on Ross." *New York Times* (12/8/1926).
1926/Texas	Miriam Amanda Wallace Ferguson	2	**W. Aven** (3/27/26) and **Alex Maxey** (8/24/26).	Texas Department of Criminal Justice. *Death Row Commutations 1923–1973.*
1927/California	C.C. Young	2	**Joseph Sandoval** and **George Watters** commuted from death to LWOP.	California. Report of Commutations and Pardons: Message of the Governor of California to the Legislature (1927–28).
1927/Florida	John Martin	3	**Annie Mae Jackson** (9/13/27), **Jim Williams** (9/17/27), and **Arthur Reed** (11/30/27). Sentences commuted by Governor John Martin.	Vandiver, Margaret. PhD diss. chart "Florida Capital Cases, 1923–1966."

1927/New York	Alfred E. Smith	7	Total number from statistical chart released to press by governor's office in 1937. Two of these were **Harry W. Cowan** (3/18/1927) and **Edward Larkman.** Gov. Smith commuted Cowan's sentence to life, citing Cowan's blindness and juror pleas for mercy. Larkman had his sentence commuted 10 hours before his execution due to doubts about his guilt. In 1929, another man confessed to the crime, but it was not until 1933 that Gov. Herbert Lehman granted Larkman a full pardon.	"Lehman Leniency Criticised in Court." *New York Times* 1/19/1937, p. 3, and "Blind Killer Saved from Death Chair." *New York Times.* (3/18/1927), and Harriman, Averill. "Mercy is a Lonely Business" *Saturday Evening Post*, March 22, 1958, pp. 24–25, 83–84.
1927–1933/Tennessee	Henry Horton	13	Henry Horton, governor of Tennessee from 1927 to 1933, commuted 13 death sentences to life imprisonment during his term in office.	Nashville Abolition Day Event (March 1st, 2002)—Opening Remarks by Randy Tatel. http://www.cuadp.org/abday2002tn-rt.html.
1927/Texas	Daniel James Moody, Jr.	1	**Pete McKinney** (9/8/27).	Texas Department of Criminal Justice. *Death Row Commutations 1923–1973*.
1928/California	C.C. Young	1	**Scott C. Stone.** Sentence commuted from death to LWOP.	California. Report of Commutations and Pardons: Message of the Governor of California to the Legislature (1927–28).

Year(s)/State	*Governor*	*Number*	*Inmate names, circumstances of the clemency, etc.*	*Source*
1928/Florida	John Martin	2	**Ralph Lang** (9/11/28) and **Roosevelt Bullard** (9/11/28). Sentences commuted by Governor John Martin.	Vandiver, Margaret. PhD diss. chart "Florida Capital Cases, 1923–1966."
1928/New York	Alfred E. Smith	3	Total number from statistical chart released to press by governor's office in 1937. One of these was **Julius Gibbs.** Originally commuted from death to life sentence in 1928 by Gov. Smith, Gibbs would receive further commutation of sentence by Gov. Harriman in 1958.	"Lehman Leniency Criticised in Court." *New York Times* 1/19/1937, p. 3 and State of New York. Public Papers of Governor Averill Harriman, 1958. "Pardons, Commutations and Reprieves." New York, 1959, pp. 839–845.
1928/Texas	Daniel James Moody, Jr.	3	**Anastacio Vargas** (3/9/28), **Pete Banks** (4/14/28), and **J. Silver** (10/25/28).	Texas Department of Criminal Justice. *Death Row Commutations, 1923–1973.*
1929/California	C.C. Young	2	**Allen Ellis** and **Joe Troche**. Sentences commuted from death to LWOP.	State of California. Report of Commutations and Pardons: Message of the Governor of California to the Legislature (1929–30).
1929/Florida	Doyle Carlton	6	**Arthur Davis** (3/12/29), **Berta Hall** (3/12/29), **Gordon Denmark** (3/20/29), **Leroy Morris** (5/9/29), **Leroy Goshea** (10/4/29), and **Abe Washington** (10/21/29). Sentences commuted by Governor Doyle Carlton.	Vandiver, Margaret. PhD diss. chart "Florida Capital Cases, 1923–1966."

1929/New York	Franklin D. Roosevelt	1	From statistical chart released to press by governor's office in 1937. No case-specifics given.	"Lehman Leniency Criticised in Court." *New York Times* 1/19/1937, p. 3.
1929–1933/North Carolina	O. Max Gardener	25	25 commutations of sentence, death to life in prison, by Governor O. Max Gardener during his term.	*Executive Clemency in Relation to Capital Punishment; A Report.* State of North Carolina (1937).
1929/Texas	Daniel James Moody, Jr.	2	**John McKenzie** (9/28/29) and **Jessie Charles** (9/13/29).	Texas Department of Criminal Justice. *Death Row Commutations, 1923–1973.*
1929/West Virginia	William Conley	1	**Clyde Beale**'s death sentence initially commuted by Gov. William Conley, after the original trial judge expressed serious doubts about the fairness of the trial and the defendants guilt. Subsequently, in 1933, Beale received a conditional pardon and was released.	Radelet, Bedau, and Putnam. *In Spite of Innocence* (1992).
1930–1963/Illinois	Louis Emmerson (1929–33); Henry Horner (1933–40); John Stelle (1940–41); Dwight H. Green (1941–49); Adlai Stevenson (1949–53) William Stratton (1953–61); Otto Kerner (1961–68)	9	10 capital commutations total by governors between 1930 and 1963 according to statistical executive clemency data compiled by Abramowitz and Paget. No specific individual information furnished, but one of these was Paul Crump's commuted by Gov. Otto Kerner in 1962 (counted separately in 1962).	Elkan Abramowitz and David Paget. *Executive Clemency in Capital Cases*. 39 *NYU L. Rev.* 191 (1964).

Year(s)/State	*Governor*	*Number*	*Inmate names, circumstances of the clemency, etc.*	*Source*
1930–1963/Iowa	Dan W. Turner (1931–33); Clyde L. Herring (1933–37); Nelson Kraschel (1937–39); George A. Wilson (1939–43); Bourke B. Hickenlooper (1943–45); Robert D. Blue (1945–49); William Beardsly (1949–54); Leo Elthon (1954–55); Leo Hoegh (1955–57); Herschel C. Loveless (1957–61); Norman Erbe (1961–63)	5	5 capital commutations total by governors between 1930 and 1963 according to statistical executive clemency data compiled by Abramowitz and Paget. No specific individual information furnished.	Elkan Abramowitz and David Paget. *Executive Clemency in Capital Cases*. 39 *NYU L. Rev.* 191 (1964).
1930/Kentucky	Flem Sampson	5	**Lloyd Williams** (12/24/30), **James Grigsby, John Keller, Lee Beckam**, and **Bluford Abbott** (12/23/30) by Gov. Flem Sampson.	*The Power, Practice and Process of Commutation of Persons Sentenced to Death* (Kentucky Department of Public Advocacy). http://dpa.ky.gov/text/cppp.pdf.
1930/New Jersey	Morgan Larson	4	From statistical summary of capital commutations in New Jersey, 1907–1960. No individualized information provided.	Bedau, Hugo. "Death Sentences in New Jersey 1907–1960." 19 *Rutgers Law Review* 1 (1964).
1930/New York	Franklin D. Roosevelt	4	Total number from statistical chart released to press by governor's office in 1937. One of these was **Milton Harris.** Leniency pleas from jurors and "hundreds of Buffalo citizens" moved Governor Roosevelt to commute Harris's sentence to life.	"Lehman Leniency Criticised in Court." *New York Times* 1/19/1937, p. 3, and Harriman, Averill, "Mercy is a Lonely Business." *Saturday Evening Post*, March 22, 1958, pp. 24–25, 83–84.

1930/Texas	Daniel James Moody, Jr.	3	**P. Howard** (5/8/30), **E. Allen** (5/13/30), and **Monty Jackson** (10/23/30).	Texas Department of Criminal Justice. *Death Row Commutations, 1923–1973.*
1930/Virginia	John Pollard	1	**Richard Phillips** spent 30 years on death row, temporarily avoiding execution only because of mental instability. In 1930, his state-appointed attorney was finally able to establish facts undeniably exonerating him. He presented these facts to Gov. Pollard, who granted Phillips an unconditional pardon.	Radelet, Bedau, and Putnam. *In Spite of Innocence* (1992).
1931/California	James Rolph	4	**Ernest A. Dias** (3/11/31), **Albert M. Stewart** (3/11/31), **Unokichi Tanaka** (6/13/31), and **Augustus A. Gingell** (9/14/31). Sentences commuted to life by Gov. Rolph.	State of California. Message of the Governor Concerning Pardons, Commutations, and Reprieves (1931–33).
1931/Florida	Doyle Carlton	1	**John Wesley** (2/26/31). Sentence commuted by Governor Doyle Carlton.	Vandiver, Margaret. PhD diss. chart "Florida Capital Cases, 1923–1966."
1931/Kentucky	Flem Sampson	6	**Oscar Pearson** (12/07/31), **Ison Gambrel, William Orndorf** (12/03/31), **George McCasland, Anderson McPerkins** (12/02/31), and **Freeman** (12/01/31) by Gov. Flem Sampson.	*The Power, Practice and Process of Commutation of Persons Sentenced to Death* (Kentucky Department of Public Advocacy). http://dpa.ky.gov/text/cppp.pdf.

Year(s)/State	*Governor*	*Number*	*Inmate names, circumstances of the clemency, etc.*	*Source*
1931/New York	Franklin D. Roosevelt	4	Total number from statistical chart released to press by governor's office in 1937. One of these was **Hyman Hirsch**. Originally commuted from death to life sentence in 1931 upon recommendation of the trial judge by Gov. Franklin Roosevelt, Hirsch would receive further commutation of sentence by Gov. Harriman in 1958.	"Lehman Leniency Criticised in Court." *New York Times* 1/19/1937, p. 3, and State of New York. Public Papers of Governor Averill Harriman, 1958. "Pardons, Commutations and Reprieves." New York, 1959, pp. 839–845.
1931/Texas	Ross Shaw Sterling	2	**Clyde Thompson** (8/6/31) and **Dave Goodwin** (8/6/31).	Texas Department of Criminal Justice. *Death Row Commutations 1923–1973.*
1932/California	James Rolph	2	**Raymond C. West** (7/12/32) and **Alexander C. Ochoa** (10/1/32). Sentences commuted by Gov. Rolph.	State of California. Message of the Governor Concerning Pardons, Commutations, and Reprieves (1931–33).
1932/Kentucky	Ruby Laffoon	1	**John Wasson** (10/13/32) by Gov. Ruby Laffoon.	*The Power, Practice and Process of Commutation of Persons Sentenced to Death* (Kentucky Department of Public Advocacy). http://dpa.ky.gov/text/cppp.pdf.

1932/New York	Franklin D. Roosevelt	13	Total number from statistical chart released to press by governor's office in 1937. Four of these commutations went to **Louis Boy, Thomas DeVore, Thomas Tobin,** and **Pietro Matera.** Boy, DeVore, and Tobin, co-participants in the same robbery-murder, had their death sentences commuted to life by Gov. Franklin Roosevelt in 1932. Boy and DeVore would have their sentences further commuted by Gov. Thomas E. Dewey in 1954. Tobin would receive further commutation of sentence by Gov. Harriman in 1958. Matera's sentence was also commuted by Gov. Roosevelt in 1932, due to doubts about his guilt.	"Lehman Leniency Criticised in Court." *New York Times* 1/19/1937, p. 3, and State of New York. Public Papers of Governor Averell Harriman, 1958. "Pardons, Commutations and Reprieves." New York, 1959. pp. 839–845, and *In Spite of Innocence* (by Radelet, Bedau, and Putnam).
1932/Florida	Doyle Carlton	1	**Sim Johnson** (9/16/32). Sentence commuted by Governor Doyle Carlton.	Vandiver, Margaret. PhD diss. chart "Florida Capital Cases, 1923–1966."
1933/California	James Rolph	1	**Ziro Kawamoto** (8/25/33). Sentence commuted by Governor Rolph to life in prison, as recommended by superior court judge due to doubts about premeditation of crime.	State of California. Report of Commutations and Pardons: Message of the Governor of California to the Legislature (1933–34).

Year(s)/State	*Governor*	*Number*	*Inmate names, circumstances of the clemency, etc.*	*Source*
1933/Florida	David Sholtz	1	**Henry Johnson** (12/6/33). Sentence commuted by Governor David Sholtz.	Vandiver, Margaret. PhD diss. chart "Florida Capital Cases, 1923–1966."
1933/Kentucky	Ruby Laffoon	4	**Boone Bowling** (11/08/33), **Allen Gray, George Lewis** (10/18/33), and **Frank Grenshaw** (04/05/33) by Gov. Ruby Laffoon.	*The Power, Practice and Process of Commutation of Persons Sentenced to Death* (Kentucky Department of Public Advocacy). http://dpa.ky. gov/text/cppp.pdf.
1933/New York	Herbert Lehman	9	Total Number from statistical chart released to press by governor's office in 1937. Three of these commutations went to Miguel Rugama, **Mateos Leylegian,** and **Nishan Sarkisian.** Convicted of felony murded, and sentenced to be executed, Ruama received a commutation to life from Gov. Herbert Lehman in 1933. Gov. Harriman would, in 1957, grant further commutation for the purposes of repatriation to Rugama's native Spain. Leylegian and Sarkisian originally had sentences commuted from death to life in 1933 by Gov. Lehman. Both men would receive further commutation of sentence by Gov. Harriman in 1958.	"Lehman Leniency Criticised in Court." *New York Times* 1/19/1937, p. 3, and State of New York. Public Papers of Governor Averill Harriman, 1957 and 1958. "Pardons, Commutations and Reprieves." New York, 1958 and 1959. Pp. 813–819 (1958) and pp. 839–845 (1959).

1933–1937/North Carolina	J.C.B. Eringhaus	28	28 commutations of sentence, death to life in prison, by Governor Eringhaus during his term.	*Executive Clemency in Relation to Capital Punishment: A Report.* State of North Carolina (1937).
1933/South Carolina	Ibra C. Blackwood	1	**Beatrice Snipes:** Sentenced to death in 1932 for killing a police officer attempting to arrest her husband. Snipes, pregnant while on death row, received national media attention. One man sentenced to life for murder in Georgia even offered publicly to swap sentences with her. Gov. Blackwood of South Carolina said such a swap could not be legally executed. He instead commuted Snipes's sentence in January of 1933.	12/31/1932 "Lifer Seeks to Die for Mrs. Snipes." *New York Times*, p. 32 1/25/1933 "Brazilians Praise Snipes Reprieve." *New York Times*, p. 6.
1933/Texas	Miriam Amanda Wallace Ferguson	8	**Guadalupe Garza** (1/9/33), **Carter Rolling** (1/6/33), **Hilton Bybee** (1/28/33), **Aaron Johnson** (2/23/33), **Castleton Whitfield** (3/13/33), **Robert Cubit** (7/21/33), **Louis Rogers** (7/21/33), and **Walter Freeney** (6/6/33).	Texas Department of Criminal Justice. *Death Row Commutations, 1923–1973.*
1934/California	James Rolph and Frank F. Mirriam	8	**Gilbert F. Collie** (1/17/34), **Jack D. Green** (1/4/34), **Odd Cornell** (1/17/34), and **Alfred Harrison** (1/15/34). Sentences commuted to LWOP by Gov. Rolph. **Manuel Larrios** (11/13/34), **Edward Shorten** (9/13/34), **Edward S. Bonilla** (12/21/34), and **Charles Tedesco** (11/15/34). Sentences commuted to life by Gov. Mirriam.	State of California. Report of Commutations and Pardons: Message of the Governor of California to the Legislature (1933–34).

Year(s)/State	*Governor*	*Number*	*Inmate names, circumstances of the clemency, etc.*	*Source*
1934/Kentucky	Ruby Laffoon	1	**Houston Jeffries** (10/25/34) by Gov. Ruby Laffoon.	*The Power, Practice and Process of Commutation of Persons Sentenced to Death* (Kentucky Department of Public Advocacy). http://dpa.ky.gov/text/cppp.pdf.
1934/Oregon	Julius Meier	1	On the recommendation of a special investigatory commission set up by the governor, **Theodore Jordan** had his sentence commuted to life in prison by Gov. Meier.	Radelet, Bedau, and Putnam. *In Spite of Innocence* (1992).
1934/New York	Herbert Lehman	5	From statistical chart released to press by governor's office in 1937. No case-specifics given.	"Lehman Leniency Criticised in Court." *New York Times* 1/19/1937, p. 3.
1934/Texas	Miriam Amanda Wallace Ferguson	4	**Leon Aubry** (1/17/34), **Paul Mitchell** (2/3/34), and **J. Hogan** (12/20/34). Also, **Bennie Young** received a full pardon after 12 years on death row. Ten years earlier, another man had confessed to the same crime, but Young was not freed until Gov. Ferguson was urged to do so by both the trial judge and the prosecutor.	Texas Department of Criminal Justice. *Death Row Commutations, 1923–1973;* also Radelet, Bedau, and Putnam. *In Spite of Innocence* (1992).

1935/Kentucky	Ruby Laffoon	1	**Stanley Mercer** (4/11/35) by Gov. Ruby Laffoon.	*The Power, Practice and Process of Commutation of Persons Sentenced to Death* (Kentucky Department of Public Advocacy). http://dpa.ky.gov/text/cppp.pdf.
1935/New Jersey	A. Harry Moore	3	From statistical summary of capital commutations in New Jersey, 1907–1960. No individualized information provided.	Bedau, Hugo. "Death Sentences in New Jersey 1907–1960." 19 *Rutgers Law Review* 1 (1964).
1935/New York	Herbert Lehman	9	Total number from statistical chart released to press by governor's office in 1937. Three of these commutations went to **Frank Graham** (1/10/1935), **George Benedatti** (1/10/1935), and **Joseph Jerossi**. Graham and Benedati received commutations of sentence to life on the same night, for different crimes. Jerossi had his death sentence commuted to life later in 1935 by Gov. Lehman, and would receive further commutation of sentence in 1957 from Gov. Harriman.	"Lehman Leniency Criticised in Court." *New York Times* 1/19/1937, p. 3, and "Commutes Two Sentences." *New York Times* (1/10/1935), and State of New York. Public Papers of Governor Averill Harriman, 1957. "Pardons, Commutations, and Reprieves." New York, 1958, pp. 813–19.
1935/Texas	James V. Allerd	3	**Cecil Short** (2/2/35), **Jose Sanchz** (3/1/35), and **Hugh McCann** (8/5/35).	Texas Department of Criminal Justice. *Death Row Commutations, 1923–1973.*

Year(s)/State	*Governor*	*Number*	*Inmate names, circumstances of the clemency, etc.*	*Source*
1936/Arkansas	Junius Futrell	1	**Ayliff Draper** had his sentence commuted to life in prison by Gov. Futrell when, hours before both he and his co-defendant were to be executed, the latter recanted his testimony, taking sole responsibility for the murder. At the urging of many original jurors and county officials, Gov. Carl Bailey granted Draper a full pardon two years later, in 1938.	Radelet, Bedau, and Putnam. *In Spite of Innocence* (1992).
1936/Florida	David Scholtz	1	**Roosevelt Daniels** (2/25/36). Sentence commuted by Governor David Sholtz.	Vandiver, Margaret. PhD diss. chart "Florida Capital Cases, 1923–1966."
1936–1961/Maryland	Harry W. Nice (1935–39); Herbert O'Conor (1939–47); William Preston Lane, Jr. (1947–51); Theodore R. McKeldin (1951–59); J. Millard Tawes (1959–67)	34	34 capital commutations total by governors between 1936 and 1961 according to statistical executive clemency data compiled by the Committee on Capital Punishment of the Legislative Council of Maryland. No specific individual information furnished.	Legislative Council of Maryland. *Report of the Committee on Capital Punishment* (1962).
1936/New Jersey	Harold Hoffman	2	From statistical summary of capital commutations in New Jersey, 1907–1960. No individualized information provided.	Bedau, Hugo. "Death Sentences in New Jersey 1907–1960." 19 *Rutgers Law Review* 1 (1964).
1936/Texas	James V. Allerd	3	**Ramiro Galvan** (2/13/36), **Willie Green** (6/12/36), and **Theo Mitchell** (5/19/36).	Texas Department of Criminal Justice. *Death Row Commutations, 1923–1973.*

1937/Florida	Fred Cone	1	**Joe Livingston** (12/10/37). Sentence commuted by Governor Fred Cone.	Vandiver, Margaret. PhD diss. chart "Florida Capital Cases, 1923–1966."
1937/New York	Herbert Lehman	6	Six death-to-life commutations granted by Gov. Lehman in the first 20 days of 1937 alone, as reported in the New York Times that same month. No case-specifics given.	"Lehman Leniency Criticized in Court." *New York Times* 1/19/1937, p. 3
1937–1954/North Carolina	Clyde R. Hoey (1937–41); J. Melville Broughton (1941–45); R. Gregg Cherry (1945–49); W. Kerr Scott (1949–53); William B. Umstead (1953–54)	54	54 commutations total were granted in capital cases in North Carolina between 1937 and 1954 according to commutation statement archives examined by Johnson in 1957. Among these was the commutation granted William Mason Wellman (1942) as documented by Radelet, Bedau, and Putnam (literally on the verge of execution—Wellman had already been strapped into the electric chair—Gov. J Melville Broughton pardoned him for apparent innocence). Names of other convicts and annual distribution not specified in Johnson article.	Elmer H. Johnson. "Selective Factors in Capital Punishment," 36 *Social Forces* 167 (1957). And Radelet, Bedau, and Putnam. *In Spite of Innocence* (1992).
1937/Texas	James V. Allerd	3	**Harry Alex** (8/16/37), **Peo Quezado** (9/30/37), and **Humphrey Henderson** (8/16/37).	Texas Department of Criminal Justice. *Death Row Commutations, 1923–1973.*
1938/Florida	Fred Cone	1	**C.J. Lowe** (3/15/38). Sentence commuted by Governor Fred Cone.	Vandiver, Margaret. PhD diss. chart "Florida Capital Cases, 1923–1966."

Year(s)/State	*Governor*	*Number*	*Inmate names, circumstances of the clemency, etc.*	*Source*
1938/New York	Herbert Lehman	1	**Richard Delany**. Death sentence commuted to life in 1938 by Gov. Herbert Lehman. Delany would receive further commutation of sentence in 1957 from Gov. Harriman.	State of New York. Public Papers of Governor Averill Harriman, 1957. "Pardons, Commutations, and Reprieves." New York, 1958. Pp. 813–819.
1938/Texas	James V. Allerd	3	**Sam Cash** (11/16/38), **Willie Caesar** (7/7/38), and **Carlos Fernandez** (9/16/38).	Texas Department of Criminal Justice. *Death Row Commutations, 1923–1973.*
1939/Florida	Fred Cone	4	**Ed Ingram** (3/28/39), **Cleo C. Wadsworth** (10/16/39), **Arthur Jordan** (10/19/39), and **Carnival Graham** (11/3/39). Sentences commuted by Governor Fred Cone.	Vandiver, Margaret. PhD diss. chart "Florida Capital Cases, 1923–1966."
1939/New Jersey	A. Harry Moore	1	Number taken from Bedau's statistical summary of capital commutations in New Jersey, 1907–1960, for which no individualized information was provided. Single commutation in 1939 likely granted to **Maguerite Dolbrow.** According to Kathleen O'Shea and *New York Times* coverage of the case, her death sentence was commuted by the governor sometime after New Jersey's highest court denied review of the case in July of 1937.	O'Shea, Kathleen. *Women and the Death Penalty in the United States 1900–1998.* (1999) and 6/2/1937 "High Court Gives Scores of Orders." *New York Times*, p.14.
1939/New York	Herbert Lehman	2	**Phillip Chaleff** and **Isidore Zimmerman's** death sentences commuted due to doubts about guilt. Zimmerman's conviction was later vacated.	Radelet, Bedau, and Putnam. *In Spite of Innocence* (1992).

1939/Texas	W. Lee O'Daniel	2	**Dan Sims** (1/16/39) and **Francis Marion** (8/15/39).	Texas Department of Criminal Justice. *Death Row Commutations, 1923–1973.*
1940/Florida	Fred Cone	4	**Tommy Lee Jordan** (8/27/40), **Willie Gray** (10/20/40), **Robert Brooks** (11/20/40), and **Solomon Milton** (12/3/40). Sentences commuted by Governor Fred Cone.	Vandiver, Margaret. PhD diss. chart "Florida Capital Cases, 1923–1966."
1940/New York	Herbert Lehman	4	**John Keough** (1/10/40), **Anthony Lategano** (1/10/40), **James Horn** (5/10/40), and **Carl Summerfield** (6/19/40) all had their death sentences commuted to life under Gov. Lehman's policy to commute in every case where at least one appellate judge dissented.	State of New York. Public Papers of Governor Herbert H. Lehman, 1940. "Pardons, Commutations and Reprieves." New York, 1941. Pp. 471–480.
1941/California	Culbert Olsen	2	**Buzzell** (no first name given), and **William Young**. Sentences commuted to life in prison by governor Culbert Olsen.	State of California. Annual Report of Executive Clemencies Granted by the Governor, 1941.
1941/Florida	Spessard Holland	2	**Willie Anderson** (12/17/41) and **Kenzie Surrency** (12/17/41). Sentences commuted by Governor Spessard Holland.	Vandiver, Margaret. PhD diss. chart "Florida Capital Cases, 1923–1966."
1941/New York	Herbert Lehman	4	**Norman J. Brabson** (2/13/41), **Lorenzo Celline** (6/2/41), **Alfred Gaetti** (6/26/41), and **Charles Rayburn Crumble** (7/30/41) all had their death sentences commuted to life under Gov. Lehman's policy to commute in every case where at least one appellate judge dissented.	State of New York. Public Papers of Governor Herbert H. Lehman, 1941. "Pardons, Commutations and Reprieves." New York, 1942. Pp. 387–397.

Year(s)/State	*Governor*	*Number*	*Inmate names, circumstances of the clemency, etc.*	*Source*
1942/California	Culbert Olsen	1	**Elie.** Sentence commuted to life in prison by governor Culbert Olsen.	State of California. Annual Report of Executive Clemencies Granted by the Governor, 1942.
1942/Florida	Spessard Holland	1	**William Alfred Sawyer** (7/9/42). Sentence commuted by Governor Spessard Holland.	Vandiver, Margaret. PhD diss. chart "Florida Capital Cases, 1923–1966."
1942/New York	Herbert Lehman	2	**Joseph Moshell** (1/5/42) and **Anthony Nadile** (3/4/42) both had their death sentences commuted to life under Gov. Lehman's policy to commute in every case where at least one appellate judge dissented.	State of New York. Public Papers of Governor Herbert H. Lehman, 1942. "Pardons, Commutations and Reprieves." New York, 1943. Pp. 475–495.
1943/Georgia	Eugene Talmadge and Ellis Gibbs Arnall	10	No individual information furnished. Impossible, based on the government record format, to discern specific distribution of capital commutations over the 17-month period covered by the report (2/10/43–6/30/44).	Georgia Board of Pardons and Paroles. *Biennial Report to the Governor and Members of the General Assembly of the State of Georgia*. Statistical Summary of Executive Actions: Feb. 10, 1943-June 30, 1944.
1943–1954/New York	Thomas E. Dewey	31	According to Christianson 72 death row inmates received commutations 1935–1963. 72 minus the 41 already documented elsewhere on this chart (1935–1942 and 1955–1963) leaves 31 capital clemencies between 1943 and 1954. One of these was Samuel Tito Williams, whose death sentence was commuted to life in prison 1949 (accounted for later this chart).	Christianson, Scott. *Condemned Inside the Sing Sing Death House* (2001).

1943/Texas	Coke R. Stevenson	1	**Fidel Contreras** (1/12/43).	Texas Department of Criminal Justice. *Death Row Commutations, 1923–1973.*
1944/California	Earl Warren	1	**Harry Fuller Goold.** Sentence commuted to LWOP by Gov. Earl Warren.	State of California. Annual Report of Executive Clemencies Granted by the Governor, 1944.
1944/Florida	Spessard Holland	1	**James Collins** (12/12/44). Sentence commuted by Governor Spessard Holland.	Vandiver, Margaret. PhD diss. chart "Florida Capital Cases, 1923–1966."
1944/New Jersey	Charles Edison	2	From statistical summary of capital commutations in New Jersey, 1907–1960. No individualized information provided.	Bedau, Hugo. "Death Sentences in New Jersey 1907–1960." 19 *Rutgers Law Review* 1 (1964).
1944/Texas	Coke R. Stevenson	3	**Willie Worlds** (5/26/44), **Harold Minor** (5/30/44), and **Ramon Munoz** (6/27/44).	Texas Department of Criminal Justice. *Death Row Commutations, 1923–1973.*
1945/California	Fredrick F. Houser	1	**William Leva Hough.** Sentence commuted to life by acting Gov. Frederick F. Houser.	State of California. Annual Report of Executive Clemencies Granted by the Governor, 1945.
1945/Florida	Millard Caldwell	2	**J.R. DeBerry** (3/20/45) and **Jerry Govan** (8/14/45). Sentences commuted by Governor Millard Caldwell.	Vandiver, Margaret. PhD diss. chart "Florida Capital Cases, 1923–1966."

Year(s)/State	*Governor*	*Number*	*Inmate names, circumstances of the clemency, etc.*	*Source*
1945/Georgia	Ellis Gibbs Amal	13	No individual information furnished. Impossible, based on the government record format, to discern specific distribution of capital commutations over the 24-month period from July 1, 1944–June 30, 1946.	Georgia Board of Pardons and Paroles. Biennial Report to the Governor and Members of the General Assembly of the State of Georgia. Statistical Summary of Executive Actions: July 1, 1944–June 30, 1946.
1945/Kentucky	Simeon Willis	2	**William Elliott** (11/03/45) and **Ernest Addington** (01/18/45) by Gov. Simeon Willis.	*The Power, Practice and Process of Commutation of Persons Sentenced to Death* (Kentucky Department of Public Advocacy). http://dpa.ky.gov/text/cppp.pdf.
1945/Texas	Coke R. Stevenson	4	**George Luke** (1/3/45), **Louis Klander** (7/7/45), **Jose Rocha** (7/30/45), and **C. Atkins** (10/2/45).	Texas Department of Criminal Justice. *Death Row Commutations, 1923–1973.*
1946/California	Fredrick F. Houser	1	**Antonio Santiago Mendez.** Sentence commuted to life by acting governor Frederick F. Houser.	State of California. Annual Report of Executive Clemencies Granted by the Governor, 1946.
1946/Florida	Millard Caldwell	1	**Leo Bailey** (7/17/46). Sentence commuted by Governor Millard Caldwell.	Vandiver, Margaret. PhD diss. chart "Florida Capital Cases, 1923–1966."

1946/Texas	Coke R. Stevenson	3	**Joseph Van Hodge** (3/6/46), **Roberto Campos** (5/25/46), **Edgar Dotson** (8/6/46).	Texas Department of Criminal Justice. *Death Row Commutations, 1923–1973.*
1947/California	Earl Warren	2	**Edward Wesley Brown** and **William Marvin Lindley** to LWOP by Gov. Earl Warren.	*In Spite of Innocence* (by Radelet, Bedau, and Putnam, and State of California, *Annual Report of Executive Clemencies Granted by the Governor,* 1947.
1947/Florida	Millard Caldwell	1	**Joe Brooks** (3/4/47). Sentence commuted by Governor Millard Caldwell.	Vandiver, Margaret. PhD diss. chart "Florida Capital Cases, 1923–1966."
1947/Georgia	Ellis Gibbs Arnall (1943–47); Herman E. Talmadge (1947); and Melvin Ernest Thompson (1947–48)	7	No individual information furnished. Impossible, based on the government record format, to discern specific distribution of capital commutations over this 24 month period July 1, 1946–June 30, 1948.	Georgia Board of Pardons and Paroles. *Biennial Report to the Governor and Members of the General Assembly of the State of Georgia*. Statistical Summary of Executive Actions: July 1, 1946–June 30, 1948.
1947/Kentucky	Simeon Willis	1	**Jack Wright** (10/9/47) by Gov. Simeon Willis	*The Power, Practice and Process of Commutation of Persons Sentenced to Death* (Kentucky Department of Public Advocacy). http://dpa.ky.gov/text/cppp.pdf.

Year(s)/State	*Governor*	*Number*	*Inmate names, circumstances of the clemency, etc.*	*Source*
1947/Texas	Beauford Jester	2	**Gaither Lovelady** (4/20/47) and **Walter Young** (6/20/47).	Texas Department of Criminal Justice. *Death Row Commutations, 1923–1973.*
1948/California	Earl Warren	1	**Hills.** Sentence commuted to life by Gov. Earl Warren.	State of California. *Annual Report of Executive Clemencies Granted by the Governor, 1948.*
1948/Texas	Beauford Jester	3	**Miguel Flores** (6/25/48), **George Gardner** (6/11/48), and **Ernest Williams** (7/23/48)	Texas Department of Criminal Justice. *Death Row Commutations 1923–1973.*
1949/California	Earl Warren	1	**Ewell Danielly.** Sentence commuted to life by Gov. Earl Warren.	State of California. *Annual Report of Executive Clemencies Granted by the Governor, 1949.*
1949/Florida	Fuller Warren	1	**Garfield Ruff** (9/13/49). Sentence commuted by Governor Fuller Warren.	Vandiver, Margaret. PhD diss. chart "Florida Capital Cases, 1923–1966."
1949/Georgia	Herman E. Talmadge	6	No individual information furnished. Impossible, based on the government record format, to discern specific distribution of capital commutations over this 24-month period from July 1, 1948–June 30, 1950.	Georgia Board of Pardons and Paroles. *Biennial Report to the Governor and Members of the General Assembly of the State of Georgia.*

				Statistical Summary of Executive Actions: July 1, 1948–June 30, 1950.
1949/New York	Thomas Dewey	1	**Samuel Tito Williams** granted commutation by Gov. Dewey for possible innocence. His conviction was later overturned.	Radelet, Bedau, and Putnam. *In Spite of Innocence* (1992).
1949/Texas	Beauford Jester	1	**Amberto Valtiero** (9/29/48).	Texas Department of Criminal Justice. *Death Row Commutations, 1923–1973*.
1950/Alabama	James E. Folsom	1	**Everett Washington**. Sentenced to death for rape. Commuted to life by governor.	State of Alabama. Legislative Report: Special Committee Investigating Pardons and Paroles, *1950*.
1950–1959/Ohio	Frank J. Lausche (1949–57); John William Brown (1957); C. William O'Neill (1957–59)	22	23 capital commutatons total between 1950 and 1959 according to aggregate statistical data compiled by Ohio legislative service staff research. Specific annual information not reported, but one of these commutations went to **Lewis Niday** (counted individually later in this chart), whose sentence was commuted by Gov. Michael DiSalle in 1959 on the grounds of mental retardation.	Ohio Legislative Service Commission, Capital Punishment, Staff Research Rep No. 46 at 62 (table 14) (1961) reprinted in Bedau, Hugo. "The Decline of Executive Clemency in Capital Cases." 18 *NYU Rev. L. & Soc. Change* 265 (1990–1991).

Year(s)/State	*Governor*	*Number*	*Inmate names, circumstances of the clemency, etc.*	*Source*
1950/Texas	Allan Shivers	1	**Cerillo Zamora** (2/3/50).	Texas Department of Criminal Justice. *Death Row Commutations, 1923–1973.*
1951/Georgia	Herman E. Talmadge	7	No individual information furnished. Impossible, based on the government record format, to discern specific distribution of capital commutations over this 24-month period July 1, 1950–June 30, 1952.	Georgia Board of Pardons and Paroles. *Biennial Report to the Governor and Members of the General Assembly of the State of Georgia.* Statistical Summary of Executive Actions: July 1, 1950–June 30, 1952.
1951/Texas	Allan Shivers	1	**Emma Oliver** (6/29/51).	Texas Department of Criminal Justice. *Death Row Commutations, 1923–1973.*
1952/Arizona	John Howard Pyle	2	Taken from statistical report. No specific individual information furnished.	Arizona Board of Pardons and Paroles. *Annual Report* (1952–53).
1952/Florida	Fuller Warren	1	**Reed Leroy Hatton** (12/10/52). Sentence commuted by Governor Fuller Warren.	Vandiver, Margaret. PhD diss. chart "Florida Capital Cases, 1923–1966."
1952/Texas	Allan Shivers	7	**Bob Wall** (3/25/52), **Billy McCune** (3/6/52), **T. Saucier** (1/8/52), **Harrell King** (3/18/52), **James Craft** (3/25/52), **Foley Gephart** (9/18/52), and **Lester Stevens** (12/2/52).	Texas Department of Criminal Justice. *Death Row Commutations, 1923–1973.*

1952/Virginia	John Battle	1	After 10 years on death row, **Silas Rogers** was granted a full pardon by Gov. Battle thanks to newly discovered exonerating evidence.	Radelet, Bedau, and Putnam. *In Spite of Innocence* (1992).
1953/California	Earl Warren	1	**John Albert Kerr, Jr.** Sentence commuted to life by Gov. Earl Warren.	State of California. Annual Report of Executive Clemencies Granted by the Governor 1953.
1953/Florida	Charley Johns	1	**Edgar Lewis Thomas** (12/16/53). Sentence commuted by Governor Charley Johns.	Vandiver, Margaret. PhD diss. chart "Florida Capital Cases, 1923–1966."
1953/Georgia	Herman E. Talmadge	4	No individual information furnished. Impossible, based on the government record format, to discern specific distribution of capital commutations over this 24-month period from July 1, 1952–June 30, 1954.	Georgia Board of Pardons and Paroles. *Biennial Report to the Governor and Members of the General Assembly of the State of Georgia*. Statistical Summary of Executive Actions: July 1, 1952–June 30, 1954.
1953–1958/Pennsylvania	John S. Fine (1951–1955); and George M. Leader (1955–1959)	14	Wolfgang et al documented 86 capital commutations between 1915 and 1958. Having already accounted for Giardiani and Farrow's 72 between 1915 and 1952, that leaves 14 more capital commutations in Pennsylvania sometime between 1953 and 1958. No year-by-year breakdown of the data was published in the Wolfgang article.	Wolfgang, Kelly, and Nolde. "Comparison of the Executed and the Commuted Among Admissions to Death Row. 53 *J. Crim. L. Criminology & Police Sci.* 301 (1962).

Year(s)/State	*Governor*	*Number*	*Inmate names, circumstances of the clemency, etc.*	*Source*
1953/Texas	Allan Shivers	1	**Robert Miers** (1/9/53).	Texas Department of Criminal Justice. *Death Row Commutations, 1923–1973.*
1954/California	Goodwin Knight	3	**John Sutic, James Francis Silva,** and **Wesley Robert Wells.** Sentences commuted case-by-case to LWOP by Gov. Goodwin Knight.	State of California. Annual Report of Executive Clemencies Granted by the Governor, 1954.
1954/Florida	Charley Johns	2	**Otis Neal Jackson, Jr.** (1954) and **Edward Webster** (9/15/54). Sentences commuted by Governor Charley Johns. Jackson, Jr. is an odd case, according to Vandiver. Convicted of rape in 1951, at the age of sixteen, he was sentenced to death, received a commutation of sentence in 1954 from Gov. Johns, escaped from prison, had his death sentence reimposed upon recapture, only to recieve another commutation, from Governor LeRoy Collins in 1956.	Vandiver, Margaret. PhD diss. chart "Florida Capital Cases, 1923–1966."
1955/Florida	LeRoy Collins	2	**Richard Floyd** (9/21/55) and **Walter Irvin** (12/16/55). Sentences commuted by Governor LeRoy Collins.	Vandiver, Margaret. PhD diss. chart "Florida Capital Cases, 1923–1966."
1955/Georgia	Herman E. Talmadge	7	No individual information furnished. Impossible, based on the government	Georgia Board of Pardons and Paroles. *Bi-*

			record format, to discern specific distribution of capital commutations over this 24-month period July 1, 1954–June 30, 1956.	*ennial Report to the Governor and Members of the General Assembly of the State of Georgia*. Statistical Summary of Executive Actions: July 1, 1954–June 30, 1956.
1955/New York	Averill Harriman	2	In 1955, **Norman Horton** (18 years old), and **Concepcion Estrada Correa** (17 years old) received two of the four capital commutations Gov. Averill Harriman granted during his term in office.	Harriman, Averill. "Mercy is a Lonely Business" *Saturday Evening Post* March 22, 1958. pp. 24–25, 83–84.
1955/Oregon	Paul L. Patterson	1	From statistical summary of capital commutations in Oregon, 1903–1964. No individualized information provided.	Bedau, Hugo. 45 *Or. L. Rev.* 8 (1965–66) "Capital Punishment in Oregon, 1903–1964."
1955/Texas	Allan Shivers	2	**Morris Addison** (2/8/55), **Gordan Morris** (2/24/55).	Texas Department of Criminal Justice. *Death Row Commutations, 1923–1973*.
1956/Florida	LeRoy Collins	2	**Ernest R. Barnes** (3/14/56) and **Fred Kinnie** (6/13/56). Sentences commuted by Governor LeRoy Collins.	Vandiver, Margaret. PhD diss. chart "Florida Capital Cases, 1923–1966."
1956–1963/West Virginia	William Marland (1953–57); Cecil Underwood (1957–61); William Wallace Barron (1961–65)	1	1 capital commutation by governors between 1956 and 1963 according to statistical executive clemency data compiled by Abramowitz and Paget. No specific individual information furnished.	Elkan Abramowitz and David Paget. *Executive Clemency in Capital Cases*. 39 *NYU L. Rev.* 191 (1964).

Year(s)/State	*Governor*	*Number*	*Inmate names, circumstances of the clemency, etc.*	*Source*
1957/Georgia	Marvin Griffin	5	No individual information furnished. Impossible, based on the government record format, to discern specific distribution of capital commutations over this 24-month period July 1, 1956–June 30, 1958.	Georgia Board of Pardons and Paroles. *Biennial Report to the Governor and Members of the General Assembly of the State of Georgia*. Statistical Summary of Executive Actions: July 1, 1956–June 30, 1958.
1957/Texas	Allan Shivers	1	**Lonnie Brinkley** (1/8/57).	Texas Department of Criminal Justice. *Death Row Commutations, 1923–1973.*
1957/Oregon	Robert Holmes	2	**Billy Junior Nunn** and one other. Because of personal opposition to the death penalty, Holmes had a blanket policy of commuting the sentences of all cases that came before him as governor. Billy Junior Nunn and one other convict received capital commutations in 1957.	Solie M. Ringold, "The Dynamics of Executive Clemency" 52 *ABA Journal* 240 (1966), and Bedau, Hugo. 45 *Or. L. Rev.* 8 (1965–66) "Capital Punishment in Oregon, 1903–1964."
1958/California	Goodwin Knight	3	**Clifford Jefferson, Remmel Wayne Brice,** and **Wilbert Felix Friend.** Sentences commuted to LWOP by Gov. Goodwin Knight.	State of California. *Annual Report of Executive Clemencies Granted by the Governor, 1958.*
1958/Florida	LeRoy Collins	2	**Marvin D. Phillips** (3/12/58) and **James H. Larry** (9/3/58). Sentences commuted by Governor LeRoy Collins.	Vandiver, Margaret. PhD diss. chart "Florida Capital Cases, 1923–1966."

1958/New Jersey	Alfred Driscoll	1	From statistical summary of capital commutations in New Jersey, 1907–1960. No individualized information provided.	Bedau, Hugo. "Death Sentences in New Jersey 1907–1960." 19 *Rutgers Law Review* 1 (1964).
1958/New York	Averill Harriman	2	**Thomas Frye** and **William A. Wynn.** (July 20, 1958.) On recommendation of the district attorney, Gov. Harriman commuted the death sentences of Frye and Wynn to life imprisonment.	State of New York. Public Papers of Governor Averill Harriman, 1958. "Pardons, Commutations and Reprieves." New York, 1959. pp. 839–845.
1958/Texas	Price Daniel	2	**Norman Kizzee** (8/26/58), **James Bell** (9/25/58).	Texas Department of Criminal Justice. *Death Row Commutations, 1923–1973.*
1959/California	Edmund G. "Pat" Brown	4	**John Crooker, Edward S. Wein, Charles E. Turville,** and **Harold A. Langdon.** Commutted case by case to LWOP by Gov. Pat Brown.	State of California. *Annual Report of Executive Clemencies Granted by the Governor, 1959.*
1959/Florida	LeRoy Collins	1	**Gilbert Francis Mead** (12/16/59). Sentence commuted by Governor LeRoy Collins.	Vandiver, Margaret. PhD diss. chart "Florida Capital Cases, 1923–1966."
1959/Georgia	Marvin Griffin	2	No individual information furnished. Impossible, based on the government record format, to discern specific distribution of capital commutations over this 24-month period July 1, 1958–June 30, 1960.	Georgia Board of Pardons and Paroles. *Biennial Report to the Governor and Members of the General Assembly of the State of Georgia.* Statisti-

Year(s)/State	*Governor*	*Number*	*Inmate names, circumstances of the clemency, etc.*	*Source*
				cal Summary of Executive Actions: July 1, 1958–June 30, 1960.
1959–1964/New York	Nelson A. Rockefeller	9	9 capital commutation by governors between 1959 and 1964 according to statistical executive clemency data compiled by Abramowitz and Paget. No specific individual information furnished.	Elkan Abramowitz and David Paget. *Executive Clemency in Capital Cases*. 39 *NYU L. Rev.* 191 (1964).
1959/Ohio	Michael DiSalle	1	**Lewis Niday:** on grounds of Niday's mental retardation.	Ellis, James W. UNM L. School article. James W. Ellis, "Mental Retardation and the Death Penalty: A Guide to State Issues," found at http://www.deathpenaltyinfo.org/MREddlisLeg.pdf.
1959/Oregon	Robert Holmes	1	From statistical summary of capital commutations in Oregon, 1903–1964. No individualized information provided.	Bedau, Hugo. 45 *Or. L. Rev.* 8 (1965–66) "Capital Punishment in Oregon, 1903–1964."
1959–1962/Pennsylvania	David Leo Lawrence	2	2 capital commutations between 1959 and 1964 according to statistical executive clemency data compiled by Abramowitz and Paget. No specific individual information furnished.	Elkan Abramowitz and David Paget. *Executive Clemency in Capital Cases*. 39 *NYU L. Rev.* 191 (1964).

1959/Texas	Price Daniel	2	**Alvaro Alcarta** (1/1/59) and **Richard McGee** (10/26/59).	Texas Department of Criminal Justice. *Death Row Commutations, 1923–1973.*
1960–1962/Alabama	John Patterson	2	2 capital commutations by the governor between 1960 and 1962 according to statistical executive clemency data compiled by Abramowitz and Paget. No specific individual information furnished.	Elkan Abramowitz and David Paget. *Executive Clemency in Capital Cases*. 39 *NYU L. Rev.* 191 (1964).
1960/California	Edmund G. "Pat" Brown	4	**Corwin, Cash, Mason,** and **James Michael Merkouris** commutted case-by-case to LWOP by Gov. Pat Brown.	State of California. *Annual Report of Executive Clemencies Granted by the Governor, 1960.*
1960/Florida	LeRoy Collins	2	**Donald Ray Askew** and **Leonard Perry Russ.** Sentences commuted by Governor LeRoy Collins.	Vandiver, Margaret. PhD diss. chart "Florida Capital Cases, 1923–1966."
1960–1962/Idaho	Robert Eben Smylie	1	1 capital commutation by the governor between 1960 and 1962 according to statistical executive clemency data compiled by Abramowitz and Paget. No specific individual information furnished.	Elkan Abramowitz and David Paget. *Executive Clemency in Capital Cases*. 39 *NYU L. Rev.* 191 (1964).
1960–1962/Louisiana	Jimmie Davis	1	1 capital commutation by the governor between 1960 and 1962 according to statistical executive clemency data compiled by Abramowitz and Paget. No specific individual information furnished.	Elkan Abramowitz and David Paget. *Executive Clemency in Capital Cases*. 39 *NYU L. Rev.* 191 (1964).

Year(s)/State	*Governor*	*Number*	*Inmate names, circumstances of the clemency, etc.*	*Source*
1960–1962/Ohio	Michael DiSalle	4	5 capital commutations total granted by the governor between 1960 and 1962 according to statistical executive clemency data compiled by Abramowitz and Paget. No specific individual information furnished, but one of these was **Edyth M. Klumpp** in 1961 (recorded separately on this chart).	Elkan Abramowitz and David Paget. *Executive Clemency in Capital Cases*. 39 *NYU L. Rev.* 191 (1964).
1960/Oklahoma	J. Howard Edmondson	1	**Louis William White** granted a full pardon, after 3 years on death row, when the actual perpetrator confessed.	Radelet, Bedau, and Putnam. *In Spite of Innocence* (1992).
1960/New Jersey	Robert Meyner	1	**Willie Butler:** sentencing disparities between Butler and his equally culpable co-defendants.	18 *N.Y.U. Rev. L. & Soc. Change* 255 Hugo Adam Bedau, "The Decline of Executive Clemency in Capital Cases."
1960–1962/Mississippi	Ross Barnett	1	1 capital commutation by the governor between 1960 and 1962 according to statistical executive clemency data compiled by Abramowitz and Paget. No specific individual information furnished.	Elkan Abramowitz and David Paget. *Executive Clemency in Capital Cases*. 39 *NYU L. Rev.* 191 (1964).
1960–1962/Missouri	James T. Blair	1	1 capital commutation by the governor between 1960 and 1962 according to statistical executive clemency data compiled by Abramowitz and Paget. No specific individual information furnished.	Elkan Abramowitz and David Paget. *Executive Clemency in Capital Cases*. 39 *NYU L. Rev.* 191 (1964).

1960–1962/Nebraska	Dwight W. Burney	1	1 capital commutation by the governor between 1960 and 1962 according to statistical executive clemency data compiled by Abramowitz and Paget. No specific individual information furnished.	Elkan Abramowitz and David Paget. *Executive Clemency in Capital Cases*. 39 *NYU L. Rev.* 191 (1964).
1960/South Carolina	Ernest F. Hollings	2	From statistical summary of capital clemencies. No individual information available.	Elkan Abramowitz and David Paget. *Executive Clemency in Capital Cases*. 39 *NYU L. Rev.* 191 (1964).
1960–1962/Tennessee	Buford Ellington	7	7 capital commutations by the governor between 1960 and 1962 according to statistical executive clemency data compiled by Abramowitz and Paget. No specific individual information furnished.	Elkan Abramowitz and David Paget. *Executive Clemency in Capital Cases*. 39 *NYU L. Rev.* 191 (1964).
1960/Texas	Price Daniel	2	**Billy Houston** (1/25/60) and **Albert Davis, Jr.** (2/12/60).	Texas Department of Criminal Justice. *Death Row Commutations, 1923–1973*.
1960–1962/Utah	George Dewey Clyde	1	1 capital commutation by the governor between 1960 and 1962 according to statistical executive clemency data compiled by Abramowitz and Paget. No specific individual information furnished.	Elkan Abramowitz and David Paget. *Executive Clemency in Capital Cases*. 39 *NYU L. Rev.* 191 (1964).

Year(s)/State	*Governor*	*Number*	*Inmate names, circumstances of the clemency, etc.*	*Source*
1960/Virginia	J. Lindsay Almond Jr.	2	1 capital commutation by the governor 1960–61 according to statistical executive clemency data compiled by Abramowitz and Paget. No specific individual information furnished.	Elkan Abramowitz and David Paget. *Executive Clemency in Capital Cases*. 39 *NYU L. Rev.* 191 (1964).
1961/California	Edmund G. "Pat" Brown	2	**Erwin M. Walker** and **Veron Atchley**. Commuted case by case to LWOP by Gov. Pat Brown.	State of California. Annual Report of Executive Clemencies Granted by the Governor, 1961.
1961/Georgia	S. Ernest Vandiver, Jr.	3	**Hilton Gardner** (11/21/60), **Morris Lee Harp** (8/11/60), and **Walter Emerson Veasey** (6/8/61) by Governor Ernert Vandiver, Jr.	Georgia Board of Pardons and Paroles. *Biennial Report to the Governor and Members of the General Assembly of the State of Georgia*. Detailed Summary of Prisoners released by Executive Action: July 1, 1960–June 30, 1962. (Number recorded for fiscal year ending June 30, 1961).
1961/Massachusetts	John Volpe	1	**Tucker Harrison** (9/28/61), on recommendation of the Advisory Board of Pardons, received the sole capital commutation in 1961 from Gov. John Volpe.	Volpe, John A. *Message From the Governor Submitting a report of the Exercise of the Pardoning Power by the Governor, 1961*. Massachusetts, 1961.

1961/Ohio	Michael DiSalle	1	**Edyth M. Klumpp.** DiSalle granted a commutation to this woman on death row after a personal interview with her. She claimed not to have fired the fatal shot in her husband's murder.	O'Shea, Kathleen. *Women and the Death Penalty in the United States 1900–1998* (1999).
1961/Texas	Price Daniel	2	**Maggie Morgan** (7/25/61) and **Ernesto Lopez** (4/7/61).	Texas Department of Criminal Justice. *Death Row Commutations, 1923–1973.*
1962/California	Edmund G. "Pat" Brown	4	**Bertrand J. Howk, Stanley William Fitzgerald, Carlos Gonzales Cisneros,** and **John Joseph Deptula.** Committed case by case to LWOP by Gov. Pat Brown.	State of California. Annual Report of Executive Clemencies Granted by the Governor, 1962.
1962/Georgia	S. Ernest Vandiver, Jr.	4	**Flexi McElroy** (11/21/61), **George Alford, Jr.** (2/13/62), **Brannon Epps** (2/13/62), and **Clifford Johnson** (2/13/61) by Gov. Ernest Vandiver, Jr.	Georgia Board of Pardons and Paroles. Biennial Report to the Governor and Members of the General Assembly of the State of Georgia. Detailed Summary of Prisoners released by Executive Action: July 1, 1960–June 30, 1962. (Number recorded for fiscal year ending June 30, 1962).
1962/Illinois	Otto Kerner	1	**Paul Crump:** according to Gov. Kerner, after seven years on death row, Crump was no longer the same ruthless man who had committed murder in 1955	18 *N.Y.U. Rev. L. & Soc. Change* 255 Hugo Adam Bedau, "The Decline of Executive

Year(s)/State	*Governor*	*Number*	*Inmate names, circumstances of the clemency, etc.*	*Source*
			and, accordingly, "it would serve no useful purpose to take this man's life."	Clemency in Capital Cases."
1962/Texas	Price Daniel	1	**Cecil Brown** (6/28/62).	Texas Department of Criminal Justice. *Death Row Commutations, 1923–1973.*
1963/California	Edmund G. "Pat" Brown	4	**Charles James Golston, Clarence Edward Ashley, William Lee Harrison,** and **Norman Arthur Whitehorn.** Commutted case by case to LWOP by Gov. Pat Brown.	State of California. Annual Report of Executive Clemencies Granted by the Governor, 1979.
1963/Florida	Farris Bryant	3	**Howard Bartlett Piccott** (3/13/63), **Nicholas Joseph Sikalis** (6/19/63), and **Leland Roy Baugus** (6/19/63). Sentence commuted by Governor Farris Bryant.	Vandiver, Margaret. PhD diss. chart "Florida Capital Cases, 1923–1966."
1963/Maryland	Millard Tawes	3	**James Giles, John Giles,** and **Joseph Johnson.** Death sentences commuted to life in prison by Gov. Tawes when public doubt was cast on the veracity of rape charges against them. Eventually a new trial was granted, and the Giles brothers were released, but Johnson, originally tried separately, had to wait for a full pardon from Gov. Spiro Agnew in 1968 before he was released.	18 *N.Y.U. Rev. L. & Soc. Change* 255 Hugo Adam Bedau, "The Decline of Executive Clemency in Capital Cases."

1963/Texas	John B. Connally	2	**Curtis Roberts** (6/17/63) and **Oscar O'Brien** (7/19/63).	Texas Department of Criminal Justice. *Death Row Commutations, 1923–1973.*
1964/Florida	Farris Bryant	2	**Tommie Lee Williams** (6/12/64) and **Dan Wilkins** (6/12/64). Sentences commuted by Governor Farris Bryant.	Vandiver, Margaret. PhD diss. chart "Florida Capital Cases, 1923–1966."
1964/Georgia	Carl Edward Sanders	1	No individual information furnished. Impossible, based on the government record format, to discern specific distribution of capital commutations over this 24-month period July 1, 1963–June 30, 1964.	Georgia Board of Pardons and Paroles. Biennial Report to the Governor and Members of the General Assembly of the State of Georgia. Statistical Summary of Executive Actions: July 1, 1963–June 30, 1964. (Number recorded for fiscal year ending June 30, 1964).
1964/Oregon	Mark Hatfield	3	Cleared death row immediately following ballot approval of a statewide repeal of capital punishment.	18 *N.Y.U. Rev. L. & Soc. Change* 255 Hugo Adam Bedau, "The Decline of Executive Clemency in Capital Cases."

Year(s)/State	*Governor*	*Number*	*Inmate names, circumstances of the clemency, etc.*	*Source*
1965/Georgia	Carl Edward Sanders	1	No individualized information provided. Impossible, based on the government record format, to discern specific distribution of capital commutations over this 24-month period July 1, 1964–June 30, 1965.	Georgia Board of Pardons and Paroles. Biennial Report to the Governor and Members of the General Assembly of the State of Georgia. Statistical Summary of Executive Actions: July 1, 1964–June 30, 1965. (Number recorded for fiscal year ending June 30, 1965).
1965/Tennessee	Frank G. Clement	5	**Rube Sims** (3/19/65), **Clayton Dawson** (3/19/65), **Richard Thomas** (3/19/65), **Freddie Green** (3/19/65), and **Henry Smith, Jr.** (3/19/65). Blanket commutation granted by Gov. Clement who, just two month earlier, had lobbied passionately in the **Tennessee** House of Representatives for abolition of capital punishment, "(I) cannot but in my heart believe that the law of capital punishment is a law unequalled and inequitably administered . . . (o)n March 26, 1915, my grandfather, Senator J.A. Clement, stood in the other body of this Tennessee General Assembly and pleaded for the abolition of capital punishment in Tennessee . . . (I)	"Gov. Clement Saves 5 From Death Chair," *New York Times (*Mar. 20, 1965) p. 1.

			beg with you to cast your vote elimination from our statutes of the capital punishment law." Governor Clement commuted the death sentences of all five men then on death row after the death penalty abolition bill failed in the State General Assembly by one vote.	
1965/Texas	John B. Connally	2	**Carolyn Lima** (4/3/65) and **Robert Freeman** (10/20/65).	Texas Department of Criminal Justice. *Death Row Commutations, 1923–1973.*
1966/California	Edmund G. "Pat" Brown	4	**Clyde Bates, William Earl Cotter, Ernest Leroy Jacobson,** and **Leo Carlton Lookadoo.** Commutted case by case to LWOP by Gov. Pat Brown.	State of California. *Annual Report of Executive Clemencies Granted by the Governor, 1966.*
1966/Florida	Haydon Burns	3	**Adolphus Brooks** (3/16/66), **Floyd A. Holzapfel** (6/23/66) and **Guy H. Eoff** (9/14/66). Sentences commuted by Governor Haydon Burns.	Vandiver, Margaret. PhD diss. chart "Florida Capital Cases, 1923–1966."
1966/Texas	John B. Connally	2	**Leslie Ashley** (1/14/16) and **Oscar Cook** (6/15/66).	Texas Department of Criminal Justice. *Death Row Commutations, 1923–1973.*
1967/California	Ronald Reagan	1	**C. Thomas** received a commutation from Gov. Ronald Reagan in June 1967.	State of California. Annual Report of Executive Clemencies Granted by the Governor, 1979.

Year(s)/State	Governor	Number	Inmate names, circumstances of the clemency, etc.	Source
1967/Georgia	Carl Edward Sanders	2	No individual information furnished. Impossible, based on the government record format, to discern specific distribution of capital commutations over this 24-month period July 1, 1966–June 30, 1967.	Georgia Board of Pardons and Paroles. Biennial Report to the Governor and Members of the General Assembly of the State of Georgia. Statistical Summary of Executive Actions: July 1, 1966–June 30, 1967. (Number recorded for fiscal year ending June 30, 1967).
1967/Kentucky	Edward Breathitt	3	**Rudolph Hamilton** (12/11/67), **Hassie Cain Martin**, and **Johnnie Smith, Jr.** by Gov. Edward Breathitt.	*The Power, Practice and Process of Commutation of Persons Sentenced to Death* (Kentucky Department of Public Advocacy). http://dpa.ky.gov/text/cppp.pdf.
1968/Georgia	Lester Maddox	5	No individual information furnished. Impossible, based on the government record format, to discern specific distribution of capital commutations over this 24-month period July 1, 1967–June 30, 1968.	Georgia Board of Pardons and Paroles. Biennial Report to the Governor and Members of the General Assembly of the State of Georgia. Statistical Summary of Executive Actions: July 1, 1967– June 30, 1968. (Number recorded for fiscal year ending June 30, 1968).

1968/Texas	John B. Connally	1	**Leon Johnston** (12/4/68).	Texas Department of Criminal Justice. *Death Row Commutations, 1923–1973.*
1969/Texas	Preston E. Smith	5	**Leon Spencer** (12/1/69), **Harold Hintz** (4/15/69), **Clifford Carroll** (5/6/69), **Jesse Ellison** (9/11/69), **Claude Edwards** (7/10/69).	Texas Department of Criminal Justice. *Death Row Commutations, 1923–1973.*
1970/Arkansas	Winthrop Rockefeller	15	**Lonnie Mitchell, Frank Harris, Daniel Montgomery, Jr., William Maxwell, Walter Lonnie Brown, Clarence Stewart, James Williams, James Scott, Albert Harris, John Henry Shepard, Allen Frank Davis, Orion Trotter, Jerry James Johnson, Franklin Basnick, Sr.,** and **Royce Vann Murphy**. Rockefeller cleared death row on his way out of office.	Dumas, Ernest. "15 Sentences Commuted by WR." *Arkansas Gazette.* 13/30/70.
1971/Arkansas	Dale Bumpers	1	Rockefeller's successor commuted one death sentence, without fanfare, his first year in office.	Rockefeller, Winthrop. "Executive Clemency and the Death Penalty." 21 *Catholic U. L. Rev.* 94 (1972–72).
1971/South Carolina	John C. West	3	**Carlos Ashbrooks** (4/12/71), **John Morris** (5/14/71), and **Edward Williams** (6/7/71).	Laughlin, McDonald. *Capital Punishment in South Carolina: The End of an Era.* 24 *S. C. L. Rev.* 762 (1972).

Year(s)/State	*Governor*	*Number*	*Inmate names, circumstances of the clemency, etc.*	*Source*
1971/Tennessee	Winifield Dunn	3	**Herbert Lee Tate, John Burmeister,** and **Ronald Ray Smith.** Sentences commuted to 99 years each by Gov. Winifield Dunn. All three would have sentences further commuted to time served in subsequent Gov. Leonard Ray Blanton's 1979 cash-for clemency scandal.	"Clemencies by Blanton Listed." *The Commercial Appeal.* Jan. 17, 1979.
1971/Texas	Preston E. Smith	5	**James Marion** (5/17/71), **Paul Crain** (12/28/71), **William Bryan** (6/9/71), **Tracey Whan** (12/28/71), and **Daniel Quintana** (11/18/71).	Texas Department of Criminal Justice. *Death Row Commutations, 1923–1973.*
1975/Florida	Reubin Askew	2	**Wilbert Lee** and **Freddie Pitts** received full pardons from Gov. Askew after twelve years of appeals during which time their convictions had been vacated, reinstated, and another man had confessed to the crime.	18 *N.Y.U. Rev. L. & Soc. Change* 255 Hugo Adam Bedau, "The Decline of Executive Clemency in Capital Cases."
1977/Georgia	George D. Busbee	1	**Charles Harris Hill:** death sentence was disproportional to the sentence given to his equally or more culpable codefendant, the actual killer.	DPIC website. (www.deathpenaltyinfo.org). Cases originally cited by Michael L. Radelet and Barbara A. Zsembik, "Executive Clemency in Post-*Furman* Capital Cases," 27 *University of Richmond Law Review* 289–314 (1993).

1979/Florida	Bob Graham	2	**Learie Leo Alford:** possible innocence. **Clifford Hallman:** death sentence deemed inappropriate for crime committed.	DPIC website. Cases originally cited by Michael L. Radelet and Barbara A. Zsembik, "Executive Clemency in Post-*Furman* Capital Cases," 27 *University of Richmond Law Review* 289–314 (1993).
1980/Florida	Bob Graham	2	**Darrell Edwin Hoy**: death sentence was disproportional to the sentence given to his equally or more culpable co-defendant, the triggerman. **Richard Henry Gibson**: death sentence was disproportional to the sentence given to his equally culpable co-defendants.	DPIC website. Cases originally cited by Michael L. Radelet and Barbara A. Zsembik, "Executive Clemency in Post-*Furman* Capital Cases," 27 *University of Richmond Law Review* 289–314 (1993).
1981/Florida	Bob Graham	1	**Michael Salvatore**: disparities in sentences between Salvatore and two others involved in the crime.	DPIC website. Cases originally cited by Michael L. Radelet and Barbara A. Zsembik, "Executive Clemency in Post-*Furman* Capital Cases," 27 *University of Richmond Law Review* 289–314 (1993).
1983/Florida	Bob Graham	1	**Jesse Rutledge**: possible innocence.	DPIC website. Cases originally cited by Michael L. Radelet and Barbara A. Zsembik,

Year(s)/State	*Governor*	*Number*	*Inmate names, circumstances of the clemency, etc.*	*Source*
				"Executive Clemency in Post-Furman Capital Cases," 27 *University of Richmond Law Review* 289–314 (1993).
1986/New Mexico	Toney Anaya	5	**David Cheadle, Joel Compton, Richard Garcia, William Gilbert, Michael Guzman:** Commuted all death row sentences at end of term.	DPIC website. Statement by Governor Toney Anaya on Crime and Capital Punishment. Santa Fe, NM. November 26, 1986.
1987/Maryland	Harry R. Hughes	1	**Doris Ann Foster:** Gov. Hughes commuted the sentence due to personal death penalty opposition and because of doubts about Foster's guilt.	DPIC website. Cases originally cited by Michael L. Radelet and Barbara A. Zsembik, "Executive Clemency in Post-*Furman* Capital Cases," 27 *University of Richmond Law Review* 289–314 (1993).
1988/Georgia	Joe Frank Harris	1	**Freddie Davis:** Board of Pardons and Paroles found that Davis's death sentence was disproportional to the life sentence given to his co-defendant.	DPIC website. Cases originally cited by Michael L. Radelet and Barbara A. Zsembik, "Executive Clemency in Post-*Furman* Capital Cases," 27 *University of Richmond Law Review* 289–314 (1993).

1988/Montana	Ted Schwinden	1	**David Cameron Keith**: Reasons reportedly included Keith's partial paralysis and blindness, remorse, religious conversion, and the possibility that he may have shot the victim as a reflex action.	DPIC website. Cases originally cited by Michael L. Radelet and Barbara A. Zsembik, "Executive Clemency in Post-*Furman* Capital Cases," 27 *University of Richmond Law Review* 289–314 (1993).
1989/Louisiana	Buddy Roemer	1	**Ronald Monroe**: Gov. Roemer had doubts about Monroe's guilt.	DPIC website. Cases originally cited by Michael L. Radelet and Barbara A. Zsembik, "Executive Clemency in Post-*Furman* Capital Cases," 27 *University of Richmond Law Review* 289–314 (1993).
1990/Georgia	Joe Frank Harris	1	**William Moore**: Board of Pardons and Paroles commuted Moore's sentence citing his exemplary prison record, remorse, religious conversion, and the pleas for clemency from the victim's family.	DPIC website. Cases originally cited by Michael L. Radelet and Barbara A. Zsembik, "Executive Clemency in Post-*Furman* Capital Cases," 27 *University of Richmond Law Review* 289–314 (1993).
1990/Virginia	Gerald L. Baliles	1	**Joseph Giarratano**: possible innocence.	DPIC website. Cases originally cited by Michael L. Radelet and Barbara A. Zsembik,

Year(s)/State	*Governor*	*Number*	*Inmate names, circumstances of the clemency, etc.*	*Source*
				"Executive Clemency in Post-*Furman* Capital Cases," 27 *University of Richmond Law Review* 289–314 (1993).
1990/Georgia	Joe Frank Harris	1	**Harold Williams**: Board of Pardons and Paroles found that Williams's death sentence was disproportional to the sentence given to his accomplice, who took full responsibility for the crime.	DPIC website. Cases originally cited by Michael L. Radelet and Barbara A. Zsembik, "Executive Clemency in Post-*Furman* Capital Cases," 27 *University of Richmond Law Review* 289–314 (1993).
1991/Ohio	Richard Celeste	8	**Debra Brown, Rosalie Grant, Elizabeth Green, Leonard Jenkins, Willie Jester, Beatrice Lampkin, Donald Maurer, Lee Seier**: Gov. Celeste commuted the sentences of eight select capital cases on his way out of office early in 1991.	DPIC Website.
1992/Virginia	Douglas Wilder	1	**Herbert Bassette**: possible innocence.	DPIC Website.
1992/North Carolina	James G. Martin	1	**Anson Avery Maynard**: possible innocence.	DPIC Website.
1993/Missouri	Mel Carnahan	1	**Bobbie Shaw**: mental disabilities.	DPIC Website.

1994/Virginia	Douglas Wilder	1	**Earl Washington**: possible innocence (Six years later, DNA tests exonerated Washington altogether. In 2000, Gov. Jim Gilmore granted Washington a full pardon.)	DPIC Website.
1996/Illinois	Jim Edgar	1	**Gwen Garcia**: death sentence deemed inappropriate for crime committed.	DPIC Website.
1996/Virginia	George Allen, Jr.	1	**Joseph Payne**: possible innocence.	DPIC Website.
1996/Idaho	Phil Batt	1	**Donald Paradis**: possible inocence (conviction was overturned five years later. Paradis was released from prison in 2001).	DPIC Website.
1997/Virginia	George Allen, Jr.	1	**William Saunders**: rehabilitation of inmate. Prosecutor and judge from trial recommended clemency.	DPIC Website.
1998/Texas	George W. Bush	1	**Henry Lee Lucas**: possible innocence.	DPIC Website.
1999/Alabama	Fob James, Jr.	1	**Judith Ann Neelley**: sentence commuted as Gov. James left office. No reason given.	DPIC Website.
1999/Missouri	Mel Carnahan	1	**Darrell Mease**: clemency granted at the request of Pope John Paul II during a visit to St. Louis.	DPIC Website.

Year(s)/State	*Governor*	*Number*	*Inmate names, circumstances of the clemency, etc.*	*Source*
1999/Arkansas	Mike Huckabee	1	**Bobby Ray Fretwell**: sentence commuted after one juror told the governor he felt pressured to vote for the death penalty, but did not actually concur with the sentence.	DPIC Website.
1999/Virginia	James S. Gilmore, III	1	**Clalvin Swann**: sentence commuted due to Swann's mental condition.	DPIC Website.
1999/North Carolina	James B. Hunt	1	**Wendell Flowers**: Governor had doubts about the extent of Flowers's involvement in the crime.	DPIC Website.
2000/Maryland	Parris N. Glendening	1	**Eugene Colvinel**: possible innocence.	DPIC Website.
2000/North Carolina	James B. Hunt	1	**Marcus Carter**: doubts about fairness of trial.	DPIC Website.
2001/Oklahoma	Frank Keating	1	**Phillip Dewitt Smith**: possible innocence.	DPIC Website.
2001/North Carolina	Mike Easley	1	**Robert Bacon, Jr.**: defense raised concerns about racial bias in sentencing, and Gov. Easley commuted Bacon's sentence to life imprisonment, stating only that it was "the appropriate sentence."	DPIC Website.
2002/North Carolina	Mike Easley	1	**Charlie Mason Alston**: defense raised concerns about possible innocence, and Gov. Easley again handed down a commutation with the only explanation being that life imprisonment "the appropriate sentence."	DPIC Website.

2002/Georgia	Roy Barnes	1	**Alexander Williams:** Board of Pardons and Paroles commuted Williams's sentence to life without parole due to his juvenile status at the time of the crime, as well as his mental illness.	DPIC Website.
2002/Nevada	Kenny Guinn	1	The Nevada Pardons Board, chaired by Governor Guinn, voted unanimously to grant clemency to **Thomas Nevius**, a mentally retarded inmate. The commuation to a sentence of life without parole came after the U.S. Supreme Court banned the practice of executing those with mental retardation.	DPIC Website.
2003/Illinois	George Ryan*	171	167 commutations (see last page of appendix C): cleared death row on his way out of office in 2003, citing a flawed legal process (Ryan's blanket commutation was preceeded on Jan 10, 2003 by 4 pardons of men wrongfully convicted: Aaron Patterson, Madison Hobley, Leroy Orange, and Stanley Howard).	DPIC Website.
2003/Louisiana	Kathleen Blanco	1	**Herbert Welcome:** Pardon and Parole Board recommendation based upon U.S. Supreme Court's decision on mental retardation.	DPIC Website.
2003/Kentucky	Paul E. Patton	1	**Kevin Stanford:** Governor Paul Patton, declaring that the justice system "perpetuated an injustice," based his decision upon Stanford's age (17) at the	DPIC Website.

Year(s)/State	*Governor*	*Number*	*Inmate names, circumstances of the clemency, etc.*	*Source*
			time of the crime. The pardon reduced Stanford's sentence to life without parole.	
2003/Ohio	Bob Taft	1	**Jerome Campell**: Pardon and Parole Board recommendation based on doubts regarding DNA evidence unavailable at trial.	DPIC Website.
2004/Georgia	Sonny Perdue	1	**Willie James Hall**. The state parole board of Georgia commuted Hall's death sentence to life without parole (1/26/2004).	DPIC Website.
2004/Texas	Rick Perry	1	**Robert Smith**. Sentence commuted from death to life due to mental retardation (IQ below 65).	DPIC Website.
2004/Oklahoma	Brad Henry	1	**Osvaldo Torres** (5/13/2004). Sentence commuted to LWOP, as recommended by the state Pardon and Parole Board. High profile case due to International Court of Justice ruling that, under the Vienna convention, the rights of Torres and 50 other Mexican nationals on death row in the U.S. had been violated.	DPIC Website.
2004/Indiana	Joe Kernan	1	**Darnell Williams** (7/2/2004). Death sentence disproportionate to life sentence of equally culpable co-defendant. Commuted by Gov. Kernan to LWOP.	DPIC Website.
			Total Commutations:	**1343**

Special thanks to the following people who provided specific data and/or helpful direction in the construction of this list: Hugo Bedau, Elmer Johnson, Jim Lucas, Linda Pine, Michael Radelet, and Margaret Vandiver.

Governor Ryan's Commutations

1. Allen, Kenneth (B)
2. Alvine, Ronald (W)
3. Armstrong, Donald (B)
4. Ashford, James (B)
5. Ballard, Mark (W)
6. Banks, Randy (B)
7. Barrow, Ronald (W)
8. Bean, Harold (W)
9. Brisbon, Henry (B)
10. Britz, Dewayne (W)
11. Brooks, Terrence (B)
12. Brown, Anthony (B)
13. Brown, Anton (B)
14. Burgess, Ray (W)
15. Burt, Ronald (W)
16. Burton, Peter (W)
17. Buss, Timothy (W)
18. Caballero, Juan (L)
19. Caffey, Fedell (B)
20. Casillas, Robert (L)
21. Casteel, Luther (W)
22. Ceja, Raul (L)
23. Chapman, Reginald (B)
24. Childress, John (B)
25. Cloutier, Robert (W)
26. Cole, Jr., John (W)
27. Coleman, Dedrick (B)
28. Cortez, Juan (L)
29. Dameron, Tony (W)
30. Daniels, Eric D. (B)
31. Davis, Chris (B)
32. Easley, Ike (B)
33. Edwards, Daniel (W)
34. Emerson, Dennis (B)
35. Enis, Anthony (B)
36. Evans, Johnnie Lee (B)
37. Evans, Jr., Robert L. (B)
38. Fair, Robert (B)
39. Fayne, Lorenzo (B)
40. Flores, Mario (L)
41. Foster, James (B)
42. Franklin, William (B)
43. Ganus, Victor (W)
44. Gilliam, Oasby (B)
45. Gosier, Harry (B)
46. Graham, Edward (B)
47. Griffin, Henry (B)
48. Griffith, Evan (B)
49. Guest, Anthony (B)
50. Hall, Anthony (B)
51. Hall, Felipe (B)

52. Harris, David (B)
53. Harris, James (B)
54. Harris, Ralph (B)
55. Haynes, Jonathan (W)
56. Heard, Delbert (B)
57. Henderson, Demetrius (B)
58. Hester, John (B)
59. Hickey, Arthur (W)
60. Hicks, Jojulien (B)
61. Holman, Tafford (B)
62. Hooper, Murray (B)
63. Hope, Edgar (B)
64. Hudson, Renaldo (B)
65. Jackson, Lawrence (B)
66. Jamison, Ernest (B)
67. Janes, Ron (W)
68. Johnson, Andrew (B)
69. Johnson, Grayland (B)
70. Johnson, Lenard (B)
71. Johnson, Mark (B)
72. Johnson, Milton (B)
73. Johnson, Montell (B)
74. Jones, Andre (B)
75. Jones, Robert K. (W)
76. Jones, William T. (B)
77. Karim, Samuel (B)
78. Keene, William (W)
79. Kidd, Leonard (B)
80. King, Derrick (B)
81. King, Maurice (B)
82. Kirchner, William B. (W)
83. Kitchen, Ronald (B)
84. Kliner, Ronald (W)
85. Lash, Dale (W)
86. Lear, Tuhran (B)
87. Lee, Eric (B)
88. Lucas, Roosevelt (B)
89. Macri, Geno (W)
90. Mahaffey, Jerry (B)
91. Mahaffey, Reginald (B)
92. Mata, Bernina (L)
93. Mccallister, Maynard (W)
94. Mcdonald, Maurice (B)
95. Mclaurin, Charles (B)
96. Mcneal, Aldwin (B)
97. Miller, Joseph (W)
98. Mitchell, Anthony (B)
99. Montgomery, Ulece (B)
100. Moore, Corey (B)

101. Moore, Edward (W)
102. Morris, Richard (B)
103. Moss, Sanantone (B)
104. Munson, James (B)
105. Neal, Jr., John (W)
106. Neilsen, Neils (W)
107. Nieves, Hector (L)
108. Oaks, Douglas (W)
109. Odle, Thomas (W)
110. Owens, Robin (B)
111. Page, Patrick (W)
112. Pecoraro, John (W)
113. Peeples, William (B)
114. Pitsonbarger, Jimmy (W)
115. Pulliam, Latasha (B)
116. Raines, Daniel (W)
117. Reynolds, Sean Clay (W)
118. Richardson, Floyd (B)
119. Riley, William (B)
120. Rissley, Jeffrey (W)
121. Sanchez, Hector (L)
122. Scott, Larry (B)
123. Shatner, Darrin (W)
124. Shurn, Keith (B)
125. Silagy, Charles (W)
126. Simms, Darryl (B)
127. Simpson, Robert (B)
128. Sims, Bobby (B)
129. Sims, Paris (B)
130. Smith, David (W)
131. Solache, Gabriel (L)
132. Spreitzer, Edward (W)
133. Strickland, Tyrone (B)
134. Szabo, John (W)
135. Taylor, Paul Eric (W)
136. Tenner, James (B)
137. Terrell, Drew (B)
138. Thomas, Walter (B)
139. Todd, Robert (W)
140. Towns, Sherrell (B)
141. Turner, Robert (W)
142. Umphrey, Thomas (W)
143. Urdiales, Andrew (W)
144. Ward, Jerry (B)
145. Watford, Marlon (B)
146. Watson, Henry (NA)
147. Westray, James (W)
148. Wiley, Howard (B)
149. Williams, Bobby (B)
150. Williams, Dorothy (B)
151. Williams, Elton (B)

152. Williams, Frank (B)
153. Williams, Jacqueline (B)
154. Williams, Michael (B)
155. Wilson, Glenn (B)
156. Woolley, Martin (W)
157. Wright, Patrick (W)

Note: Governor Ryan also granted clemency to the following inmates on death row who had had their sentences vacated and were awaiting a new sentence hearing.

158. Bracey, William (B)
159. Brown, Cortez (B)
160. Collins, Roger L. (B)
161. Erickson, Paul S. (W)
162. Fuller, Tyrone (B)
163. Kantu, Juius (B)
164. Madej, Gregory (W)
165. Morgan, Samuel (B)
166. St. Pierre, Robert (W)
167. Thompkins, Willie (B)

(W) = white; (B) = black; (L) = Latino/Latina; (NA) = not available

Notes

Chapter 1
Mercy, Clemency, and Capital Punishment:
The Illinois Story

1. As a result of the *Furman* decision, approximately six hundred death sentences across the nation were reduced to life in prison. See *Furman v. Georgia*, 408 U.S. 238 (1972).

2. For a discussion of the new abolitionism, see Austin Sarat, *When the State Kills: Capital Punishment and the American Condition* (Princeton: Princeton University Press, 2001), chapter 9.

3. For a discussion of the president's emergency powers, see Bruce Ackerman, "The Emergency Constitution," 113 *Yale Law Journal* (2004), 1029. For criticism of Ackerman's views, see David Cole, "The Priority of Morality: The Emergency Constitution's Blind Spot," 113 *Yale Law Journal* (2002), 1753; and Lawrence Tribe and Patrick Gudridge, "The Anti-Emergency Constitution," 113 *Yale Law Journal* (2004), 1801.

4. Bruce Shapiro, "A Talk with Governor Ryan," *The Nation* (December 21, 2000), http://www.thenation.com/doc.mhtml%3Fi=20010108&s=shapiro.

5. Ibid.

6. Recommendation 107, ABA House of Delegates, February 3, 1997.

7. The report and recommendation both call for a permanent halt to the execution of juveniles and the mentally retarded.

8. Stephen Bright, "Counsel for the Poor: The Death Sentence Not for the Worst Crime, but for the Worst Lawyer," 103 *Yale Law Journal* (1994), 1835.

9. Charlotte Holdman, "Is There Any Habeas Left in This Corpus?" 27 *Loyola University of Chicago Law Journal* (1996), 524.

10. Report of the ABA, Submitted with Recommendation 107, 5.

11. Ibid., 11, 13.

12. David Baldus, George Woodworth, and Charles Pulaski, *Equal Justice and the Death Penalty: A Legal and Empirical Analysis* (Boston: Northeastern University Press, 1990).

13. See Samuel Gross and Robert Mauro, *Death and Discrimination: Racial Disparities in Capital Sentences* (Boston: Northeastern University Press, 1989).

14. See Jesse Jackson Jr., "Why I Support the Illinois Death Penalty Moratorium Campaign," found at Congressman Jesse Jackson Jr., Web Site (April 21, 1997), http://www.jessejacksonjr.org/issues/i042197264.html

15. "Bill Would Stay Executions Pending Review," *Chicago Daily Law Bulletin* (April 27, 1997), p. 1.

16. Douglas Holt and Steve Mills, "Double Murder Case Unravels," *Chicago Tribune* (February 4, 1999), 1.

17. Among those urging such action were Illinois State Supreme Court justices Moses Harrison and Charles Freeman. See John Flynn Rooney, "Death Penalty Issue Engages All Three Branches," *Chicago Daily Law Bulletin* (February 10, 1999), 1.

18. See Christopher Wills, "Despite Porter Case, Death Penalty Moratorium Faces Strong Opposition," *AP State and Local Wire* (February 5, 1999).

19. "Doubts about Death Penalty," *Chicago Tribune* (February 7, 1999), 1, 8.

20. Rick Pearson and Cornelia Grunman, "A Change of Heart on Execution Cases," *Chicago Tribune* (February 11, 1999), 1, 27.

21. Shapiro, "A Talk with Governor Ryan." See also Norman Greene et al., "Governor Ryan's Capital Punishment Moratorium and the Executioner's Confession: Views from the Governor's Mansion to Death Row," 75 *St. John's Law Review* (2001), 401, 409.

22. Cornelia Grunman and Rick Pearson, "Ryan Agonized, but Confident He 'Did the Right Thing,'" *Chicago Tribune* (March 18, 1999), 1, 20. That same month legislative efforts to establish a death penalty moratorium came to a halt when a state senate committee failed by one vote to move a resolution to the full chamber.

23. Dave McKinney, "Kokoraleis Executed Despite Late Appeals," *Chicago Sun-Times* (March 17, 1999), 7. Kokoraleis would be the only person executed in Illinois during Ryan's term.

24. Kate Marquess, "Judges to Look at Death Penalty," *Chicago Lawyer* (May, 1999), 10.

25. Shapiro, "A Talk with Governor Ryan."

26. Ken Armstrong and Steve Mills, "Part 1: Death Row Justice Derailed," *Chicago Tribune* (November 14, 1999), 1.

27. As Ryan put it, referring to the Armstrong and Mills series, "It is pretty startling." See Greene et al., "Governor Ryan's Capital Punishment Moratorium and the Executioner's Confession: Views from the Governor's Mansion to Death Row," 411. Three and a half years later, as he announced pardons for several death row inmates who were wrongfully prosecuted and sentenced to die Ryan again credited the Armstrong and Mills series, noting, "I've repeated many times the findings of reporters Steve Mills and Ken Armstrong." See Steve Mills and Christi Parsons, "'The System Has Failed': Ryan Condemns Injustice, Pardons 6," *Chicago Tribune* (January 11, 2003), 1, 18.

28. At the time he announced the moratorium and the creation of the new panel, numerous other reviews of the state's capital punishment system were already under way, including the Supreme Court's Special Committee on Capital Cases, the House Task Force on the Death Penalty, the House Special Committee on Prosecutorial Misconduct, and the Task Force on Criminal Justice of the State Senate. See Aaron Chambers, "Ryan Halts All Executions in Illinois," *Chicago Daily Law Bulletin* (January 31, 2000), 1.

29. For a discussion of reactions, see Darryl Van Duch, "The ABA, Rome, React to Gov. Ryan's Moratorium," *American Lawyer Media* (February 3, 2000). Some critics questioned Ryan's motivation. "It seems apparent to me that this was an attempt to deflect attention from his other problems," argued Peoria County state's attorney Kevin Lyons. See Omar Sofradzija, "Peoria County State's Attorney Blasts Ryan on Death Penalty," *Copley News Service* (February 1, 2000). For an example of other criticism, see "Execution Moratorium Illegal, State Justice Says," *Chicago Sun-Times* (October 4, 2000), 2.

30. "Editorial: Reprieve for Justice," *Chicago Sun-Times* (February 1, 2000), 19.

31. Paul Krawzak, "Inmates Nearing Death Sway Ryan's View," *State Journal-Register* (Springfield, IL) (February 1, 2000), 1.

32. Ken Armstrong and Steve Mills, "Ryan: 'Until I Can Be Sure'" *Chicago Tribune* (February 1, 2000), 1, 4.

33. See Tim Novak, "Select Panel Won't Be Alone in Studying Death Penalty," *Chicago-Sun Times* (March 10, 2000), 22.

34. See Greene et al., "Governor Ryan's Capital Punishment Moratorium and the Executioner's Confession: Views from the Governor's Mansion to Death Row," 406.

35. Mark Brown, "Guts Not Real Issue in Ryan-Philip Spat," *Chicago Sun-Times* (April 26, 2001), 2.

36. See Nathaniel Hernandez, "Rules Changes in Death Penalty Cases Seen as a Beginning," *Chicago Lawyer* (March, 2001), 10.

37. Steve Mills and Christi Parsons, "Death Penalty Report Readied," *Chicago Tribune* (February 1, 2002), 1.

38. Michael Sneed and Dave Newbart, "Ryan Studies Death Row Cases," *Chicago Sun-Times* (March 3, 2002), 3.

39. " 'I'm surprised that he says 'some' rather than 'all' or 'most,' said a board member of the Illinois Coalition Against the Death Penalty. 'None of these 163 [*sic*] people had the benefit of (whatever reforms are put forth by) the Governor's Commission.' " Ibid.

40. See Maurice Possley and Eric Ferkenhoff, "Daley, Cops Question Death Penalty Reform Plan," *Chicago Tribune* (April 17, 2002), 1.

41. "Reactions to the Governor's Death Penalty Commission Report," *Associated Press State and Local Wire* (April 12, 2002).

42. Dave McKinney, " 'Why Let Them Live?' Asks Boy Upset by Bids for Clemency," *Chicago Sun-Times* (August 29, 2002), 8.

43. See Mary Mitchell, "Governor Ryan Steamrolls Murder Victims' Families," *Chicago Sun-Times* (September 5, 2002), 14.

44. "Editorial: Blanket Amnesty Would Rob Justice," *Chicago Sun-Times* (September 8, 2002), 33.

45. Dan Rozek, "Ryan Sees Clemency for All or None," *Chicago Sun-Times* (September 7, 2002), 2.

46. John Patterson, "Clemency Hearings Open Old Wounds," *Chicago Daily Herald* (October 15, 2002), 1.

47. Steve Mills and Christi Parsons, "Tears Send a Message: Hearings' Emotional Impact Surprises Death Penalty Foes," *Chicago Tribune* (October 27, 2002), 1.

48. See Steve Mills, "Life-or-Death Debate Rages at Hearings," *Chicago Tribune* (October 16, 2002), 1, 14.

49. Mills and Parsons, "Tears Send a Message: Hearings' Emotional Impact Surprises Death Penalty Foes," 1.

50. Steve Neal, "Editorial: Governor Is Out of Control," *Chicago Sun-Times* (October 22, 2002), 27.

51. "Editorial: Ryan's Hearings Cruel and Unusual," *Chicago Sun-Times* (October 22, 2002), 27.

52. "Editorial: Crime, Punishment and Politics," *Chicago Tribune* (November 20, 2002), 26.

53. In May 2003 the legislature finally passed a reform package that, among other things, ended the execution of the mentally retarded, established a pilot program to begin police videotaping of homicide interrogations and confessions, increased the ability of the state supreme court to overturn death sentences, and gave defendants greater access to DNA testing. See "Editorial: Not a Flawless Fix, but We Can Work with It," *Chicago Sun-Times* (June 1, 2003), 39.

54. John Keilman, "Clemency Pleas Rile Panelists," *Chicago Tribune Tribwest* (October 17, 2002), 1.

55. Charles Keeshan, "Family Blasts Clemency Hearings," *Chicago Daily Herald* (October 18, 2002), 1. Also John Keilman, "Anger over Ryan Grows," *Chicago Tribune Tribwest* (October 18, 2002), 1.

56. Steve Mills, "650 Lawyers Offer Ryan Case for Blanket Commutation," *Chicago Tribune* (November 19, 2002), 1; also "No Blanket Clemency, Prosecutors Urge Ryan," *Chicago Tribune* (December 13, 2002), and John McCormick, "Letter Prods Ryan on Clemency: Law Teachers Urge Weighing Blanket Commutation," *Chicago Tribune* (December 30, 2002).

57. John Patterson, "What Will the Governor Do? On Clemency Issue Ryan's Hard to Predict," *Chicago Daily Herald* (October 23, 2002), 1. On other occasions Ryan said that he "probably won't" issue a blanket clemency after the hearings. Gary Wisby and Carlos Sadovi, "Governor Flips, Says He'll Talk to Victims' Kin," *Chicago Sun-Times* (November 2, 2002), 5. At the time he announced his clemency decision Ryan acknowledged his vacillation saying about the families of murder victims, "They have a right to feel betrayed. . . . I have probably misled them." John Keilman, "Relatives of Victims Feel 'Cheated,'" *Chicago Tribune* (January 12, 2003).

58. Michel Foucault, *The History of Sexuality*, vol. 1. *An Introduction*. Robert Hurley, trans. (New York: Viking, 1990), 135.

59. *Calvin's Case* 77 E.R. 377 (Exchequer, 1608), at 398. For more on this tradition and the development of the Roman law maxim in common law, see Nasser Hussain, *The Jurisprudence of Emergency: Colo-*

nialism and the Rule of Law (Ann Arbor: University of Michigan Press, 2004), 45–46.

60. Michel Foucault, "Governmentality," in *The Foucault Effect*, Graham Burchell, Colin Gordon, and Peter Miller, eds. (Chicago: University of Chicago Press, 1991).

61. See Sylvia Ostry, "Globalization and Sovereignty," James R. Mallory Annual Lecture in Canadian Studies, McGill University (March 19, 1999), http://www.misc-iecm.mcgill.ca/publications/ostry.pdf. The hallmark of globalization as it is generally understood is the worldwide spread of corporate capitalism and neoliberal values. In other words, globalization should not be equated with the construction of an open, apolitical, and beneficent global village. Instead it is first and foremost a vast project in political economy that is restructuring the global order in ways that maximize its compatibility with the values and interests of multinational corporate enterprise and reorient dominant political ideologies. See also Susan Strange, *The Retreat of the State: The Diffusion of Power in the World Economy* (New York: Cambridge University Press, 1996).

The global economic system has been institutionalized in organizations like the World Bank, the International Monetary Fund, the World Trade Organization, and the North American Free Trade Area, to name only a few. These institutions seek to impose the discipline of the market on economics that have been, it is claimed, corrupted by crony capitalism, welfare-state social policy, and other autarchic tendencies. Accordingly, the mission of institutional messengers of globalized capitalism is to dismantle barriers to the free flow of populations, commerce, information, and especially capital—all in the service of economic growth and industrial development. To an extent hardly foreseeable ten or fifteen years ago, this venture has been successful.

62. William Connolly, *Identity/Difference* (Ithaca: Cornell University Press, 1991), 24.

63. Timothy Kaufman-Osborn, *From Noose to Needle: Capital Punishment and the Late Liberal State* (Ann Arbor: University of Michigan Press, 2002), 208.

64. Foucault, *The History of Sexuality*, 88–89.

65. Nikolas Rose, *Powers of Freedom* (Cambridge: Cambridge University Press), 1999, 18.

66. Kaufman-Osborn, *From Noose to Needle*, 189.

67. Rose, *Powers of Freedom*, 162.

68. Ibid., 171, 172.

69. See, for example, Sarat, *When the State Kills: Capital Punishment and the American Condition.*

70. Robert Cover, "Violence and the Word," 95 *Yale Law Journal* (1986), 1601. See also Austin Sarat, ed., *Pain, Death, and the Law* (Ann Arbor: University of Michigan Press, 2001).

71. For important discussions and illustrations of this prerogative, see Natalie Zemon Davis, *Fiction in the Archives: Pardon Tales and Their Tellers in Sixteenth-Century France* (Stanford: Stanford University Press, 1987); and Douglas Hay, "Property, Authority, and the Criminal Law," in *Albion's Fatal Tree: Crime and Society in Eighteenth-Century England*, Douglas Hay et al., eds. (New York: Pantheon Books, 1975).

72. Executive clemency is, of course, not coterminous with "sparing life." Pardons are used for the most mundane of crimes. Also it could be argued that the potential to "spare life" is not exclusively reserved to executive clemency: A jury that declines to impose capital punishment when it has the choice to do so could equally be considered sparing life—as indeed could an appeals court that overturns a death sentence. "As a matter of fact," James Barnett contends, "many others exercise virtually the same function—judges, juries, prosecuting attorneys, informers, police officers, victims of the offense." See James Barnett, "The Grounds of Pardon," 17 *Journal of the American Institute of Criminal Law and Criminology* (1927), 490.

73. *Clemency for Battered Women in Michigan: A Manual for Attorneys, Law Students and Social Workers,* at http://www.umich.edu/~clemency/clemency_manual/manual_chapter02.html.

74. See Robert Weisberg, "Apology, Legislation, and Mercy," 82 *North Carolina Law Review* (2004), 1415, 1421.

75. William Blackstone, *Commentaries on the Laws of England: A Facsimile of the First Edition of 1765–1769* (Chicago: University of Chicago Press, 1979), 4:389. As Montesquieu notes, "So many are the advantages which monarchs gain by clemency, so greatly does it raise their fame, and endear them of their subjects, that it is generally happy for them to have an opportunity of displaying it." See Baron de Charles de Secondat Montesquieu, *The Spirit of the Laws* [1748]. Anne M. Cohler et al., eds. and trans. (Cambridge: Cambridge University Press, 1989), bk. 6: 21.

76. Typical are the claims of Daniel Markel. "Note, then," Markel argues, "what mercy is not: it is not forgiveness. The two are distinct. Mercy is an act, whereas forgiveness is an attitude. That is, mercy contains a publicly observable aspect that is distinct from forgiveness: mercy could be granted without any change in the grantor's feeling toward the wrongdoer. Conversely, as Murphy has noted, one can forgive someone, even oneself, but still wish for him to experience the full extent of punishment. Forgiveness needs no observable action." Daniel Markel, "Against Mercy," 88 *Minnesota Law Review* (2004), 1421, 1439. Also Jeffrie Murphy and Jean Hampton, *Forgiveness and Mercy* (Cambridge: Cambridge University Press, 1988). Also Alwynne Smart, "Mercy," in *The Philosophy of Punishment*, ed. H. B. Acton (New York: St. Martin's Press, 1969), 212–27.

77. See Markel, "Against Mercy," and Linda Helyar Meyer, Grace and Justice, PhD dissertation, Jurisprudence and Social Policy, University of California, Berkeley, 1991.

78. For example, Claudia Card, "On Mercy," *Philosophy Review* 43 (1972), 182.

79. Robert Misner, "A Strategy for Mercy," 41 *William and Mary Law Review* (2000), 1303, 1322. Weisberg urges scholars to consider "what mercy actually does." He answers, "it can vacate a conviction, release a person from prison, protect the convicted from the collateral consequences of conviction, or spare the condemned from death." See Weisberg, "Apology, Legislation, and Mercy," 1416. Also Stephen Garvey, "Is It Wrong to Commute Death Row? Retribution, Atonement, and Mercy," 82 *North Carolina Law Review* (2004), 1319.

80. I am grateful to Patricia Ewick for pointing this out and sharing this formulation.

81. See J. H. Baker, *An Introduction to English Legal History* (London: Butterworths: 1990), 122–28.

82. Breslin and Howley argue that in clemency cases executives "are beholden to no particular rules, precedents or institutions. . . . they stand alone in their deliberations." See Beau Breslin and John J. P. Howley, "Defending the Politics of Clemency," 81 *Oregon Law Review* (2002), 231, 239. As Rapaport puts it, "Broad discretionary authority has survived . . . only in the office of the prosecutor and in the plenary power of executives in clemency decisions; unlike prosecutors, the discretion of executives in clemency is constitutionally insulated from

legislative reform and judicial review." Elizabeth Rapaport, "Staying Alive: Executive Clemency, Equal Protection, and the Politics of Gender in Women's Capital Cases," 4 *Buffalo Criminal Law Review* (2001), 967, 974–75. Also, Abramowitz and Paget, "Executive Clemency in Capital Cases," 177.

83. John Locke, *Second Treatise on Civil Government*, C. B. Macpherson, ed. (Indianapolis, IN: Hackett Publishing, 1980), sections 159–60.

84. John Harrison, "Pardon as Prerogative," 13 *Federal Sentencing Reporter* (2000–2001), 147. In his view "[Pardons] should be like lightning bolts . . . because their incidence . . . cannot be accounted for in advance by the imperfect approximations on which legal rules are based." Harrison, "Pardon as Prerogative," 148.

85. William Miller, "Clint Eastwood and Equity: Popular Culture's Theory of Revenge," in *Law in the Domains of Culture*, Austin Sarat and Thomas R. Kearns, eds. (Ann Arbor: University of Michigan Press, 1998), p. 175.

86. Blackstone, *Commentaries on the Laws of England*, 4:389, 390.

87. Robert Salladay, "Clemency: Slim Chance These Days," *San Francisco Examiner* (November 29, 1998), http://www.sfgate.com/cgi-bin/article.cgi%3Ff=/examiner/archive/1998/11/29/NEWS8622.dtl&type=printable.

88. Alan Berlow, "The Texas Clemency Memos," *Atlantic Monthly* (July/August 2003), http://www.theatlantic.com/issues/2003/07/berlow.htm.

89. Cited in "Clemency Becoming Rare as Executions Increase," *Corrections Digest* (July 8, 1987), 2.

90. Two recent clemency decisions, one commuting a death sentence to life in prison and one denying a commutation, give further evidence of the currency of these views. In the former, Indiana governor Joe Kernan commuted the sentence of Michael Daniels. In a statement issued at the time he made his decision, the governor explained,

> Clemency may be appropriate when there is credible evidence that would indicate a miscarriage of justice—evidence that was never presented to the courts or that can no longer be presented to the courts. Clemency also may be appropriate when there is a defect in

> the judicial process that would erode our confidence in integrity of those proceedings. Daniels's case presents these circumstances.

See "Grant of Commutation for Michael Daniels," *Indianapolis Star* (January 7, 2005), http://www.indystar.com/images/graphics/2005/01/0107_kernan_statement.pdf. In the latter, California governor Arnold Schwarzenegger refused to grant clemency to Donald Beardslee. Schwarzenegger said, "The state and federal courts have affirmed his conviction and death sentence, and nothing in his petition or the record of his case convinces me that he did not understand the gravity of his actions or that these heinous murders were wrong." See "California Executes First Inmate in Three Years," *New York Times* (January 19, 2005), http://www.nytimes.com/reuters/news/news_crime-executioncalifornia.html.

These views have a long history, reaching back at least to the early nineteenth century. However, "the actual record of gubernatorial pardons . . . (in that period) shows that in practice the pardon process was not so cut and dried." See Richard Brown, *The Hanging of Ephraim Walker: A Story of Rape, Incest, and Justice in Early America* (Cambridge, MA: Harvard University Press, 2003), 191.

91. See Breslin and Howley, "Defending the Politics of Clemency," 239. Also, Alyson Dinsmore, "Clemency in Capital Cases: The Need to Ensure Meaningful Review," 49 *UCLA Law Review* (2202), 1825, 1842; and Daniel Kobil, "Chance and the Constitution in Capital Clemency Cases," 28 *Capital University Law Review* (2002), 567, 572. Love notes a similar reluctance at the federal level. Beginning with the Reagan Administration, she says, "the number of pardons each year began to drop off." Margaret Colgate Love, "Fear of Forgiving: Rule and Discretion in the Theory and Practice of Pardoning," *Federal Sentencing Reporter* 13 (2000–2001), 125, 126. Rita Radostitz, codirector of the Capital Punishment Clinic at the University of Texas and an attorney for Henry Lee Lucas, who was granted clemency in Texas, says about clemency: "I think that clearly a miscarriage of justice should be raised, but in other cases, mercy could also come into play. . . . That's what clemency has historically been about—mercy." Quoted in Salladay, "Clemency: Slim Chance These Days."

It may be, however, that clemency is less about mercy today than it has been in the past, in part because of substantial changes that have taken place in the death penalty system since 1972, changes that have resulted in juries being "presented with the same evidence that is designed to evoke a merciful response, in the form of mitigating factors, that will be reviewed later by the clemency authority. . . . In the pre-*Furman* era, replete with unitary guilt-sentencing trials and the consequent limitations on presenting reasons not to sentence an offender to death (not to mention the jurisdictions that retained the practice of mandatory capital punishment), the sentencer presumably was denied the chance even to consider factors that would suggest mercy. Thus, pre-*Furman*, the clemency authority could be considered as the first one to be fully apprised of mitigating or merciful factors relevant to a sentence of death. In the post-*Furman* era, the clemency authority (at least in cases where no new evidence is presented) essentially must define itself as "overriding" the sentencer's informed decision not to be merciful. In the pre-*Furman* era we at least could pretend that the governor was not saying that the jury got it 'wrong'—just that the jury did not have as complete information and thus was denied a fair opportunity to be merciful." Communication from James Acker to the author (December 30, 2004).

92. See Jonathan Simon, *Governing through Crime: The War on Crime and the Transformation of American Governance, 1960–2000* (New York: Oxford University Press, forthcoming). See also Joseph E. Kennedy, "Monstrous Offenders and the Search for Solidarity through Modern Punishment," 51 *Hastings Law Journal* (2000), 829, 832. Kennedy argues, "The breadth and depth of the political consensus behind . . . increases in the severity of criminal sentences may be without parallel in contemporary political history."

93. See Simon, *Governing through Crime*, chapter 5.

94. This quotation is taken from Jonathan Simon's review of a proposal for this book.

95. Early in the statement he made when he issued his clemency, Ryan focused attention on problems in the death penalty system: "How many more cases of wrongful conviction have to occur before we can all agree that *the system is broken*." Governor George Ryan, "I Must Act," January 11, 2003. Speech at the Northwestern University College of Law. Ryan's speech is reprinted in appendix A.

96. See *Herrera v. Collins*, 506 U.S. (1993), 390, 412.

97. Controversies surrounding particular grants of clemency, the punishments for which clemency should be issued, and/or the proper

allocation of power between legislatures and executives are almost as old as the practice of granting clemency itself. See Elkan Abramowitz and David Paget, "Executive Clemency in Capital Cases," 39 *New York University Law Review* (1964), 136, 138–40. For a discussion of some of those controversies in England, see William Duker, "The President's Power to Pardon: A Constitutional History," 18 *William and Mary Law Review* (1977), 475, 476–97. For a case study of controversy surrounding the granting of clemency in Ohio, see Daniel Kobil, "Do the Paperwork or Die: Clemency, Ohio Style," 52 *Ohio State Law Journal* (1991), 655, 671–82. For a comparable study of the pardons in the Iran-Contra Affair, see James Jorgensen, "Federal Executive Clemency Power: The President's Prerogative to Escape Accountability," 27 *University of Richmond Law Review* (1992–93), 345. See also chapter 2 of this book.

98. This was, of course, not true of all his supporters. Thus, law professors from around the country encouraged Ryan to issue a blanket commutation. "We feel compelled to share with you our considered judgment that, in our country, the power of executive clemency is not so limited," their letter said. "To the contrary, where circumstances warrant, executive clemency should be and has in fact been used as a means to correct systemic injustice." From "An Open Letter to Governor Ryan" (December 30, 2002), http://www.law.northwestern.edu/depts/clinic/wrongful/documents/LawProfLet1.pdf. Some lawyers in Illinois agreed with this position. "We who have signed this letter are convinced that you would best serve the Illinois criminal justice system and the citizens of this State by commuting the sentences of all of the petitioners. A system of capital punishment so fundamentally flawed as ours—one that has sentenced *at least* 13 innocent persons to death cannot be permitted to inflict the ultimate punishment." From "Open letter signed by more than 650 Illinois attorneys" (November 18, 2002), http://www.law.northwestern.edu/depts/clinic/wrongful/documents/LawyerLet1.pdf.

99. Claire O'Brien, "Ryan: Life over Death: Over Protests of Victims' Families, Governor Commutes All Sentences," *Southern Illinoisan* (January 11, 2003), at http://www.stopcapitalpunishment.org/coverage/45.html.

100. Dominic Evans, "Amnesty Urges Bush 'Moral Stand' on Death Penalty," *Reuters* (January 12, 2003), at http://www.stopcapitalpunishment.org/coverage/48.html.

101. See "Illinois Governor's Blanket Pardon Spares Lives of 167 Condemned Inmates," Fox News (January 11, 2003), http://www.foxnews.com/story/0,2933,75170,00.html.

102. O'Brien, "Ryan: Life Over Death."

103. John Keilman, "Relatives of Victims Feel 'Cheated,'" *Chicago Tribune* (January 12, 2003), 1, 15.

104. Rick Pearson and Ray Long, "History—and Federal Prosecutors—Will Write Final Chapter in How Ryan Is Remembered," *Chicago Tribune* (January 13, 2003), 1, 12.

105. O'Brien, "Ryan: Life Over Death."

106. Rod Blagojevich, Ryan's successor, said, "I support the governor's decision on the moratorium. I think he is right to review all of the cases on a case-by-case basis. I think that is a moral obligation. He's been right to do that. But I disagree with his decision to provide blanket clemency. I think a blanket anything is usually wrong. There is no one-size fits all approach to this. We're talking about convicted murderers. And I just think that—that is a mistake." Don Babwin, "Illinois Governor Empties Death Row" (January 12, 2003), found at http://www.stopcapitalpunishment.org/coverage/56.html. In addition, Cook County state's attorney Richard Devine joined the attack on Ryan, saying, "All of these cases would have been best left for consideration by the courts which have the experience, the training and the wisdom to decide innocence or guilt. Instead, they were ripped away from the justice system by a man who is a pharmacist by training and a politician by trade. . . . By his actions today the governor has breached faith with the memory of the dead victims, their families and the people he was elected to serve." Robert Anthony Phillips, "Ryan Commutes All Death Sentences in Illinois," *TheDeathHouse.com* (January 11, 2003), http://www.thedeathhouse.com/deathhousenewfi_352.htm (link no longer active).

107. Editorial, *Chicago Sun-Times* (January 12, 2003), 29.

108. Sean Hamill and Kevin Lynch, "Debate Is Urged on Execution Law," *Chicago Tribune* (January 13, 2003), section 2, 1. Legislation was introduced to "require the Prisoner Review Board to review all commutations and make recommendations before a governor could exercise his power to mandate blanket clemency." See "Editorial: It Is Unconscionable that Elected Official Would Rather Restrict Clemency than Fix a System that Is Broken," *Chicago Sun Times* (January 29, 2003), 37.

109. Abdon Pallasch, "Madigan Joins Case against Clemency," *Chicago Sun-Times* (February 5, 2003), 18. A year later, the Illinois Supreme Court upheld Ryan's actions. See *People ex rel. Lisa Madigan v. Snyder*, 208 Ill. 2d (2004) 457.

110. Steve Whitworth, "Haine Enraged by Governor's Move," *The Telegraph* (Alton, IL) (January 12, 2003), at http://www.stopcapitalpunishment.org/coverage/44.html.

111. Ibid.

112. George Will, "Death Row Clemency Shows a Contempt for Democracy," *Chicago Sun-Times* (January 19, 2003), Editorial, 33. See also John O'Sullivan, "Editorial: Clemency Is Cause to Mourn Not Cheer," *Chicago Sun-Times* (January 14, 2003), 23. "Ryan," O'Sullivan claimed, "abused his power of commutation not to save innocent men, but to repeal a law passed by the Illinois legislature and supported by the voters of Illinois that he and his political allies are unable to repeal by democratic debate and electoral struggle. We might call that a miscarriage of democracy."

113. Whitworth, "Haine Enraged by Governor's Move."

114. See Patricia Goff, "Invisible Borders: Economic Liberalization and National Identity," *International Studies Quarterly* 44 (December 2000), 533. As Jacobsen notes, "Particularly striking is the fading role of a territory in defining a people (as in the nation-state), at least in the West, and the subsequent 'deterritorialization of identity.'" David Jacobson, "New Frontiers: Territory, Social Spaces, and the State," *Sociological Forum* 12 (1997), 121, 124.

115. "The borders of a settled nation-state substantially define our sense of political identity and justify a marked ethical partiality towards our fellow nationals." Michael Kenny, "Global Civil Society: A Liberal-Republican Argument," *Review of International Studies* 29 (2003), 119.

116. Margaret Montoya, "Border/ed Identities: Narrative and the Social Construction of Legal and Personal Identities," in *Crossing Boundaries: Traditions and Transformations in Law and Society Research*, Austin Sarat, Marianne Constable, David Engel, Valerie Hans, and Susan Lawrence, eds. (Evanston: Northwestern University Press, 1998), 131.

117. For a discussion of the uncertainty and anxiety as well as possibility and opportunity found in borderlands, see Thomas W. Wilson,

ed. *Border Identities: Nation and State at International Borders* (Cambridge: Cambridge Press, 1998).

Chapter 2
Capital Clemency in the Twentieth Century: Putting Illinois in Context

At this point I again want to acknowledge Penelope Van Tuyl whose work provided much of the substance of this chapter.

1. See "Presidential Pardons," at http://jurist.law.pitt.edu/pardons5a.htm.

2. "By the Numbers: Huckabee's Clemency Record," KFSM News (July 28, 2004), http://www.kfsm.com/global/story.asp?s=2102254&ClientType=Printable. Perhaps not surprisingly, Huckabee's pardon practices have turned out to be controversial. As one commentator reports, "Huckabee's record is so high that Arkansas families who have been victims of serious crimes and fear that the offender might be quickly turned loose insist that prosecuting attorneys try the offender for the maximum punishment." Bob McCord, "Huckabee's Pardons," *Arkansas-Times* (July 29, 2004), http://www.arktimes.com/mccord/072904mccord.html.

3. "Through the 1970s, Democratic governors oversaw the handing out of 1,527 pardons, including a high of 477 pardons in 1970 under Gov. Francis W. Sargent. Through the 1990s, Republican governors pardoned just 90 people, a 95 percent drop from two decades earlier." See Jason B. Grosky, "Critics: Pardons Are Too Political," *Eagle-Tribune* (October 13, 2002), http://www.eagletribune.com/news/stories/20021013/LN_001.htm.

4. See "Pardon Inquiry Moves Forward," ABC News (February 15, 2001), http://abcnews.go.com/sections/politics/DailyNews/clinton_pardon010215.html.

5. See Joe Conason, "The Bush Pardons," *Salon* (February 27, 2001), http://dir.salon.com/news/col/cona/2001/02/27/pardons/index.html. Conason explains,

> The widely and justly criticized pardons of Caspar Weinberger and other Iran-Contra defendants by George Herbert Walker Bush

should have been just the beginning of that story. Yet, for reasons best known to the incorruptible watchdogs of the Washington press corps, Poppy's self-interested mercy upon Weinberger instigated no searching examination of the other pardons granted by the departing president. Indeed, the final dozen pardons given by Bush—including the unexplained release of a Pakistani heroin trafficker—received virtually no coverage at all.

The elder Bush delivered a few highly questionable pardons well before his last days in office. The very first of his presidency went to Armand Hammer, the legendary oilman best known for his relationships with Soviet leaders dating back to Lenin. In an investigation that grew out of Watergate, Hammer had pleaded guilty in 1975 to laundering $54,000 in illicit contributions to Nixon's reelection war chest. By the summer of 1989, when Bush gave Hammer what he wanted, the aging chief of Occidental Petroleum had been pestering government officials on his own behalf for several years.

6. See Steve Neal, "Editorial: Governor Is Out of Control," *Chicago Sun-Times* (October 22, 2002), 27.

7. In an effort to track the decline of capital clemency, I tried to identify every instance of its use from 1900 to 2004. Because no systematic compilation of clemency data prior to 1972 exists, this required gathering information from various published and unpublished sources and doing research state by state. The results of this effort are reported in appendix B. They are, I believe, more comprehensive than any currently available data. Nonetheless, given the difficulty of gathering this information, I cannot claim that they are complete and error free.

However, the pattern revealed by my data is similar to what others have found. Thus, using different figures, Michael Heise reaches a similar conclusion about the recent history of capital clemency. He notes that "after 1984, the ratio of successful clemency petitions to executions dropped dramatically. Before 1984, the number of successful clemency petitions was slightly more than three times greater than the number of executions (105 to 32). After 1984, however, the ratio reversed: The number of executions (556) was seven times larger than the number of removals through clemency." See Michael Heise, "Mercy by the Numbers: An Empirical Analysis of Clemency and Its

Structure," 89 *Virginia Law Review* (2003), 239, 309. For another source of data on capital clemency, see "Executive Clemency Process and Execution Warrant Procedure In Death Penalty Cases," *National Coalition to Abolish the Death Penalty* (1993, with updates by the Death Penalty Information Center), at http://www.deathpenaltyinfo.org/article.php?did=126&scid=13#news.

Whatever source one uses, it is clear that as Radelet and Zsembik put it, "clemency in a capital case is extremely rare." See Michael Radelet and Barbara Zsembik, "Executive Clemency in Post-*Furman* Capital Cases," 27 *University of Richmond Law Review* (1992–93), 289, 304.

8. Susan Martin, "Commutation of Prison Sentences: Practice, Promise, and Limitation," *Crime and Delinquency* 4 (1983), 593, 596.

9. Looking at 1998, for example, reveals that sixty-eight people were executed. Only one death row inmate was granted clemency, a Texas man who "confessed" to six hundred murders but was found to be in Florida during the one killing for which he received a death sentence. See appendix B.

10. As Banner notes, "For centuries governors commuted death sentences in significant numbers. That pattern continued for the first two-thirds of the twentieth century. Florida commuted nearly a quarter of its death sentences between 1924 and 1966; North Carolina commuted more than a third between 1909 and 1954. Those figures dropped close to zero under new sentencing schemes." See Stuart Banner, *The Death Penalty: An American History* (Cambridge, MA: Harvard University Press, 2002), 291–92.

11. This information was provided by James Marcus, a lawyer in the Texas Defender Service. Marcus explained that post-*Furman* Texas death penalty statutes went through some legal growing pains in the early 1980s and again in the 1990s. Following two particular court rulings that mandated statutory changes, sizeable waves of death row inmates appealed their convictions and were resentenced to terms of years. Excluding cases such as these, where commutation was granted for the sake of judicial expediency, Marcus said that exactly two death row inmates were granted executive clemency in Texas between 1974 and 2004—Henry Lee Lucas in 1998 by Governor Bush, and Robert Smith in 2004 by Governor Perry. For a discussion of the situation in Texas and elsewhere, see Robert Salladay, "Clemency: Slim Chance These Days," *San Francisco Examiner* (November 29, 1998),

http://www.sfgate.com/cgi-bin/article.cgi%3Ff=/examiner/archive/1998/11/29/NEWS8622.dtl&type=printable. See Bruce Ledewitz and Scott Staples, "The Role of Executive Clemency in Modern Death Penalty Cases," 27 *University of Richmond Law Review* (1993), 227. So routine are denials of clemency in Texas that its Board of Pardon and Parole does not bother to meet. Members vote by fax, phone, or letter. A defendant never gets an opportunity to plead his or her case with them personally. And, even when the Board urges commutation, the climate in Texas is so hostile to clemency that the governor may not follow its recommendation. Thus,

> on the eve of Kelsey Patterson's scheduled execution in Texas, the state's Board of Pardons and Paroles voted 5-1 to recommend that Governor Rick Perry commute Patterson's death sentence to life in prison. In its rare recommendation for clemency, the Board noted that if Governor Perry refuses to grant clemency, Patterson, a mentally ill man who is scheduled to be executed on Tuesday, May 18th, should receive a 120-day reprieve. The Board's actions mark the first time in more than two decades that members have recommended a commutation to the governor at such a late state in a condemned inmate's case. Patterson has been diagnosed as a paranoid schizophrenic who, in the years leading up to his capital murder conviction, was ruled mentally incompetent to stand trial on unrelated charges. However, despite the recommendation of the Pardons and Paroles Board, Governor Perry denied the clemency request, and Patterson was executed on May 18, 2004.

(See Death Penalty Information Center, "Clemency News and Developments," http://www.deathpenaltyinfo.org/article.php?scid= 13&did= 850.)

12. Washington State Office of the Attorney General, *Reprieves, Pardons and Commutations in Death Penalty Cases*, http://www.atg.wa.gov/deathpenalty/pardons.shtml.

13. See appendix B.

14. See James Acker and Charles Lanier, "May God—or the Governor—Have Mercy: Executive Clemency and Executions in Modern Death-Penalty Systems," 36 *Criminal Law Bulletin* (2000), 200.

15. Samuel Gross and Phoebe Ellsworth, "Second Thoughts: Americans' Views of the Death Penalty at the Turn of the Century," in *Be-*

yond Repair? America's Death Penalty (Durham: Duke University Press, 2003), 7, 13.

16. Quoted in Salladay, "Clemency: Slim Chance These Days." As Fiskesjo puts it, "In light of 'domestic' opinion, it is very often not the decision to pardon but the decision not to pardon that best furthers the political standing of the power-holder" See Magnus Fiskesjo, *The Thanksgiving Turkey Pardon, The Death of Teddy's Bear, and the Sovereign Exception of Guantanamo* (Chicago: Prickly Paradigm Press, 2003), 46.

17. As Cobb argues, "Political considerations have figured prominently in the unwillingness of many governors to be merciful. The popularity of the death penalty suggests to these officials that the safest course of action is to avoid the exercise of their clemency powers." See Paul Cobb, "Reviving Mercy in the Structure of Capital Punishment," 99 *Yale Law Journal* (1989), 389, 394.

This is not to say that capital clemency has completely disappeared. It has not. For example, in 2002, "[h]ours before Charlie Alston was scheduled to be executed in North Carolina, Governor Mike Easley commuted Alston's sentence to life without parole. Although Easley did not give a specific reason for the reprieve, he stated, 'After long and careful consideration of all the facts and circumstances of this case in its entirety, I conclude that the appropriate sentence for the defendant is life in prison without parole.' Alston's commutation marks the 2nd time Easley has granted clemency, and the 5th time a North Carolina governor has done so since 1976. During that same time, 47 death row inmates nationally have had their sentences commuted for humanitarian reasons." See Death Penalty Information Center, "Clemency News and Developments."

In Oklahoma, Governor Brad Henry recently granted a request for clemency in the case of Osvaldo Torres, a Mexican foreign national on Oklahoma's death row, in part because of a recent International Court of Justice decision ordering the United States to review the cases of 51 Mexican foreign nationals because they were denied their right to seek consular assistance following their arrest. Henry's

> decision to commute Torres' sentence to life in prison without parole marks the first time that the Governor has granted clemency to an individual on death row. In his statement, Henry said the International Court of Justice ruling is binding on U.S. courts, and that the U.S. State Department had contacted his office to urge

that he give careful consideration to the fact that the U.S. signed the 1963 Vienna Convention on Consular Relations, which ensures access to consular assistance for foreign nationals who are arrested. "The treaty is also important to protecting the rights of American citizens abroad," Henry noted. (Death Penalty Information Center, "Clemency News and Developments.")

18. Terry Sanford, "On Executive Clemency," in *Messages, Addresses and Public Papers of Governor Terry Sanford, 1961–1965*, at 552 (1966).

19. Craigg Hines, "A Heartening Rain as We Await the Flood," *Houston Chronicle.com* (January 14, 2003), http://www.chron.com/content/Archives.

20. Cruce's action and his reasoning were the subject of scathing criticism by Oklahoma's Court of Criminal Appeals. See *Henry v. State* 10 Okla. Crim. (1913), 369, 385. For a discussion of this case, see chapter 3 of this book.

21. Hines, "A Heartening Rain." For a more complete discussion of his views, see Winthrop Rockefeller. "Executive Clemency and the Death Penalty," 21 *Catholic University Law Review* (1971), 94.

22. "Five, Lives Spared, Hail Anaya's Move," *New York Times* (November 28, 1986), A18.

23. Hines, "A Heartening Rain."

24. I chose these governors because of their embrace of a broad view of capital clemency. They were not chosen randomly. They come from states deep in the "death belt," one southern, one a border state, and one from the southwest. While others could have been chosen, and indeed I discuss two others—Governors Brown of California and DiSalle of Ohio—in chapter 6, these three give a rich flavor of the uses and political risks associated with capital clemency in the twentieth century.

25. Obren Casey, "Oklahoma's Governor Cruce Abolished Death Penalty," Oklahoma Historical Society Archive. 95.51, Box 2, File 4.

26. Bobby Dean Smith, "Lee Cruce: Governor of Oklahoma, 1911–1915." In *Oklahoma's Governors, 1907–1929: Turbulent Politics*. Leroy H. Fischer, ed. (Oklahoma Historical Society. Oklahoma City, 1981).

27. Lee Cruce, "State of the State Address" (January 8, 1913), at http://edl.ok.us/oar/governors/addresses/cruce1913.pdf.

28. Joe O'Brien, "He 'Killed' Oklahoma's Death Penalty," *Daily Oklahoman* (July 31, 1927), D1.

29. Ibid.

30. Ibid.

31. Smith, "Lee Cruce: Governor of Oklahoma, 1911–1915."

32. Casey, "Oklahoma's Governor Cruce Abolished Death Penalty."

33. "Governor Criticized for Commuting Sentence." *Harlan's* (January 4, 1913). Oklahoma Historical Society Archives, 95.51, Box 3, Filed 6.

34. Casey, "Oklahoma's Governor Cruce Abolished Death Penalty." A few years later Oklahoma would indeed witness one of this nation's worst race riots, the Tulsa riot in 1921. See James Langton, "Mass Graves Hold the Secrets of American Race Massacre" (March 29, 1999), http://www.ritesofpassage.org/df99-articles/mass.htm.

35. Casey, "Oklahoma's Governor Cruce Abolished Death Penalty." In the first twenty-two years after the Oklahoma Territory was opened, citizens lynched eighty-five black men, far more than Texas's second place standing with forty during the same period.

36. Ibid.

37. Cruce, "State of the State Address."

38. Ibid.

39. Ibid.

40. O'Brien, "He 'Killed' Oklahoma's Death Penalty."

41. Ibid.

42. Cruce, "State of the State Address."

43. O'Brien, "He 'Killed' Oklahoma's Death Penalty."

44. Ibid.

45. "No Holiday for Governor Cruce: Finds Convicts Pardoned and Contracts Signed in His Absence." *New York Times* (August 4, 1913), 1.

46. O'Brien, "He 'Killed' Oklahoma's Death Penalty."

47. Ibid.

48. "Governor Criticized for Commuting Sentence."

49. Leroy H. Fischer, *Oklahoma's Governors, 1907–1929: Turbulent Politics*. Oklahoma Historical Society (Oklahoma City, OK, 1981).

50. Editorial. "The Governor's Message." *Hollis Post-Herald* (Hollis, OK) (December 19, 1912).

51. "Governor Criticized for Commuting Sentence."

52. Ibid.

53. Casey, "Oklahoma's Governor Cruce Abolished Death Penalty."

54. Ibid.

55. O'Brien. "He 'Killed' Oklahoma's Death Penalty."

56. "Fifteen Death Sentences Commuted by Winthrop Rockefeller: Legislators Are Dismayed." *Arkansas Gazette* (December 30, 1970), 3A.

57. "Arkansas Spares All on Death Row." *New York Times* (December 30, 1970), A9.

58. The Supreme Court did not rule on capital punishment in 1968, and more than six hundred men on death row nationwide sat in limbo four more years before *Furman v. Georgia* spared their lives.

59. Editorial. "Mr. Rockefeller and the Death Sentences." *Arkansas Gazette* (December 27, 1970), 3D.

60. Ibid.

61. The ratio of Democrats to Republicans was 97 to 3 during that period.

62. Letter from Rev. J. F. Cooley to Winthrop Rockefeller (November 17, 1970). Winthrop Rockefeller Papers, Record Group III, Box 443, Folder 2.

63. Editorial. "Mr. Rockefeller and the Death Sentences."

64. Ernest Dumas, "Winthrop Rockefeller Will Discuss His Plans Today on Fifteen Death Terms." *Arkansas Gazette* (December 23, 1970), 1A.

65. "Winthrop Rockefeller Selects Five to Offer Advice on Fifteen Death Terms." *Arkansas Gazette* (December 24, 1970), 3D.

66. Ernest Dumas, "What a Governor May Do About Fifteen on Death Row." *Arkansas Gazette* (December 27, 1970), 3D.

67. Ibid.

68. "Arkansas Spares All on Death Row."

69. Dumas, "Fifteen Death Sentences Commuted by Winthrop Rockefeller."

70. Ibid., "Winthrop Rockefeller Will Discuss His Plans Today on Fifteen Death Terms."

71. "Fifteen Death Sentences Commuted by Winthrop Rockefeller: Legislators Are Dismayed." *Arkansas Gazette* (December 30, 1970), 3A.

72. Editorial. "Mr. Rockefeller and the Death Sentences." Editorial. "Mr. Rockefeller's Act of Conscience." *Arkansas Gazette* (December 31, 1970), 6A.

73. Editorial. *Jacksonville Daily News* (December 30, 1970), 8.

74. Memo, count of letters for and against governor's commutations (January 21, 1971), Winthrop Rockefeller Papers, Record Group III, Box 646, Folder 1.

75. "Fifteen Death Sentences Commuted by Winthrop Rockefeller: Legislators Are Dismayed."

76. "Arkansas Spares All on Death Row."

77. "Fifteen Death Sentences Commuted by Winthrop Rockefeller: Legislators Are Dismayed."

78. "Arkansas Spares All on Death Row."

79. Letter from Ed Bethune to Winthrop Rockefeller (December 30, 1970), Winthrop Rockefeller Papers, Record Group III, Box 339, Folder 4.

80. Ray Randell, letter to the Editor of the *Arkansas Gazette* (January 2, 1971), 3D.

81. "Fifteen Death Sentences Commuted by Winthrop Rockefeller: Legislators Are Dismayed."

82. Wayne Jordan, "Prosecutors Admit Fifteen Commutations Legal: Hint Law Should Be Changed." *Arkansas Gazette* (December 31, 1970), 1A. While George Ryan would face criticism for dragging the families of victims through a long and emotionally draining month of hearings in order to make his decision, Rockefeller did not include the voices of the victims' families in his clemency deliberation at all.

83. Mrs. Ralph Thomas, letter to the Editor of the *Arkansas Gazette* (January 2, 1971), 3D.

84. Jordan, "Prosecutors Admit Fifteen Commutations Legal."

85. "Fifteen Death Sentences Commuted by Winthrop Rockefeller: Legislators Are Dismayed."

86. Mike Harmon, letter to the Editor of the *Arkansas Gazette* (January 2, 1971), 3D.

87. "Fifteen Death Sentences Commuted by Winthrop Rockefeller: Legislators Are Dismayed."

88. Jordan, "Prosecutors Admit Fifteen Commutations Legal: Hint Law Should Be Changed."

89. "Winthrop Rockefeller Tours Prisons, Is Thanked." *Arkansas Gazette* (January 2, 1971).

90. Winthrop Rockefeller, "Executive Clemency and the Death Penalty." 21 *Catholic University Law Review* (1971), 97.

91. Death Penalty Information Center. Found at www.deathpenaltyinfo.org.

92. "Statement by Governor Toney Anaya on Crime and Capital Punishment" (Santa Fe, New Mexico. November 26, 1986).

93. Richard E. Meyer, "New Mexico Death Sentences Commuted." *Los Angeles Times* (November 27, 1986), A1.

94. Ibid.

95. Toney Anaya, "Clemency and Pardons Symposium: Statement by Toney Anaya on Capital Punishment." 27 *University of Richmond Law Review* (1992), 177.

96. Meyer, "New Mexico Death Sentences Commuted."

97. Ibid.

98. "Statement by Governor Toney Anaya on Crime and Capital Punishment."

99. Robert Reinhold, "Outgoing Governor in New Mexico Bars the Execution of Five." *New York Times* (November 27, 1986), A1.

100. David Staats, "Anaya Cuts Death Sentences to Life. Groups Praise Move; Carruthers Denounces 'Violation of Duty.'" *Albuquerque Journal* (November 27, 1986), A1.

101. Kate Nelson, "What Can One Man Do? Be Haunted by the Death Penalty." *Albuquerque Tribune* (February 15, 2003), at http://www.stopcapitalpunishment.org/coverage/170.html.

102. Meyer, "New Mexico Death Sentences Commuted."

103. "Statement by Governor Toney Anaya on Crime and Capital Punishment."

104. Ibid.

105. Anaya, "Clemency and Pardons Symposium: Statement by Toney Anaya on Capital Punishment."

106. Ibid.

107. "Statement by Governor Toney Anaya on Crime and Capital Punishment."

108. Memoranda and individual correspondence received by the governor, press clippings. Papers of Toney Anaya, Center for Southwest Research, Collection 575, Box 17, Folders 14, 16–18.

109. Meyer, "New Mexico Death Sentences Commuted," A22.

110. Anaya, "Clemency and Pardons Symposium: Statement by Toney Anaya on Capital Punishment."

111. Editorial. "Anaya's Meddling Has Gone Too Far." *The New Mexican* (December 7, 1986), A4.

112. David Staats,"Attorney General Cites Way to Fight Commutation." *Albuquerque Journal* (November 28, 1986), A1.

113. David Staats, "High Court Turns Back District Attorney's Appeal." *Albuquerque Journal* (December 23, 1986), A3.

114. Susan Hansen, "Governor's 'Beliefs' Stop Executions." *National Catholic Reporter* (December 12, 1986), A1.

115. Nelson, "What Can One Man Do? Be Haunted by the Death Penalty."

116. Papers of Toney Anaya, Center for Southwest Research, Collection 575, Box 17, Folder 14.

117. Anaya, "Clemency and Pardons Symposium: Statement by Toney Anaya on Capital Punishment."

118. Quoted in Grosky, "Critics: Pardons Are Too Political."

Chapter 3
The Jurisprudence of Clemency: What Place for Mercy?

1. Steve Whitworth, "Haine Enraged by Governor's Move," *The Telegraph* (Alton, IL) (January 12, 2003), http://www.stopcapital punishment.org/coverage/44.html.

2. Coleen Klasmeier, "Towards a New Understanding of Capital Clemency and Procedural Due Process," 75 *Boston University Law Review* (1995), 1507.

3. Paul Ricouer, *The Just*, David Pellauer, trans. (Chicago: University of Chicago Press, 1995), 144. As Hugo Adam Bedau puts it, "Clemency decisions—even in death penalty cases—are standardless in procedure, discretionary in exercise, and unreviewable in result." See Hugo Adam Bedau, "The Decline of Executive Clemency in Capital Cases," 8 *New York University Review of Law and Social Change* (1990–91), 252, 255.

4. Henry Weihofen, "Pardon as an Extraordinary Remedy," 12 *Rocky Mountain Law Review* (1940), 112, 114. See also Victoria

Palacios, "Faith in Fantasy: The Supreme Court's Reliance on Commutation to Ensure Justice in Death Penalty Cases," 49 *Vanderbilt Law Review* (1996), 311, 331–32. Palacios says that clemency "operates in derogation of the law. It is the antithesis of the rule of law because it is called upon when legal rules have failed to do justice. It is inherently paradoxical because it enhances justice in general by overriding the justice system in a specific case." As the government of Mexico recently contended in an argument before the International Court of Justice, in the United States, "clemency review is standardless, secretive, and immune from judicial oversight." See Memorial of Mexico (June 20, 2003), submitted in the *Case concerning Avena and Other Mexican Nationals, Mexico v. United States of America*, at http://www.icj-cij.org/icjwww/idocket/imus/imusframe.htm.

5. Peter Fitzpatrick, "Life, Death, and the Law—and Why Capital Punishment Is Legally Insupportable," 47 *Cleveland State Law Review* (1999), 483, 484, 486, 487.

6. U.S. Department of Justice, 3 *Attorney General's Survey of Release Procedures* (1939), 209, 295.

7. Kobil calls this "the enduring paradoxical nature of clemency." See Daniel Kobil, "Chance and the Constitution in Capital Clemency Cases," 28 *Capital University Law Review* (2002), 567, 569.

8. Giorgio Agamben, *Homo Sacer: Sovereign Power and Bare Life*, Daniel Heller-Roazen, trans. (Stanford: Stanford University Press, 1998).

9. Carl Schmitt, *Political Theology: Four Chapters on the Concept of Sovereignty*, 2nd ed., George Schwab trans. (Cambridge, MA: MIT Press, [1932] 1985), 5.

10. For a different view, see Bruce Ackerman, "The Emergency Constitution," 113 *Yale Law Journal* (2004), 1029.

11. Schmitt, *Political Theology*, 13.

12. Writing about Carl Schmitt's conception of sovereignty Kahn suggests that Schmitt's opposition of law to sovereignty is too stark. In a constitutional democracy, Kahn argues,"The sovereign power is not just at the border of law, but deep within the law as well." See Paul Kahn, "The Question of Sovereignty," 40 *Stanford Journal of International Law* (2004), 263.

13. Agamben, *Homo Sacer*, 17–18. For a discussion of Agamben's concept of the exception, see Nasser Hussain, "Thresholds: Sovereignty and the Sacred," *Law and Society Review* 34 (2000), 495, 500–501.

14. Agamben, *Homo Sacer*, 18 As Derrida puts it, "The pardon is not, it should not be normal, normative, normalizing. It should remain exceptional and extraordinary, by proof of the impossible: as if it could interrupt the ordinary course of historic temporality." See Jacques Derrida, "The Century and the Pardon," *Le Mondes des Debats*, no. 9 (December, 1999), 3; online at http://fixion.sytes.net/pardonEng.htm.

15. Andrew Norris, "Introduction: Giorgio Agamben and the Politics of the Living Dead," in *Politics, Metaphysics, and Death: Essays on Giorgio Agamben's* Homo Sacer, unpublished ms., 2003, p. 15. "Each time that the pardon is effectively exercised, it seems to suppose some sovereign power. That can be the sovereign power of a noble or strong soul, but also a power of state with uncontestable legitimacy at its disposal, the power necessary for organizing a trial, an applicable judgment or, eventually, the acquittal, amnesty, or pardon." Derrida, "The Century and the Pardon," 16. As Fiskesjo puts it, "To dream of a world without pardons is to dream of a world without sovereign power." See Magnus Fiskesjo, *The Thanksgiving Turkey Pardon, The Death of Teddy's Bear, and the Sovereign Exception of Guantanamo* (Chicago: Prickly Paradigm Press, 2003), 51.

16. Baron de Charles de Secondat Montesquieu, *The Spirit of the Laws* [1748]. Anne M. Cohler et al., eds. and trans. (Cambridge: Cambridge University Press, 1989) bk. 11, 147.

17. William Blackstone, *Commentaries on the Laws of England: A Facsimile of the First Edition of 1765–1769* (Chicago: University of Chicago Press, 1979), 4:389.

18. Derrida, "The Century and the Pardon," 5, 9.

19. Ibid., 6. Blackstone, writing about the effect of pardon on the legal and political status of its recipients, said "the effect of such pardon by the king . . . is to make the offender a new man . . . as to give him a new credit and capacity." *Commentaries*, 4, 16.

20. Derrida, "The Century and the Pardon," 6.

21. Ibid., 9. "[T]he right of grace is . . . the exception of the right, the exception of the right is situated at the summit or the foundation of the juridicio-political. In the body of the sovereign, it incarnates that which founds, sustains or raises, more highly, with the unity of the nation, the guaranty of the constitution, the conditions and the exercise of the law." Ibid., 10.

22. Clemency is of course not the only place where law recognizes such a power. Other examples of this recognition include a prosecutor's decision not to charge someone with a crime or a jury's decision not to convict.

23. Derrida, "The Century and the Pardon." See also Fiskesjo, *The Thanksgiving Turkey Pardon*, 3. Pardon, Fiskesjo says, is "a state of willed emergency where raw power roams free, no longer bound by the constraints or directions of any formal law or legislation."

24. "[T]he non-juridical dimension of forgiveness, and of the unforgivable—there where it suspends and interrupts the usual order of law—has not in fact come to inscribe itself, inscribe its interruption in law itself." See Jacques Derrida, "Part I: Forgiving," 25–26.

25. Ibid., 9. "The only inscription of forgiveness in law," Derrida says, ". . . is no doubt the right to grant clemency, the kingly right of theological-political origin that survives in modern democracies." See "Part I: Forgiving," 32.

26. Blackstone, *Commentaries*, 4:397–402.

27. James Wilson, "Executive Department," *Lectures on Law* in *The Works of James Wilson*, vol. 2, Robert McCloskey, ed. (Cambridge, MA: Harvard University Press, [1791] 1967): 442–44.

28. Joseph Story, *Commentaries on the Constitution of the United States*, 3 vols. (Cambridge: Brown, Shattuck, 1833), section 1491.

29. James Wilson, "Executive Department," 442–44.

30. See, for example, Palacios, "Faith in Fantasy," 335–36.

31. Typical is the remark of Justice Frankfurter, who said, "It is not for this Court even remotely to enter into the domain of clemency reserved by the Constitution exclusively to the President." See *Rosenberg et al. v. United States*, 346 U.S. (1953), 322.

32. The amazing trick, as Fish defines it, is "the trick by which the law rebuilds itself in mid-air without ever touching down." See Stanley Fish, "The Law Wishes to Have a Formal Existence," in *The Fate of Law*, Austin Sarat and Thomas R. Kearns, eds. (Ann Arbor: University of Michigan, 1991), 196.

33. See *United States v. Wilson*, 32 U.S. 150, 160 (1833); 159.

34. Ibid., 160. As we will see below, many have taken issue with the conception of clemency as grace. For example, Winthrop Rockefeller says that this view is "totally wrong. In a civilized society such as ours, executive clemency provides the state with a final deliberative

opportunity to reassess the moral and legal propriety of the awful penalty which it intends to inflict." Winthrop Rockefeller, "Executive Clemency and the Death Penalty," 21 *Catholic University Law Review* (1971), 94, 95.

35. Blackstone *Commentaries on the Laws of England*, 4:397–402.

36. *United States v. Wilson*, 160–161. Similarly, the Supreme Court of Virginia, writing in 1872, said that the validity of a pardon depends on its "acceptance." "It may be rejected," the court held, "and if rejected, there is no power to force it upon him." See *Lee v. Murphy*, 63 Va. (1872) 789, 798.

37. On the force of law, see Jacques Derrida, "Force of Law: The Mystical Foundation of Authority," 11 *Cardozo Law Review* (1990), 919.

38. In the words of contrary authority, "For it is the king's will that he shall not be [hanged], and the king has an interest in the life of his subject." See *United States v. Wilson*, 162, 163.

39. For discussions of such judicial deference, see Daniel Kobil, "The Quality of Mercy Strained: Wresting the Pardoning Power from the King," 69 *Texas Law Review* (1991), 569, 595–604; and Beau Breslin and John J. P. Howley, "Defending the Politics of Clemency," 81 *Oregon Law Review* (2002), 231, 240–42.

40. *Ex Parte Wells*, 59 U.S. (1856) 307.

41. For a discussion of their constitutional roots as well as a qualified defense of conditional pardons, see Harold Krent, "Conditioning the President's Conditional Pardon Power," 89 *California Law Review* (2001), 1665, 1719–21.

42. *Ex Parte Wells*, 309–310.

43. Ibid., 310. Embracing Wayne's view of the distinction between clemency and forgiveness, former Ohio governor Richard Celeste explained his commutation of eight death sentences by saying that while he spared the lives of those whose sentences were changed to life in prison, he "didn't forgive them. I did not forgive them." See "Celeste at Ease with Commutations," *Cleveland Plain Dealer* (January 5, 1997), National, 12A. Or, as Moore notes, "Forgiveness and pardon are logically independent. . . . A pardon is an act one can perform only in a social or legal role. This characteristic distinguishes it from forgiveness and mercy, which are virtues that persons exhibit as individuals." See Kathleen Dean Moore, *Pardons: Justice, Mercy, and the Public Interest* (New York: Oxford University Press, 1989), 185, 193.

44. *Ex Parte Wells*, 310.

45. Emilios Christodoulidis, "The Irrationality of Merciful Legal Judgment: Exclusionary Reasoning and the Question of the Particular," 18 *Law and Philosophy* (1999), 215, 218. Christodoulidis contends that mercy demonstrates an "irreconcilability with law" in that it is "located in the space between law—law's justice—and particularity." Mercy, he says, "must provide its own criteria for judgment." Mercy, Johnson notes, allows "for the individuation between cases where the universal law cannot." Also see Clara Ann Hage Johnson, "Entitled to Clemency: Mercy in the Criminal Law," 10 *Law and Philosophy* (1991), 109, 115.

46. I think that Daniel Kobil captures the basis for this anxiety when he says, "Historically, the institution of clemency seems to have had more to do with power than justice." See Kobil, "The Quality of Mercy Strained," 583.

47. *Ex Parte Garland*, 71 U.S. (1866), 333, 336, 376.

48. Ibid., 371. See also *Armstrong v. United States*, 80 U.S. (1872) 154, 155–56 (upholding the validity of Andrew Johnson's proclamation of pardon and amnesty of December 25, 1868) and *United States v. Klein*, 80 U.S. (1872), 128, 142 (upholding the president's power to "annex to his offer of pardon any conditions and qualifications he should see fit").

49. *Ex Parte Garland*, 380–81. In Fields's words,

> A pardon reaches both the punishment prescribed for the offence and the guilt of the offender; and when the pardon is full, it releases the punishment and blots out of existence the guilt, so that in the eye of the law the offender is as innocent as if he had never committed the offence. If granted before conviction, it prevents any of the penalties and disabilities consequent upon conviction from attaching; if granted after conviction, it removes the penalties and disabilities, and restores him to all his civil rights; it makes him, as it were, a new man, and gives him a new credit and capacity.

50. *Ex Parte Grossman*, 120–21. As Taft put it, "It is a check entrusted to the executive for special cases. To exercise it to the extent of destroying the deterrent effect of judicial punishment would be to pervert it; but whoever is to make it useful must have full discretion to ex-

ercise it." See Mortimer R. Kadish and Sanford H. Kadish, *Discretion to Disobey: A Study of Lawful Departures from Legal Rules* (Stanford: Stanford University Press, 1973).

51. *Ex Parte Grossman*, 121.

52. *Biddle v. Perovich* 274 U.S. (1927) 480, 485.

53. Ibid., 486.

54. See P. E. Digeser, "Justice, Forgiveness, Mercy, and Forgetting: The Complex Meaning of Executive Pardoning," 31 *Capital University Law Review* (2003), 161, 165. Digeser says pardon is a form of "political forgiveness . . . [that] is wholly public."

55. *Biddle v. Perovich*, 486–87.

56. On the adequacy of Holmes's reasoning, see Mark Straaer, "Limits of the Clemency Power on Pardons, Retributivists, and the United States Constitution," 41 *Brandeis Law Journal* (2002), 85, 111–12.

57. See *Henry v. State*, 136 P. (1913), 982, 987.

58. Ibid., 988.

59. Ibid.

60. Ibid., 990, 989.

61. *Schick v. Reed*, 483 F2d (1973) 1266, 1267.

62. *Hoffa v. Saxbe*, 378 F. Supp. (1974) 1221, 1231.

63. *Jamison v. Flanner*, 116 Kan (1924), 624, 630, 632. As the Supreme Court of Tennessee put it, "Executive clemency operates outside the letter of the law." See *Workman v. Tennessee*, 22 S.W. 3d (2000), 807, 812. Or in the words of Judge Arnold of the U.S. District Court for the Eastern District of Arkansas, grants of clemency "are by definition acts of grace, bestowed on no fixed basis and according to no ascertainable standards. They are manifestations of mercy, not of the operation of law." See *Rogers v. Britton*, 476 F. Supp (1979), 1036, 1039.

64. *Eacret v. Holmes*, 333 P. 2d (1958), 741, 742.

65. Ibid., 744. See also *Maurer v. Sheward*, 71 Ohio St. 3d (1994), 513, 525. The governor's clemency power may be subject to procedural regulations governing, for example, the manner of applying for a pardon, but the governor "has ultimate substantive discretion over whether to grant or deny a pardon." *Woratzeck v. Arizona Board of Executive Clemency*, 117 F3d (1997), 400, 401. "Arizona places no substantive limitations on official discretion over the ultimate decision to grant or deny clemency."

66. See *State v. Jones*, 639 So. 2d (1994), 1144, 1150.

67. *Sullivan v. Askew*, 348 So. 2d (1977) 312, 315.

68. *In re Sapp*, 118 F. 3d (1997), 460, 465. See *Otey v. Nebraska*, 485 N.W. 2d (1992), 153, 166. (The Nebraska Board of Pardons has "unfettered discretion" to grant or deny a commutation "for any reason or no reason at all.") Also *Joubert v. Nebraska Board of Pardons*, 87 F.3d (1996), 966 (8th Cir.).

69. *Ex Parte Crump*, 135 P. (1913), 428.

70. Ibid., 430.

71. Ibid.

72. *Herrera v. Collins*, 506 U.S. (1993), 390.

73. See Kobil, "Chance and the Constitution," 572. Also Kathleen Ridolfi, "Not Just an Act of Mercy: The Demise of Post-Conviction Relief and a Rightful Claim to Clemency," 24 *New York Review of Law and Social Change* (1998), 43, 47.

74. *Herrera v. Collins*, 412.

75. This conception is important to those who see clemency through the lens of retributive justice. See, for example, Moore, *Pardons*.

76. *Herrera v. Collins*, 412. The adequacy of clemency as a fail-safe mechanism in the death penalty process was recently subject to adjudication under provisions of international law, namely Artcle 36 (2) of the Vienna Convention, which requires that nations provide meaningful and effective review and reconsideration of convictions and sentences. The International Court of Justice ruled that "the clemency process, as currently practiced within the United States criminal justice system does not appear to meet those requirements." See *Case Concerning Avena and Other Mexican Nationals, Mexico v. United States of America* (March 31, 2004), 54. Found at http://www.icj-cij.org/icjwww/idocket/imus/imusframe.htm.

77. *Ohio Adult Parole Authority v. Woodard*, 523 U.S. (1998), 272.

78. See Adam Gershowitz, "The Diffusion of Responsibility in Capital Clemency," 17 *Journal of Law and Politics* (2001), 669, 673.

79. "Rarely, if ever (are clemency decisions) appropriate subjects for judicial review." See *Ohio Adult Parole Authority v. Woodard*, 276.

80. Ibid., 279. Contra Rehnquist, Strach argues that the Court should treat clemency "as a special subset of the entire procedural due

process controversy. Implicit in this treatment would be the recognition that an individual's life interest is not divisible or extinguishable in the same way that a liberty interest is typically held to be." Phillip John Strach, "*Ohio Adult Parole v. Woodard*: Breathing New 'Life' Into an Old Fourteenth Amendment Controversy," 77 *North Carolina Law Review* (1999), 891, 929. See also Daniel Kobil, "Due Process in Death Penalty Commutations: Life, Liberty, and the Pursuit of Clemency," 27 *University of Richmond Law Review* (1992–93), 201, 216.

81. *Ohio Adult Parole Authority v. Woodard*, 280–81; 285.

82. Various commentators disagree on what *Woodard* stands for, some seeing Rehnquist's no due process as the correct reading of the holding, others insisting that O'Connor's minimal due process garnered a majority. See David Olson, "Second-Guessing the Quality of Mercy: Due Process in State Executive Clemency Proceedings," *Harvard Journal of Law and Public Policy* 22 (1999), 1009. Also Kenneth Williams, "The Deregulation of the Death Penalty," 40 *Santa Clara Law Review* (2000) 677, 719; Kobil, "Chance and the Constitution," 573. Some courts have also taken notice of the division in *Woodard*. See *Duvall v. Keating*, 162 F. 3d 1058, 1060; and *Workman v. Bell*, 245 F.3d (2001), 849, 852.

83. *Ohio Adult Parole Authority v. Woodard*, 289.

84. Ibid. For an earlier elaboration of what the requirements due process in capital clemency cases might be, see "A Matter of Life and Death: Due Process Protection in Capital Clemency Proceedings," 90 *Yale Law Journal* (1980–81), 889, 908–11.

85. *Ohio Adult Parole Authority v. Woodard*, 292 (Stevens dissenting). See Mark Strasser, "Some Reflections on the President's Pardon Power," 31 *Capital University Law Review* (2003), 143, 153–59. Strasser argues that Stevens's imagined cases are "not the kinds of cases that might reasonably be expected to occur."

86. See, for example, *Sellers v. Oklahoma*, 973 P. 2d (1999), 894, 896; *Anderson v. Davis*, 279 F.3d 674, 676; *Faulder v. Texas*, 178 F. 3d (1999), 343–44; and *Duvall v. Keating*. For an important exception, see *McGee v. Arizona State Board of Pardons and Paroles*, 376 P. 2d 779, 781. (Board of Pardons ordered to hold a hearing at which McGee would be allowed to present evidence in support of his application for clemency.)

87. *Bacon v. Lee*, 353 N.C. (2001) 696, 712.

88. *People ex rel. Lisa Madigan v. Snyder*, 208 Ill. 2d (2004) 457, 473, 480.

89. See Patrick Buchanan, "George Ryan's Pathetic Farewell," *Human Events* 59 (2003), 1. Buchanan labeled Ryan's commutation "arbitrary, capricious, immoral and anti-democratic."

90. References to the rule of law are notoriously vague. As George Fletcher puts it, "Of all the dreams that drive men and women into the streets, from Buenos Aires to Budapest, the 'rule of law' is the most puzzling. We have a pretty good idea what we mean by 'free markets' and 'democratic elections.' But legality and the 'rule of law' are ideals that present themselves as opaque even to legal philosophers." George Fletcher, *Basic Concepts of Legal Thought* (New York: Oxford University Press, 1996), 11. Yet the rule-of-law ideal points toward a set of concepts, ideas, ideals summarized in the idea that, as Cass puts it, "something other than the mere will of the individual deputized to exercise government powers must have primacy." Ronald Cass, *The Rule of Law in America* (Baltimore: The Johns Hopkins University Press, 2001), 3. See also Richard Fallon, "'The Rule of Law' as a Concept in Constitutional Discourse," 97 *Columbia Law Review* (1997), 1.

91. William F. Buckley Jr., "Strange Uses of Tolerance," *San Diego Union-Tribune* (January 27, 1985), C2.

92. Alexis de Tocqueville, *Democracy in America*, vol. 1 (New York: Knopf, 1945), 278.

93. See *Planned Parenthood v. Casey*, 505 U.S. 833, 868 (1992).

94. Cass, *The Rule of Law in America*, xii. Political scientist Samuel Huntington notes, "Western concepts differ fundamentally from those prevalent in other civilizations. Western ideas of individualism, liberalism, constitutionalism, human rights, equality, liberty, the rule of law . . . often have little resonance in Islamic, Confucian, Japanese, Hindu, Buddhist, or Orthodox culture." Samuel Huntington, *The Clash of Civilizations and the Remaking of World Order* (New York: Simon and Schuster, 1996), 311.

95. Michael Oakeshott, *Rationalism in Politics and Other Essays* (Indianapolis: Liberty Press, 1991), 389.

96. Henry Cisneros, "Extra Spice for American Culture," *Financial Times of London* (May 24, 2004), 17. See also Marci Hamilton, "The Rule of Law: Even as We Try to Export the Ideal of Justice by Law,

Not Whim, Some in America Resist That Very Ideal" (October 23, 2003), at http://writ.news.findlaw.com/hamilton/20031023.html.

97. See Jonathan Lippman, "Preserving Safety and Access to the Courts," 83 *New York Law Journal* (April 30, 2004), 9.

98. Ann Parks, "Former Secretary of Defense Shares Views on War, Business and the Rule of Law," *Daily Record* (May 17, 2004). See also Law Tribune Advisory Board, "Are We Still the Land of the Free," *Connecticut Law Tribune* (April 12, 2004), 19.

99. Ron Paul's *Texas Straight Talk*, "War in Iraq, War on the Rule of Law?" (August 26, 2002), http://www.house.gov/paul/tst/tst2002/tst082602.htm. See also "Our Opinions: Ignoring Detainees Rights Weakens U.S. Principles," *Atlanta Journal Constitution* (May 18, 2004), 10a; and John Hutson, "Rule of Law: Guantanamo Offers U.S. a Chance to Showcase Ideal of Due Process," *The Recorder* (January 16, 2004), 4.

100. See Brian Hoffstadt, "Normalizing the Federal Clemency Power," 79 *Texas Law Review* (2001), 561, 562.

101. Nasser Hussain, *The Jurisprudence of Emergency: Colonialism and the Rule of Law*. Ann Arbor: University of Michigan Press, 2004. Also Magnus Fiskesjo, *The Thanksgiving Turkey Pardon, The Death of Teddy's Bear, and the Sovereign Exception of Guantanamo* (Chicago: Prickly Paradigm Press, 2003), 53.

102. *The Federalist* No. 74. New York: The Modern Library, 1956, 483.

103. For a recent repudiation of that effort, see *Hamdi v. Rumsfeld*, 124 S. Ct. 2633 (2004).

Chapter 4
Governing Clemency: From Redemption to Retribution

1. Francis Allen, *The Decline of the Rehabilitative Ideal: Penal Policy and Social Purpose* (New Haven: Yale University Press), 1981.

2. See *Williams v. New York*, 337 US 241, 247–49 (1949).

3. David Garland, *The Culture of Control: Crime and Social Order in Contemporary Society* (Chicago: University of Chicago Press, 2001), 36.

4. See Andrew Von Hirsch, *Doing Justice: The Choice of Punishments* (New York: Hill and Wang, 1976), xxix. See also Karl Menninger, *The Crime of Punishment* (New York, Viking Press, 1969).

5. For a description and critique of the practices of indeterminate sentencing, see Marvin Frankel, *Criminal Sentences: Law Without Order* (New York; Hill and Wang), 1976.

6. See, for example, Keally McBride, "Hitched to the Post: Prison Labor, Choice, and Citizenship," 30 *Studies in Law, Politics, and Society* (2004), 107.

7. Elizabeth Rapaport, "Retribution and Redemption in the Operation of Executive Clemency," 74 *Chicago-Kent Law Review* (2000), 1501.

8. Rehabilitative approaches to punishment are less interested in giving the offender what he or she deserves than they are in assigning punishment on the basis of what an offender needs.

9. As Daniel Markel puts it, mercy "refers primarily to leniency afforded to criminal offenders on the basis of characteristics that evoke compassion or sympathy but that are morally unrelated to the offender's competence and ability to choose to engage in criminal conduct." See Daniel Markel, "Against Mercy," 88 *Minnesota Law Review* (2004), 1041, note 1.

10. Rapaport, "Retribution and Redemption in the Operation of Executive Clemency," 1501. Redemption is, of course, not the only grounds on which clemency can be based. Among other reasons are, as we have seen, considerations of justice, that is, pardoning to correct miscarriages of justice, and principled opposition to an entire type of punishment, for instance the death penalty.

11. Ibid., 1523, 1528.

12. On the significance of this last factor, see Stephen Garvey, "Punishment as Atonement," 46 *UCLA Law Review* (1999), 1801.

13. Rapaport, "Retribution and Redemption in the Operation of Executive Clemency," 1530.

14. The Supreme Court in *U.S. v. Booker*, 125 S. Ct. 1006 (2005), found that, insofar as they were regarded as mandatory, the Federal Sentencing Guidelines violated the Sixth Amendment. The Court held that the guidelines could be used in an advisory fashion without suffering such a constitutional defect. The result of the Court's decision is to restore greater sentencing discretion to federal judges.

15. Fox Butterfield, "U.S. 'Correctional Population' Hits New High," *New York Times* (July 26, 2004), http://www.nytimes.com/2004/07/26/national/26parole.html.

16. See Jonathan Simon, *Governing through Crime: The War on Crime and the Transformation of American Governance, 1960–2000* (New York: Oxford University Press, forthcoming).

17. James Whitman, *Harsh Justice: Criminal Punishment and the Widening Divide between American and Europe* (New York: Oxford University Press, 2003), 14–15.

18. See Stuart Scheingold, *The Politics of Law and Order: Street Crime and Public Policy* (New York: Basic Books, 1984).

19. This so-called myth presents punitiveness as both a necessary and sufficient solution to complicated and otherwise intractable problems of social order, including but not restricted to crime. Its appeal is greater where people's apprehensions and insecurities are more pronounced, apart from the realities of crime and the risks of victimization. See William Connolly, *The Ethos of Pluralization* (Minneapolis: University of Minnesota Press, 1995), chapter 2. The emphasis on punishment as the solution is rooted in America's cultural themes of "frontier justice" and "individual responsibility," according to Scheingold; they are, in his words, "more expressive than instrumental." See Scheingold, *The Politics of Law and Order*, 64.

20. Scheingold, *The Politics of Law and Order*, 60. Also William Connolly, "The Will, Capital Punishment, and Cultural War," in *The Killing State: Capital Punishment in Law, Politics, and Culture*, Austin Sarat, ed. (New York: Oxford, 1999), 200.

21. Since the claim that punishment is now too lenient is embedded in cultural understandings rather than experience with crime, the implication that we are not now imposing enough punishment is a cultural tenet, a value judgment not subject to empirical refutation. See Scheingold, *The Politics of Law and Order*, 226–27. Thus incontestible documentation that the United States is unrivaled among Western democracies in severity of sentences and time served for criminal violence is ignored or deemed irrelevant.

22. Studies have documented public obsession with the ability of the criminal justice system to keep offenders off the streets (see Julian V. Roberts and Anthony N. Doob, "News Media Influences on Public Views of Sentencing" 14 *Law and Human Behavior* [1991], 451).

Several other studies describe the media's predilection for (murder) stories of criminal violence against the person. (See Doris A. Graber, *Crime News and the Public* [New York; Praeger, 1980]; Richard Victor Ericson, Patricia M. Baranek, and Janet B. L. Chan, *Representing Order: Crime, Law, and Justice in the News Media* [Toronto: University of Toronto Press, 1991]; Philip Schlesinger and Howard Tumber, *Reporting Crime: The Media Politics Of Criminal Justice* [New York: Oxford University Press, 1994]; especially for serial killers, Philip Jenkins, *Using Murder: The Social Construction of Serial Homicide* [New York: A. de Gruyter, 1994].)

23. James F. Hodgson and Debra S. Kelley, eds., *Sexual Violence: Policies, Practices, and Challenges in the United States and Canada* (Westport, CT.: Praeger, 2002).

24. See Katherine Beckett and Theodore Sasson, *The Politics of Injustice: Crime and Punishment in America* (London: Sage Publications, 1999).

25. Ellsworth and Gross traced this effect during the 1988 presidential campaign. In the May and July 1988 polls, most people did not know how the candidates stood on capital punishment. Specifically, when asked which candidate "comes closer to your way of thinking" on the death penalty, 21 percent said Bush, 19 percent said Dukakis, and 60 percent said there was no difference or had no opinion. In late summer, after the Bush campaign emphasized the theme that Dukakis was soft on crime because he was against the death penalty and was responsible for the furlough of Willie Horton, there was a short-term spike in general support for capital punishment. Polls in September and October 1988 both found 79 percent support for capital punishment, an all-time high for death penalty support in the national polls. In October, 71 percent of a national poll correctly chose Dukakis as the candidate who opposed the death penalty, 12 percent mistakenly chose Bush, and 17 percent did not know. See Phoebe Ellsworth and Samuel R. Gross, "Hardening of the Attitudes: Americans' Views on the Death Penalty," *Journal of Social Issues* 50 (1994), 44.

26. The Horton narrative provides both the underpinnings for a punitive response to social change and disorder, and the rationale for stereotyping and scapegoating categories or classes of people as the "criminal element." *The Politics of Law and Order*, 226. According to Scheingold the desire for harsh punishment is imbedded in cultural

understandings rather than experience with crime. This "myth" represents punitiveness as a necessary and sufficient solution to complicated and otherwise intractable problems, including but not restricted to crime. Its appeal is greater where people's apprehensions and insecurities are more pronounced, apart from the realities of crime and risks of victimization. The attractions of punishment are, in his words, "more expressive than instrumental." Ibid., 226–27.

27. The theme of the Horton ads was apparently replicated in concurrent media crime coverage. Over the period 1985–89, Jamieson reports that she found that in crime stories of 1998 there was a significant increase in news of black alleged offenders and female victims, with no corresponding increase in reported crime. Katherine Jamieson, *Dirty Politics* (Oxford University Press: New York, 1992), 134.

28. As a characterization of Dukakis's furlough policy, the Horton ad was a gross misrepresentation of a prisoner work program that had proved to be relatively free of abuses and compared quite favorably to such policies in most other states, including California under the governorship of Ronald Reagan. Jamieson observes that the Horton incident was a freakishly rare event in Dukakis's furlough program.

> Of the 268 furloughed convicts [out of 11,497 individuals given a total of 67,378 furloughs] who jumped furlough during Dukakis's first two terms, only four had ever been convicted first-degree murderers not eligible for parole. Of those four not "many" but *one* [emphasis added] went on to kidnap and rape. That one was William Horton. (Ibid., 19)

29. Ibid., 31–33.

30. Ibid., 34.

31. Ibid., 35.

32. Ibid., 31–32.

33. The "larger than life" character of the Horton incident is underscored by Gore Vidal in the following facetious comment: "Certainly no reality intrudes upon our presidential elections. They are simply fast moving fiction, empty of content at a cognitive level, but at a visceral level very powerful indeed, as the tragic election of Willie Horton to the governorship of Massachusetts demonstrated in 1988." See Gore Vidal, *Palimpsest: A Memoir* (New York: Random House, 1992).

34. See Von Hirsch, *Doing Justice*, 12, 29. "The most obvious drawback of allowing wide-open discretion . . . is the disparity it permits."

35. Robert Martinson, "What Works?—Questions and Answers about Prison Reform," *The Public Interest* 10 (1974), 22. As Von Hirsch argues, "In our day-to-day experience, and in our preliminary research findings, it seemed that rehabilitation was far less often achieved than our predecessors would have believed. . . . Despite every effort and every attempt, correctional treatment programs have failed." See *Doing Justice*, xxxii, xxxviii.

36. See, for example, Jessica Mitford, *Kind and Usual Punishment: The Prison Business* (New York: Knopf, 1973).

37. Von Hirsch, *Doing Justice*.

38. See Ernest van den Haag, *Punishing Criminals: Concerning a Very Old and Painful Question* (New York: Basic Books, 1975).

39. Herbert Morris, "Persons and Punishment," in *Human Rights*, Abraham Melden, ed. (Belmont, CA: Wadsworth, 1970).

40. Ibid., 112.

41. Ibid., 126.

42. Ibid., 120, 127.

43. Von Hirsch, *Doing Justice*, xxix.

44. Morris, "Persons and Punishment," 115, 118.

45. Ibid., 116.

46. "To say someone 'deserves' to be rewarded or punished is to refer to his *past* conduct, and assert that its merit or demerit is reason for according him pleasant or unpleasant treatment." Von Hirsch, *Doing Justice*, 46.

47. Morris, "Persons and Punishment," 118.

48. Von Hirsch observes that "if one asks how severely a wrongdoer deserves to be punished a familiar principle comes to mind: Severity of punishment should be commensurate with the seriousness of the wrong. . . . Disproportionate penalties are undeserved." *Doing Justice*, 66. See also Andrew Von Hirsch, *Past or Future Crimes: Deservedness and Dangerousness in the Sentencing of Criminals* (New Brunswick, NJ: Rutgers University Press, 1985), chapter 3.

49. Morris, "Persons and Punishment," 119.

50. Ibid., 117.

51. Similarly Von Hirsch observes that "the rehabilitative model, despite its emphasis on understanding and concern, has been more

cruel and punitive than a frankly punitive model would probably be. Medicine is allowed to be bitter; inflicted pain is not cruelty, if it is treatment rather than punishment. Under the rehabilitative model, we have been able to abuse our charges, the prisoners, without disabusing our consciences." See *Doing Justice*, xxxviii. Of course the radical expansion of the prison population and the increase in the severity of punishments that retributive theories encouraged during the last two decades suggest that the problem of harsh punishment cannot be laid solely at the door of rehabilitative theory.

52. Morris, "Persons and Punishment," 114.

53. Von Hirsch, *Doing Justice*, xxxix.

54. Morris, "Persons and Punishment," 123.

55. *Herrera v. Collins*, 506 U.S. (1993), 390, 412.

56. See Daniel Kobil, "The Quality of Mercy Strained: Wrestling the Pardoning Power from the King," 69 *Texas Law Review* (1991), 569, 575. Also Daniel Kobil, "The Evolving Role of Clemency in Capital Cases," in *America's Experiment with Capital Punishment: Reflections on the Past, Present, and Future of the Ultimate Penal Sanction*, James Acker, Robert Bohm, and Charles Lanier, eds. (Durham, NC: Carolina Academic Press, 1998), 531–42.

57. Kathleen Dean Moore, *Pardons: Justice, Mercy, and the Public Interest* (New York: Oxford University Press, 1989), 91. Linda Meyer provides a very different perspective on this issue as well as an important critique of retributivism when she contends that every act of punishment is also "a form of forgiveness." See Linda Meyer, "Forgiveness and Public Trust," 27 *Fordham Urban Law Journal* (2000), 1515, 1530.

58. Moore, *Pardons*, 91.

59. Ibid., 129, 91–92.

60. Kathleen Dean Moore, "Pardon for Good and Sufficient Reasons," 27 *University of Richmond Law Review* (1992–93), 281.

61. Ibid., 286–87.

62. Moore, *Pardons*, 11.

63. Moore, "Pardon for Good and Sufficient Reasons," 284.

64. Moore, *Pardons*, 225.

65. Daniel Kobil, "How to Grant Clemency in Unforgiving Times," 31 *Capital University Law Review* (2003), 219, 223.

66. Markel, "Against Mercy," 1429, note 23.

67. Ibid., 1425. "If I were conscious that I ever advised the president to exercise clemency for no better reason than because I felt sorry for the prisoner or those interested in him, I should feel that my conduct had differed, indeed, in degree, but not in kind, from what it would have been had I given such advice for a bribe in money." Attorney General James Bonaparte, quoted in *Proceedings of the Annual Congress of the National Prison Association* (1907), 201.

68. Markel, "Against Mercy," 1472.

69. Ibid.

70. Ibid., 1429.

71. Ibid., 1432.

72. Ibid., 1447.

73. As Markel notes, it would not be mercy but rather "the exercise of equitable or justice enhancing discretion." Ibid., 1456.

74. Ibid. James Whitman notes what he sees as a distinctively American criticism of clemency in the name of egalitarianism. As he puts it, "American officials needed pardoning and they used it. But doing so touched a raw egalitarian nerve among Americans as it would continue to do down to the Clinton pardons in 2000." James Whitman, *Harsh Justice*, 183.

75. Markel, "Against Mercy," 1456.

76. See, for example, L. Gregory Jones, *Embodying Forgiveness: A Theological Analysis* (New York: Eerdmans Publishing Company, 1995).

77. These efforts are discussed in Andrew Von Hirsch, *Restorative Justice and Criminal Justice: Competing or Reconcilable Paradigms?* (Oxford: Hart Publishing, 2003).

78. Hugo Adam Bedau, "A Retributive Theory of the Pardoning Power," 27 *University of Richmond Law Review* (1992–93), 185, 200. Bedau develops a systematic critique of the retributivist position that points him to mercy as providing the basis for clemency.

79. See, for example, P. E. Digeser, "Justice, Forgiveness, Mercy, and Forgetting: The Complex Meaning of Executive Pardoning," 31 *Capital University Law Review* (2003), 161, 166.

80. Rapaport offers an interesting portrait of clemency when she says that making clemency decisions

> involves weighing incommensurables—weighing, for example, equity against rehabilitation through some process of judgment

> employing standards, intuition, precedents, experience, and background knowledge. The use of discretion in clemency decisions can only be denied at the cost of creating a fiction that standards and their nearly mechanical application alone govern, or through the exclusion of legitimate considerations in the service of a reductionist program like retributivism. When we seek to banish discretion, we impoverish justice and consort with comforting fictions.

See Rapaport, "Retribution and Redemption in the Operation of Executive Clemency," 1534–35.

81. See Margaret Colgate Love, "Of Pardons, Politics and Collar Buttons: Reflections on the President's Duty to Be Merciful," 27 *Fordham Urban Law Journal* (2000), 1483, 1502.

82. Love, "Fear of Forgiving," 127.

83. Love, "Of Pardons," 1503.

84. Love, "Fear of Forgiving," 126.

85. Love, "Of Pardons," 1503; 1506. For the elaboration of a related concept, "political forgiveness," see Digeser, "Justice, Forgiveness," 166. In addition, Digeser holds open the idea that clemency can represent an "official act of amnesia" whose purpose is "to further the peace and security of the state," 176.

Chapter 5
Clemency without Mercy: George Ryan's Dilemma

1. See Robert Ferguson, "The Judicial Opinion as a Literary Genre," 2 *Yale Journal of Law and the Humanities* (1990), 201.

2. Ferguson describes the rhetoric of judicial opinions as a response to "the judiciary's nonmajoritarian status in a democratic republic." Ibid., 205, 207.

3. Ibid., 205.

4. A recent Fox News poll found that 69 percent of Americans favor the death penalty for persons convicted of premeditated murder, a drop of 7 percentage points from the number of respondents supporting capital punishment in 1997. The poll revealed that 23 percent of respondents opposed capital punishment, and 8 percent were not sure. In previous years, support for the death penalty registered 76 percent in 1997, 74 percent in 1998, 68 percent in 2000, and 2001. (Fox News,

June 10, 2003), at http://www.deathpenaltyinfo.org/article.php?scid=23&did=210#foxnews7/03.

5. "We live in a culture where more and more people are claiming their own holocaust . . . etc. The victim culture creates a compassion fatigue, which interferes with helping those who truly need and deserve our help." See Ofer Zur, "Psychology of Victimhood: Reflections on a Culture of Victims" (1994), at http://www.drozur.com/victimhood.html. Also Susan D. Moeller, *Compassion Fatigue: How the Media Sell Disease, Famine, War and Death* (New York: Routledge, 1999).

6. See Daniel Markel, "Against Mercy," 88 *Minnesota Law Review* (2004), 1421.

7. Charles Sykes, *A Nation of Victims: The Decay of the American Character* (New York: St. Martin's Press, 1992).

8. Thomas Jipping, "Extending Mercy to the Wrong Group" (January 17, 2003), http://www.worldnetdaily.com/news/article.asp?ARTICLE_ID=30536. As John Douglas remarked, "The bottom line is that Governor Ryan showed mercy to the merciless." See John Douglas, "Mercy to the Merciless: Governor Ryan's Blanket Commutation," *Newsletter* (January 28, 2003), http://www.johndouglasmindhunter.com/newsletter/030128.php. For a contrary view, see Thomas J. Broderick, "Commutation Is Justice, Not Mercy," *New Ground 84* (September–October 2002), http://www.chicagodsa.org/ngarchive/ng84.html.

9. This and other quotations from Governor Ryan's "I Must Act Speech" may be found in appendix A.

10. Stephen Garvey argues that

> Mercy as equity might be able to justify a decision to commute the sentences of everyone on death row in the name of justice, but not in the name of mercy. Mercy as imperfect obligation can justify a decision to commute the sentences of some on death row in the name of mercy, but not the sentences of them all. With each act of mercy comes a corresponding injustice until at some point the demands of justice must prevail against those of mercy. The moral logic changes when one switches from retribution to atonement. For atonement, unlike for retribution, deserved punishment is not an end in itself. It is merely a means, although a necessary means, to the end of reconciliation. But when the punishment an offender deserves is death, the means and end of atonement come

> apart. Death precludes the possibility of atonement, but without death atonement depends on the supererogatory forgiveness of victims. What to do? Commute or not commute? The answer, I think, is properly delegated to the conscience. A governor is free to do as he or she in good faith sees fit. A governor is free to commute the death sentences of all, some, or none of those on death row in mercy's name. But if a governor chooses to commute the sentences of everyone on death row, such a choice can be understood as a morally permissible act of mercy only if we abandon retribution and embrace atonement.

See "Is It Wrong to Commute Death Row? Retribution, Atonement, and Mercy," 82 *North Carolina Law Review* (2004), 1319, 1343.

11. Martha Nussbaum, "Equity and Mercy," *Philosophy and Public Affairs* 22 (1993), 86, 103.

12. As noted in chapter 2 of this book, Lee Cruce of Oklahoma explained his commutations by saying, "I am today more confirmed than ever in my opposition to this ancient and uncivilized form of human punishment." See Joe O'Brien, "He Killed Oklahoma's Death Penalty," *Daily Oklahoman* (July 31, 1927), D1. Or, as Governor Anaya of New Mexico said in announcing his blanket commutation, "I call for the abolition of the death penalty because it is inhumane, immoral, anti-God, and is incompatible with an enlightened society." "Statement by Governor Toney Anaya on Crime and Punishment," Santa Fe, New Mexico. November 26, 1986.

13. The closest Ryan came to such an outright condemnation of the death penalty was when he quoted former governor Pat Brown of California who said about capital punishment, "Beyond its honor and incredibility, it has neither protected the innocent nor deterred the killers. Publicly sanctioned killing has cheapened human life and dignity without the redeeming grace which comes from justice metered out swiftly, evenly, humanely."

14. Zur, "Psychology of Victimhood: Reflections on a Culture of Victims."

15. For a description of the retributive theory of clemency, see chapter 4. Also Kathleen Dean Moore, "Pardon for Good and Sufficient Reasons," 27 *University of Richmond Law Review* (1992–93), 281; and Daniel Kobil, "The Quality of Mercy Strained: Wresting the Pardoning Power from the King," 69 *Texas Law Review* (1991), 569.

16. His critique of capital punishment is systemic not moral; his justification oddly evocative of a seventeenth-century view of sovereign prerogative.

17. Jennifer Culbert, "The Body in *Payne*: The Rhetoric of Victims' Rights and the Predicament of Judgment." Paper presented to the 1995 Annual Meeting of the Law and Society Association, Toronto, Canada, 8.

18. Ryan relied, Kobil only somewhat inaccurately claims, "entirely on retributive arguments." Daniel Kobil, "How to Grant Clemency in Unforgiving Times," 31 *Capital University Law Review* (2003), 219, 227. Stephen Garvey recently has argued that mass clemency of the kind that Ryan issued cannot be squared with retributive principles. Garvey, "Is It Wrong to Commute Death Row? Retribution, Atonement, and Mercy," 1319. For a contrasting view, see Daniel Markel, "Commuting Death Row," unpublished manuscript, 2004.

19. "Clemency," Rehnquist said, "is deeply rooted in our Anglo-American tradition of law, and is the historic remedy for preventing miscarriages of justice where judicial process has been exhausted." *Herrera v. Collins*, 506 U.S. (1993), 390, 412. For a more complete discussion of Rehnquist's position, see chapter 3 of this book.

20. See Susan Bandes, "Introduction," in *The Passions of Law*, Susan Bandes, ed. (New York: New York University Press, 1999), 1, 7.

21. See Susan Jacoby, *Wild Justice: The Evolution of Revenge* (New York: Harper & Row, 1983), 115. "Insofar as humanly possible . . . law attempts to remove personal animus from the process of apportioning blame and exacting retribution. It is the removal of personal animus . . . that distinguishes the rule of law from the rule of passion." On just deserts, see Richard Singer, *Just Deserts: Sentencing Based on Equality and Desert* (Cambridge, MA: Ballinger Publishing Company, 1979); and Andrew von Hirsch, *Past or Future Crimes: Deservedness and Dangerousness in the Sentencing of Criminals* (New Brunswick, NJ: Rutgers University Press, 1985).

22. Kant, *Metaphysical Elements of Justice*, 101.

23. See Terry Aladjem, "Revenge and Consent," unpublished manuscript, 1990, 9.

24. For a discussion of the role of emotion in justice, see Samuel Pillsbury, "Emotional Justice: Moralizing the Passions of Criminal Justice," 74 *Cornell Law Review* (1989), 655.

25. St. Augustine, *The Writings of St. Augustine* (New York: Fathers of the Church, 1947), 168–69.

26. Lawrence Becker, "Criminal Attempt and the Theory of the Law of Crimes," *Philosophy & Public Affairs* 3 (1974), 262.

27. Quoted in J. Ferrer, *Crimes and Punishments* (London: Chatto and Windus, 1880), 190.

28. See Markus Dirk Dubber, *Victims in the War on Crime: The Use and Abuse of Victims' Rights* (New York: New York University Press, 2002).

29. "President Calls for Crime Victims' Rights Amendment" (April 16, 2002), http://www.whitehouse.gov/news/releases/2002/04/20020416-1.html. See also Ezzat A. Fattah, "Victim's Rights: Past, Present and Future" (2001), at http://www.enm.justice.fr/centre_de_ressources/dossiers_reflexions/oeuvre_justice/victims_rights1.htm. As Fattah puts it,

> Crime victims are a disenfranchised group that has been far too long forgotten by the general public, neglected by legislators and ignored or mistreated by those who operate the criminal justice system. Their legitimate rights were usurped by the State and they were left to suffer in silence and to endure the consequences of their victimization without redress, compensation, help or assistance. Over the years, victims were gradually relegated to the shadow and ceased to be active participants enjoying a formal legal status or playing a dominant role in the justice process.

30. In 1981 President Reagan proclaimed the week of April 19 the first "National Victims Rights Week." See Proclamation No. 4831, 3 C.F.R. 18 (1982). Each president has proclaimed a Crime Victims Week annually since. Legislation now exists that grants victims a role in the plea bargaining process and in sentencing decisions as well as a right to be notified about the release of the offenders who victimized them. All fifty states have passed victims rights laws, and more than half the states have amended their constitutions to guarantee rights for crime victims. See Leroy Lamborn, "Victim Participation in the Criminal Justice Process: The Proposal for a Constitutional Amendment," 34 *Wayne Law Review* (1987), 125. Moreover, "Today, the constitutions of at least 20 states now contain 'victims' rights amendments,' and similar legislation has been introduced at the federal level."

Wayne Logan, "Through the Past Darkly: A Survey of the Uses and Abuses of Victim Impact in Capital Trials," 41 *Arizona Law Review* (1999), 144, note 4. See also Maureen McLoed, "Victim Participation at Sentencing," 22 *Criminal Law Bulletin* (1986), 501; Frank Carrington and George Nicholson, "The Victims' Movement: An Idea Whose Time Has Come," 11 *Pepperdine Law Review* (1984), 1; and Lynne Henderson, "The Wrongs of Victims' Rights," 37 *Stanford Law Review* (1985), 937.

31. See Paul Cassell and Robert F. Hoyt, "The Tale of Victims-Rights," *Legal Times* (12/23 and 12/30, 1996), http://www.law.utah.edu/faculty/websites/cassellp/Tale_of_Victims_Rights.htm.

32. See Sykes, *A Nation of Victims*.

33. Stuart Scheingold, Toska Olson, and Jana Pershing, "Sexual Violence, Victim Advocacy, and Republican Criminology: Washington State's Community Protection Act," 28 *Law & Society Review* (1994), 734, 736.

34. Zur, "Psychology of Victimhood: Reflections on a Culture of Victims."

35. On the requirements of retributive justice, see Immanuel Kant, *Metaphysical Elements of Justice*, John Ladd, trans. (Indianapolis: Bobbs-Merrill, 1965). See also Jeffrie G. Murphy, *Retribution, Justice, and Therapy: Essays in the Philosophy of Law* (Dordrecht, Holland, and Boston: D. Reidel Publishing Company, 1979); and Marvin Henberg, *Retribution: Evil for Evil in Ethics, Law, and Literature* (Philadelphia: Temple University Press, 1990).

36. Danielle Allen, "Democratic Dis-ease: Of Anger and the Troubling Nature of Punishment," in *The Passions of Law*, Susan Bandes, ed. (New York: New York University Press, 1999), 191, 204.

37. Wendy Kaminer, *It's All the Rage: Crime and Culture* (Reading, MA: Addison-Wesley, 1995). "To a victim," Kaminer writes, "the notion that crimes are committed against society, making the community the injured party, can seem both bizarre and insulting: it can make them feel invisible, unavenged, and unprotected." p. 75. Also Angela Harris, "The Jurisprudence of Victimhood," 1991 *Supreme Court Review* (1991), 77.

38. For a discussion of rituals of grieving, see Lou Taylor, *Mourning Dress: A Costume and Social History* (London: Allen and Unwin, 1983).

39. Terry Aladjem, "Vengeance and Democratic Justice: American Culture and the Limits of Punishment," unpublished manuscript, 1992, 3.

40. Quoted in Jonathan Simon, *Governing through Crime: The War on Crime and the Transformation of American Governance, 1960–2000* (New York: Oxford University Press, forthcoming), chapter 3, 5–7, 27. We become what Berlant calls "infantile citizens." In this version of citizenship, "a citizen is defined as a person traumatized by some aspect of life in the United States. Portraits and stories of citizen-victims . . . now permeate the political public sphere." See Lauren Berlant, *The Queen of America Goes to Washington City: Essays on Sex and Citizenship* (Durham: Duke University Press, 1997).

41. Ryan's decision, as I argued in chapter 1, followed closely on the heels of an extraordinary series of hearings by the Illinois Prison Review Board, hearings that were dominated by victims and their family members. During these hearing, as one newspaper described them, "hour after hour, victims and family members of dead victims have been forced to come before a panel and revisit the most horrific event in their lives. These people had to retell their stories and beg, sobbing, for the panel to let the current sentence of death stand." Katie Walsh, "Clemency Hearings Unjust to Victims' Families," *Columbia Chronicle Online*, http://www.ccchronicle.com/back/2002-10-21/opinions4.html.

For a useful analysis of the role of the families of the victims in those hearings, see Jonathan Simon, "Fearless Speech in the Killing State: The Power of Capital Crime Victim Speech," 82 *North Carolina Law Review* (2004), 1377. As Jennifer Culbert puts it, in our era, "[t]he pain and suffering expressed by the murder victim's survivors can serve as an absolute in a society in which every other kind of claim is subject to contestation, doubt, and criticism." See Jennifer Culbert, "The Sacred Name of Pain: The Role of Victim Impact Evidence in Death Penalty Sentencing Decisions," in *Pain, Death, and the Law*, Austin Sarat, ed. (Ann Arbor: University of Michigan Press, 2001), 104. In addition to their role as anchors of social values, Scheingold, Olson, and Pershing suggest that victims also pursue instrumental goals that may make them less not more punitive in their attitudes. See "Sexual Violence, Victim Advocacy, and Republican Criminology," 736.

42. Peter Fitzpatrick, "Life, Death, and the Law—and Why Capital Punishment Is Legally Insupportable," 47 *Cleveland State Law Review* (1999), 483, 484, 486, 487.

43. The small-town imagery is reminiscent of what Minow says about victim-impact statements. They "persuade, when they do, because they invoke widely shared images of goodness, Christian piety . . . the 'little guy,' and American patriotism, all of which are talismans of the deserving person. Some degree of simplification is inevitable and no one should be surprised to find that victim impact statements do not reveal the uniqueness of the human being victimized by crime." Martha Minow "Surviving Victim Talk," 40 *UCLA Law Review* (1993), 1432.

44. "With the death penalty—an act of sovereignty—the State, the Prince or the Dictator claims an extraordinary power of calculation: the right to determine when life expires. The President, Governor or the Judge, who hold the right to grant pardon, the right to forgive and thus to make exceptions, are meant to know and be able to calculate the time of death, the moment which abruptly puts an end to the other's finitude." Stafano Crosara, "I'm Against the Death Penalty," *Trieste Contemporanea* (November 2000), at http://www.tscont.ts.it/pag20-e.htm.

45. Culbert, "The Sacred Name," 104–5.

46. "[F]orgiveness in general should only be permitted on the part of the victim. The question of forgiveness as such should only arise in the head-to-head or the face-to-face between the victim and the guilty party, never by a third party for a third. . . . [Y]et forgiveness perhaps implies, from the outset . . . the appearance on the scene of a third party whom it nonetheless must, should, exclude." See Jacques Derrida, "Part I: Forgiving," in *Questioning God*, eds. John Caputo et al. (Bloomington: Indiana University Press, 2001), 34.

47. Jacques Derrida, "The Century and the Pardon," *Le Mondes des Debats*, no. 9 (December 1999), 9, 16, at http://fixion.sytes.net/pardonEng.htm.

48. As the cultural critic Lauren Berlant notes, the result is to produce a "special form of tyranny that makes citizens like children, infantilized, passive, and over dependent on the 'immense and tutelary power' of the state." Berlant, *The Queen of American*, 27.

49. See the discussion of *Ohio Adult Parole Authority v. Woodard*, 523 U.S. (1998), 272, in chapter 3 of this book.

50. "In the absence of an overarching principle or absolute to which to refer for sense and guidance in a multicultural, morally pluralist society, the survivor is embraced as a unique figure with the power to liberate people from the chains of a well-meaning but paralyzing relativism." See Culbert, "The Sacred Name," 134.

51. Culbert contends that it is "counter-intuitive to think of a subjective experience like pain as establishing a publicly valid authority." "The Body in *Payne*," 8.

52. At this point Ryan associates his act with a "political" conception of clemency described by Hamilton. See Alexander Hamilton, *The Federalist* No. 74 (New York: The Modern Library, 1956), 483. Other examples of the political conception include President Gerald Ford's pardon of Richard Nixon. See President Gerald R. Ford's Remarks on Signing a Proclamation Granting Pardon to Richard Nixon (September 8, 1974), at http://www.ford.utexas.edu/library/speeches/740060.htm.

As Ford explained his decision he said,

> After years of bitter controversy and divisive national debate, I have been advised, and I am compelled to conclude that many months and perhaps more years will have to pass before Richard Nixon could obtain a fair trial by jury in any jurisdiction of the United States under governing decisions of the Supreme Court. I deeply believe in equal justice for all Americans, whatever their station or former station. The law, whether human or divine, is no respecter of persons; but the law is a respecter of reality. During this long period of delay and potential litigation, ugly passions would again be aroused. And our people would again be polarized in their opinions. And the credibility of our free institutions of government would again be challenged at home and abroad. . . . But it is not the ultimate fate of Richard Nixon that most concerns me, though surely it deeply troubles every decent and every compassionate person. My concern is the immediate future of this great country.

For another example, see President Carter's pardon of Vietnam War resisters in 1977: Proclamation 4483—granting pardon for violations of the Selective Service Act (August 4, 1964, to March 28, 1973), at http://www.archives.gov/federal_register/codification/proclamations/04483.html.

53. In Kaminer's view, talk about closure "partakes of a popular confusion of law and therapy and the substitution of feelings for facts. But if feelings are facts in a therapist's office . . . feelings are prejudices in a court of law. . . . Justice is not a form of therapy, meaning that what is helpful to a particular victim . . . is not necessarily just and what is just may not be therapeutic." See Kaminer, *It's All the Rage*, 84.

54. Kobil, "How to Grant Clemency in Unforgiving Times," 228.

55. See *Ex Parte Garland*, 71 U.S. (1866), 333, 371. Also *Ex Parte Grossman* 267 US (1925), 87, 120–21. "Executive clemency," Chief Justice Taft said,

> exists to afford relief from undue harshness or evident mistake in the operation or enforcement of the criminal law. The administration of justice by the courts is not necessarily always wise or certainly considerate of circumstances which may properly mitigate guilt. To afford a remedy, it has always been thought essential in popular governments, as well as in monarchies, to vest in some other authority than the courts power to ameliorate or avoid particular criminal judgments. It is a check entrusted to the executive for special cases. To exercise it to the extent of destroying the deterrent effect of judicial punishment would be to pervert it; but whoever is to make it useful must have full discretion to exercise it.

56. *McCleskey v. Kemp*, 481 U.S. 279 (1987), 281.

57. For a useful analysis of the implications of this refusal for our understanding of narrative and rhetoric, see Patricia Ewick and Susan Silbey, "Subversive Stories, Hegemonic Tales: Toward a Sociology of Narrative," 29 *Law and Society Review* (1995), 197, 215–16.

58. Ryan's journey is chronicled in a documentary film entitled *Deadline*, directed by Katy Chevigny and Kirsten Johnson (Big Mouth Productions, 2004). *Deadline* was broadcast on NBC's *Dateline* on July 30, 2004.

59. Austin Sarat, *When the State Kills: Capital Punishment and the American Condition* (Princeton: Princeton University Press, 2001), chapter 9.

60. Kobil, "How to Grant Clemency in Unforgiving Times," 227–28, 240.

61. Derrida, "The Century and the Pardon," 9.

62. "Energy in the Executive is a leading character in the definition of good government." *Federalist* No. 70, 454.

63. Kobil, "How to Grant Clemency in Unforgiving Times," 227, 228, 240.

64. See Robert Nozick, *Philosophical Explanations* (Cambridge, MA: Harvard University Press, 1981). See also Hugo Adam Bedau, "Retribution and the Theory of Punishment," *Journal of Philosophy* 75 (1978), 601; John Cottingham, "Varieties of Retribution," *Philosophical Quarterly* 29 (1979), 241; and Joel Feinberg, *Doing and Deserving* (Princeton: Princeton University Press, 1970).

65. Nozick, *Philosophical Explanations*, 366.

66. Ibid., 367.

67. See Michael Davis, "Harm and Retribution," in *Punishment*, A. John Simmons et al., eds. (Princeton: Princeton University Press, 1995), 191. Kant says of the law of retribution that "any undeserved evil that you inflict on someone else among the people is one that you do to yourself." *Metaphysical Elements of Justice*, 101–2.

68. Nozick, *Philosophical Explanations*, 367.

69. Ibid.

70. William Miller, "Clint Eastwood and Equity: Popular Culture's Theory of Revenge," in *Law in the Domains of Culture*, Austin Sarat and Thomas R. Kearns, eds. (Ann Arbor: University of Michigan Press, 1998), 167.

71. Ibid.

72. Nozick, *Philosophical Explanations*, 368.

Chapter 6
Conclusion:
On Mercy and Its Risks

1. Timothy Kaufman-Osborn, *From Noose to Needle: Capital Punishment and the Late Liberal State* (Ann Arbor: University of Michigan Press, 2002), 172–73, 208–9.

2. William Connolly, "The Will, Capital Punishment, and Cultural War," in *The Killing State: Capital Punishment in Law, Politics, and Culture* (New York: Oxford, 1999), 200.

3. Seneca, *Moral and Political Essays*, John Cooper and J. F. Procope, eds. and trans. (Cambridge: Cambridge University Press), 132.

4. Alexander Hamilton, "Federalist 74," *The Federalist: A Commentary on the Constitution of the United States* (New York: The Modern Library, 1956), 482.

5. To the Framers, the power to pardon was necessary because in the England of their day it was common for minor offenses to carry a sentence of death, with pardon by the king being the only way to avoid that punishment. Judges often applied a death sentence, having no choice, but at the same time applied for a royal pardon in the same breath.

6. Hamilton, "Federalist 74," 482.

7. Marvin Scott and Stanford Lyman, "Accounts," *American Sociological Review* 33 (1968), 46. Accounts, like pardon tales, are linguistic devices "employed whenever an action is subject to valuative inquiry . . . to explain unanticipated or untoward behavior. . . . [They] recognize a general sense in which the act in question is impermissible, but claim that the particular occasion permits or requires the very act." In clemency what is untoward or impermissible, in need of explanation and defense, is its lawless quality, its status as "the power of doing good without a rule."

8. Natalie Zemon Davis, *Fiction in the Archives: Pardon Tales and Their Tellers in Sixteenth-Century France* (Stanford: Stanford University Press, 1987), 4.

9. Edmund G. (Pat) Brown with Dick Adler, *Public Justice, Private Mercy: A Governor's Education on Death Row* (New York: Weidenfeld & Nicolson, 1989).

10. See appendix A.

11. Ibid., xii, 45.

12. Ibid., 106.

13. Ibid., 142.

14. Ibid., 36, 142.

15. Ibid., 10.

16. Ibid., 135.

17. Ibid., 121.

18. Ibid., 121, 135.

19. See, for example, Averell Harriman, "Mercy Is a Lonely Business," *Saturday Evening Post* (March 28, 1958), 24–25, 83–84. "Sitting alone in his office with the ancient, awesome power of clemency," Harriman writes, "the governor must take on the most difficult task of all: he must become the conscience of the people of his state."

20. Ibid., 163. Harriman disagrees with Brown's suggestion. He argues that "there are strong arguments in favor of leaving such decisions in the hands of a governor." See Harriman, "Mercy Is a Lonely Business," 25, 105, 163.

21. Pat Brown, *Public Justice, Private Mercy*, 105, 163.

22. Ibid.

23. Ibid., xvii.

24. Jack Lessenberry, "Book Review: DiSalle's True Potential Unfulfilled," *Toledo Blade* (May 16, 2004), http://www.toledoblade.com/apps/pbcs.dll/ article?AID=/20040516/ART02/405160312.

25. Michael V. DiSalle with Lawrence G. Blochman, *The Power of Life or Death* (New York: Random House, 1965), 6.

26. As a commentator noted sometime later, while conservatives attacked DiSalle for his opposition to the death penalty, "there were more executions carried out in Mr. DiSalle's one term than in the administrations of the next four governors combined!" Lessenberry, "Book Review: DiSalle's True Potential Unfulfilled."

27. Ibid.

28. DiSalle with Blochman, *The Power of Life or Death*, 27, 39.

29. Ibid., 54.

30. Ibid., 4.

31. Ibid., 28.

32. Ibid.

33. Ibid., 5.

34. In any case, when victims do enter DiSalle's pardon tale, they appear mostly as an abstract category. Thus, early in the book DiSalle says, "[T]he time to show concern for the victims of crime is long before the shot is fired or the blow struck—by seeking a sensible way of eliminating the causes of crime rather than by trying as we now do, futilely, after the fact, to eradicate crime by punishing the perpetrator." Ibid., 4.

35. Ibid., 52.

36. Ibid., 80, 87.

37. Ibid., 3, 83.

38. Ibid., 6, 83.

39. Ibid., 5.

40. James Whitman illustrates these concerns when he describes what he calls a "characteristically American . . . anxiety" concerning executive grants of mercy, "that pardons were being used to benefit

persons with good connections. . . . Pardons, it was argued, were inevitably inegalitarian." See James Whitman, *Harsh Justice: Criminal Punishment and the Widening Divide between America and Europe* (New York: Oxford University Press, 2003), 184.

41. *Furman v. Georgia*, 408 U.S. 238 (1972).

42. Ibid., 253, 254, 257.

43. Ibid., 413.

44. Ibid., 398.

45. Justice Stewart, writing in *Gregg v. Georgia*, drew an explicit parallel between jury discretion and clemency. "The petitioner's argument," Stewart said,

> is nothing more than a veiled contention that *Furman* indirectly outlawed capital punishment by placing totally unrealistic conditions on its use. In order to repair the alleged defects pointed to by the petitioner, it would be necessary to require that prosecuting authorities charge a capital offense whenever arguably there had been a capital murder and that they refuse to plea bargain with the defendant. If a jury refused to convict even though the evidence supported the charge, its verdict would have to be reversed and a verdict of guilty entered or a new trial ordered, since the discretionary act of jury nullification would not be permitted. Finally, acts of executive clemency would have to be prohibited. Such a system, of course, would be totally alien to our notions of criminal justice. (*Gregg v. Georgia*, 428 U.S. 153, 199, note 50 [1976])

46. *Korematsu v. United States*, 323 U.S. 214, 244, 248 (1944). Jackson also argues that

> It would be impracticable and dangerous idealism to expect or insist that each specific military command in an area of probable operations will conform to conventional tests of constitutionality. When an area is so beset that it must be put under military control at all, the paramount consideration is that its measures be successful, rather than legal. The armed services must protect a society, not merely its Constitution. The very essence of the military job is to marshal physical force, to remove every obstacle to its effectiveness, to give it every strategic advantage. . . . [A]

commander in temporarily focusing the life of a community on defense is carrying out a military program; he is not making law in the sense the courts know the term. He issues orders, and they may have a certain authority as military commands, although they may be very bad as constitutional law. . . . But if we cannot confine military expedients by the Constitution, neither would I distort the Constitution to approve all that the military may deem expedient. (Ibid., 244.)

47. Hamilton, *The Federalist* 74, 482.
48. *Korematsu v. United States*, 248.

Index

The following index does not include all data appearing in this book's appendixes. Appendix B ("Capital Clemency, 1900–2004: Commutations by State," pages 181–87) and appendix C ("Chronology of Capital Clemency, 1900–2004: Commutations by Governor," pages 189–258) are intended to supplement this index by providing historical and comparative perspective on capital clemency.